The Politics of Policy Change

Selected Titles in the American Governance and Public Policy Series
Series Editors: Gerard W. Boychuk, Karen Mossberger, and Mark C. Rom

Branching Out, Digging In: Environmental Advocacy and Agenda Setting
Sarah Pralle

Brussels Versus the Beltway: Advocacy in the United States and the European Union
Christine Mahoney

City-County Consolidation: Promises Made, Promises Kept?
Suzanne M. Leland and Kurt Thurmaier, Editors

Collaborative Public Management: New Strategies for Local Governments
Robert Agranoff and Michael McGuire

Competitive Interests: Competition and Compromise in American Interest Group Politics
Thomas T. Holyoke

The Congressional Budget Office: Honest Numbers, Power, and Policymaking
Philip G. Joyce

Custodians of Place: Governing the Growth and Development of Cities
Paul G. Lewis and Max Neiman

The Government Taketh Away: The Politics of Pain in the United States and Canada
Leslie A. Pal and R. Kent Weaver, Editors

Healthy Voices, Unhealthy Silence: Advocacy and Health Policy for the Poor
Colleen M. Grogan and Michael K. Gusmano

Investing in the Disadvantaged: Assessing the Benefits and Costs of Social Policies
David L. Weimer and Aidan R. Vining, Editors

Lessons of Disaster: Policy Change after Catastrophic Events
Thomas A. Birkland

Making Policy, Making Law: An Interbranch Perspective
Mark C. Miller and Jeb Barnes, Editors

Medical Governance: Values, Expertise, and Interests in Organ Transplantation
David L. Weimer

*National Health Insurance in the United States and Canada: Race,
Territory, and the Roots of Difference*
Gerard W. Boychuk

Out and Running: Gay and Lesbian Candidates, Elections, and Policy Representation
Donald P. Haider-Markel

The Politics of Ideas and the Spread of Enterprise Zones
Karen Mossberger

The Politics of Unfunded Mandates: Whither Federalism?
Paul L. Posner

Scandalous Politics: Child Welfare Policy in the States
Juliet F. Gainsborough

School's In: Federalism and the National Education Agenda
Paul Manna

Welfare Policymaking in the States: The Devil in Devolution
Pamela Winston

The Politics of Policy Change

Welfare, Medicare, and Social Security Reform in the United States

Daniel Béland and Alex Waddan

GEORGETOWN UNIVERSITY PRESS / WASHINGTON DC

Georgetown University Press, Washington, D.C.
www.press.georgetown.edu
© 2012 by Georgetown University Press. All rights reserved. No
part of this book may be reproduced or utilized in any form or
by any means, electronic or mechanical, including photocopying
and recording, or by any information storage and retrieval system,
without permission in writing from the publisher.

Library of Congress Cataloging-in-Publication Data

Béland, Daniel.
 The politics of policy change : welfare, medicare, and social
security reform in the United States / by Daniel Béland and Alex
Waddan.
     p. cm. — (American governance and public policy series)
 Includes bibliographical references and index.
 ISBN 978-1-58901-884-6 (pbk. : alk. paper)
 1. United States—Social policy. 2. Public welfare—United States.
3. Medicare. 4. Social security—United States. 5. United States—
Politics and government. I. Waddan, Alex, 1964- II. Title.
 HN65.B423 2012
 361.6'10973—dc23

                         2011035688

∞ This book is printed on acid-free paper meeting the
requirements of the American National Standard for
Permanence in Paper for Printed Library Materials.

18 17 16 15 14 13 12   9 8 7 6 5 4 3 2
First printing

Printed in the United States of America

This book is dedicated to Angela and Cheryl

Contents

Preface   ix

Introduction   1

Chapter One: Welfare Reform, 1996   24

Chapter Two: Medicare Reform, 2003   74

Chapter Three: The Failed Attempt at Social Security
                   Privatization, 2005   125

Conclusion   167

References   179

Index   213

Preface

In March 2010 President Barack Obama signed the most comprehensive health care reform in the United States since the enactment of Medicare and Medicaid forty-five years earlier. In order to increase coverage to the uninsured and control rising health care costs, among other things, this reform brings comprehensive change to some aspects of America's complex public–private health insurance system and revises other parts in a more incremental manner. The heated nature of the debate surrounding this key legislation and the compromises necessary for the president and the Democratic majorities in Congress to enact a reform in the first place showed once again how the politics of policy change is both risky and complicated, especially when it involves dealing with powerful vested interests and a nervous public. This in turn illustrates the need for scholars and other commentators on public affairs to have a proper understanding of the dynamics of the process of policy change. What motivates political actors and policymakers to pursue a reform agenda? And what are the opportunities and challenges they face? To help deepen understanding of these processes, this book explores the politics of policy change in the United States through a systematic comparison of three major policy areas and policy episodes: the 1996 welfare reform, the 2003 Medicare reform, and the 2005 failed attempt to privatize Social Security.

These three cases had quite distinct immediate outcomes. First, there was a sharp, conservative reform of welfare as the Aid to Families with Dependent Children program, initially established in the 1930s, was ended and replaced by a new program called Temporary Assistance to Needy Families (with an emphasis on "Temporary"). Second, during the George W. Bush years, legislation was enacted to reform Medicare but, as a social policy reform, this was less radical and more ideologically ambiguous. This is true because the introduction of a prescription drug benefit for seniors was accompanied by a series of less publicized but potentially significant conservative minded changes. Finally, the attempt to reform Social Security ended in dismal legislative failure. Despite these different outcomes, the three cases share common themes, particularly with regard to the importance of ideas and their interaction with other causal factors such as issue ownership and institutional legacies. Placing our discussion of the three episodes and their aftermath in the context of these factors allows us to develop an empirically grounded and integrated analytical framework that should help others to better grasp the politics of policy change in the field of social policy and well beyond.

In putting forward this framework, this book explicitly contributes to the debate about the nature and the sources of policy change in advanced industrial societies associated with the work of scholars such as Jacob Hacker and Kathleen Thelen. Yet, because our book is deliberately written in a clear and accessible manner, we hope that informed, nonacademic readers interested in federal social policy reform in the United States will find our empirical analysis and our general remarks about policy change insightful. The development of the federal welfare state is and will remain a major issue in the politics of the United States, and we strongly believe that systematically comparing specific yet important policy areas is an important way to further explore what Paul Pierson famously called "the new politics of the welfare state." As we show, much has changed in social policy since the Clinton years, and our framework, we believe, offers a compelling way to explain both incremental and sharp policy changes that have taken place in the federal welfare state since 1993. Although our book focuses on the Bill Clinton and the George W. Bush years, our analysis of the three policy episodes listed earlier leads to remarks about more recent developments, including the 2010 health insurance reform. Overall, our book should help the reader better understand and explain major social policy developments in contemporary federal politics.

This project began in 2005, when Daniel Béland met series coeditor Gerry Boychuk at the annual American Political Science Association meeting in Washington, DC. Gerry mentioned the possibility of writing a book on US social policy for his series, something that Daniel found very exciting. Immediately after the meeting, he contacted his friend and long-time collaborator, Alex Waddan, to see whether they could collaborate on this project. Alex had already published extensively on welfare reform and Daniel had just published a book on the history and politics of Social Security, so they decided to compare the two policy areas while bringing in a field of inquiry that was relatively new to both of them: health care and, more specifically, Medicare reform. From the start, the main goal was to engage with the most recent literature on institutional and policy change to shed new light on the politics of welfare state reform in the United States. Later, the authors conducted a series of interviews with policy actors involved in the welfare, Medicare, and Social Security debates, respectively. They also surveyed the literature on the three reform episodes while studying media and political discourse surrounding them.

Many people helped us in preparing this book. At Georgetown University Press, Don Jacobs, as well as the three editors of the American Governance and Public Policy series, Gerry Boychuk, Karen Mossberger, and Mark Rom, provided much-needed advice along the road. We warmly thank the three anonymous reviewers, as well as Ed Berkowitz, Larry DeWitt, Sascha Muennich, and Patrick Sachweh for their comments and suggestions. We would like to thank research assistants Crystal Boeur and Ruben Sierra for their support and enthusiasm. Daniel Béland acknowledges support from the Canada Research Chairs Program, the University of Saskatchewan, the Johnson-Shoyama Graduate School of Public Policy, and the Woodrow Wilson International Center for

Scholars, where he spent five months as a public policy scholar from January to May 2008. Alex Waddan would like to thank colleagues at the University of Leicester for their help and support. Finally, we are both grateful to the many people who gave their time and agreed to be interviewed for this book. We dedicate this book to our respective spouses, Angela and Cheryl, who have been very supportive, as always.

Introduction

S ince the New Deal, social policy reform has remained a key and controversial aspect of federal politics. The sheer scope of the major federal programs created since the 1930s makes it inevitable that policymakers will revisit these programs because they are so central to American social and economic life. In turn, this means that social policy developments have a direct impact on American politics as political actors position themselves as being in support of, or in opposition to, particular programs. Today, programs such as Medicare and Social Security, which have enormous fiscal and political weight, are subject to intense scrutiny and their long-term future provokes heated dispute. As for debates on issues such as universal health coverage, they divide citizens, interests groups, and politicians alike. Interestingly, as the 2009–10 health care debate illustrated, the contemporary politics of social policy reform in the United States, as in other developed countries, has different and contradictory facets, partly because cost control imperatives and attempts to improve social protection in a changing economic and social context come into conflict (Howard 2006; Quadagno and Street 2006).

Considering the size of the federal deficit and the accumulated debt that the United States faces, such contradictory patterns are likely to remain a key feature of federal politics in the years to come. The election of Barack Obama to the presidency in 2008 amid an ongoing and major economic downturn exaggerated these challenges as the president's supporters on the left urged bold action to extend social protections to Americans in need while conservatives protested that the country could simply not afford extra spending on social programs and that, furthermore, expanding the federal welfare state was fundamentally the wrong answer to the problems the country faced. Yet, importantly, these types of debates and struggles are anything but new in American politics, and looking at past policy episodes can provide insight into the contemporary politics of federal social policy change.

Drawing on international scholarly literatures about the conditions and the sources of policy change in developed societies, this book compares and contrasts developments in three major federal policy areas: welfare, Medicare, and Social Security. The main goal of this study is to improve our understanding of the politics of policy change in contemporary federal politics. Crucially, we argue that it is necessary to pay close attention to ideas when explaining concrete episodes of policy change, including incremental change. Yet the argument of the book is not simply to state that "ideas matter." Instead, the study presents an integrated ideational and institutional framework to explore *how* ideas matter (Béland and Cox 2011; Jacobs 2009a; Mehta 2011) in relationship to particular forms of policy change and to other potential causal factors, namely institutions and issue ownership. To show the added value of this framework, the book concentrates on three cases of social policy reform (or attempted reform) that took place during the presidencies of Bill Clinton and George W. Bush.

The federal policy areas mentioned earlier, welfare, Medicare, and Social Security, were selected for scrutiny because of their importance in the everyday lives of many millions of Americans, which in turn makes the debates concerning their future highly controversial. Furthermore, the discussion of three distinct programs and policy episodes allows us to offer a more systematic empirical analysis aimed at testing important analytical claims about the nature and the sources of policy change. Drawing on the integrated framework sketched in the following discussion, the book offers new insights about the varying dynamics affecting federal social policy through its focus on three reform cases: the 1996 welfare reform, the 2003 Medicare legislation, and the 2005 attempt to privatize Social Security. These three cases have been subject to individual study (e.g., Altman 2005; Jaenicke and Waddan 2006b; Weaver 2000), but the systematic comparison presented here provides new insight, and, taken together, these episodes illustrate the applicability of our integrated framework while stressing the diversity of the reform paths that have emerged in federal social policy since the 1990s.[1] Moreover, the book does not simply stop its examination of the three policy domains as if the events of 1996, 2003, and 2005 were end points. Little understood but important changes were made to the 1996 welfare reform when it was reauthorized in 2005 that had the effect of further reinforcing the direction of the earlier reform. As part of the 2010 federal overhaul of health care arrangements, the Medicare program was again reformed while the debate over the sustainability of the Social Security program has been ongoing. By taking into account what happened in the years following our three reform episodes, we offer new insight into their meaning and long-term impact, an approach consistent with the analytical framework outlined below.

By using this integrated framework, our study sheds new light on these three areas of policymaking and contributes to the debates about the sources of policy change in developed societies, and about reform possibilities in contemporary federal social policy. For example, how do we explain that, over the last two decades, conservative ideas have proved highly influential in the reform of welfare, moderately so with regard to Medicare reform yet less so in Social Security reform? Also, why did a Democratic president, Bill Clinton, sign into law a bill that reduced access to welfare benefits? Why did a Republican president, George W. Bush, successfully push for the largest Medicare expansion for seniors since the creation of the program? And why did a Republican Congress fail to support a Republican president's efforts to introduce a degree of privatization to the Social Security system? These questions raise important analytical issues about the nature of policy change and the factors that can explain change—or the absence of meaningful change—in the first place.

Overall, our book explores two broad sets of issues: how to identify different levels of policy change, and, once we have accurately described change, how to explain policy outcomes through the analysis of concrete political cases. This type of analytical yet empirically grounded perspective on programs and political episodes also helps us assess the prospects for change in contemporary federal social policy.

Institutions

From an analytical perspective, the starting point of our book is historical institutionalism, an approach pointing to the political impact of formal and informal political institutions, which generally refer to the historically embedded "rules of the game" that shape the behavior of individual and collective actors.[2] These institutions range from constitutional rules and political parties to informal norms and concrete policy legacies (Amenta 1998; Bonoli 2000; Campbell 2004; Hacker 2002; Hall and Taylor 1996; Immergut 1998; Lecours 2005; Maioni 1998; Orloff 1993; Orren and Skowronek 2004; Pierson 1994, 2001; Skocpol 1992; Steinmo, Thelen, and Longstreth 1992; Weaver and Rockman 1993).[3] In the United States, historical institutionalism is related to an even broader intellectual tradition known as American Political Development (Orren and Skowronek 2004).

To improve our understanding of American politics, this book draws explicitly on two contributions from historical institutionalism. First, like other students of American politics, we start from the perspective that political institutions create major constraints and opportunities that, often in combination with other factors, directly impact the behavior of political actors. For example, in the United States, the separation of powers, the system of checks and balances, and the related fragmentation of federal authority often make it difficult for reformers to successfully promote the implementation of path-departing social and economic programs (Pierson 1994). As evidenced by the New Deal in the United States, massive and sharp path-departing reforms are possible, but institutional fragmentation and the lack of formal party discipline reduce their prospect, at least under normal economic and political circumstances (Skocpol 1992). Although this book rejects overly deterministic frameworks that focus almost exclusively on formal political institutions to predict policy outcomes (e.g., Steinmo and Watts 1995; for a critique, see Hacker 1997), it recognizes the impact of institutional fragmentation and the lack of formal party discipline on federal welfare-state politics.[4]

Second, our book draws on the concept of policy feedback, which points to the weight of previously enacted policies and the institutional obstacles and opportunities these policies create (Hacker 1998; Immergut 1998; Orloff 1993; Pierson 1994, 2000; Steinmo, Thelen, and Longstreth 1992; Weaver and Rockman 1993).

In general, policy feedback is about how existing social and economic programs are likely to shape future policy decisions by affecting the perceptions and strategies of policymakers as well as their capacity to bring about policy change in a specific area. For instance, massive social programs such as Medicare and Social Security have created large constituencies that political actors must take into account when they seek to reform such programs (Campbell 2003; Pierson 1994). In this book, faithful to the historical institutionalist tradition, we pay systematic attention to the feedback effects produced by existing social programs, especially the constituencies and vested interests they may create over time. Yet we also recognize that policy institutions (in our case social programs) do not reproduce themselves automatically; active support and mobilization is often necessary to maintain them over time (Mahoney and Thelen 2009). Equally important, although less apparent in much of the existing literature, we recognize the potential role of negative feedback effects, a concept referring to the fact that policy institutions do not always benefit from self-reproduction mechanisms, as some of their intrinsic features can weaken them over time (Weaver 2010).

Authors such as Jacob Hacker have argued that key historical institutionalist claims regarding the impact of policy legacies on welfare state development also apply to private benefits (Béland 2007b; Béland and Hacker 2004; Hacker 2002).[5] According to these authors, well-established private schemes create constraints and opportunities for policymakers that are similar to the ones stemming from public social programs. Moreover, private schemes promoted through federal incentives and regulations can ironically serve as an explicit model for the reform of public benefits (Hacker 2004; Teles 1998). The example of the push for personal savings accounts as part of the Social Security system discussed in chapter 3 provides ground to this claim. From this angle, the development of government-sponsored private provision is not always an obstacle to reform because, under specific circumstances, it may also provide an impetus for policy change. As evidenced in this book, in order to understand what is going on inside the federal welfare state, the study of policy feedback should focus on both public and private benefits (Béland and Hacker 2004). Many older Americans, for example, have their Medicare coverage supplemented by continuing coverage from a former employer, or they take out a so-called Medigap insurance package to help cover the cost of the deductibles and copayments built in to the Medicare program. Over time this has reduced the pressure to expand Medicare to cover those costs.

In the social policy literature, the concept of policy feedback is also crucial to understand what Paul Pierson (1994, 1996) calls the "new politics of the welfare state." According to Pierson the "politics of expansion" that characterized the postwar era has been supplanted by the "politics of retrenchment." This latter period constitutes a different political reality because it is marked by direct and indirect attempts to control social spending and curtail social programs in the name of fiscal austerity. Pierson argues, "The welfare state now faces a context of essentially permanent austerity" (2001, 411).[6] Conversely, feedback effects from existing programs have largely shaped the options available to political actors in the era of retrenchment. That is, in the postwar era, new social programs—and the expansion of existing ones such as Social Security—created "armies of beneficiaries" that typically mobilize to protect the programs that served them (Pierson 1996, 146).

To pursue their retrenchment agenda while reducing the electoral risks they face, politicians pursue various "blame avoidance strategies" that can make painful changes less visible or diffuse blame for "bad news" among various actors (Pierson 1996; Weaver 1986).[7] Overall, social policy development is described as a path-dependent process in which "external shocks" are the most likely sources of major, path-departing change leading to the elimination or the creation of large economic and social programs (Pierson 2000).

Although it is true that existing policy legacies do impact political decisions about the future of social policy programs, there are several aspects of Pierson's framework that we find problematic. First, there is evidence that, in the United States, as in most other developed countries, contemporary welfare state politics is not only about retrenchment. Although controlling social spending is a key issue in most policy areas, the last thirty years have witnessed a combination of changes reflecting not only retrenchment but also other changes that favor an expansion or a redefinition of state action that transcends the idea of retrenchment (e.g., Béland 2010b; Gilbert 2002; Howard 2006; Palier 2002). In the American context, this is well illustrated by the example of health care reform. Although cost control is a key imperative in the United States, it is not the only aspect of the contemporary health care debate in which the plight of the uninsured and the attempt to increase coverage is a central concern. In fact, in the United States, the last two decades have witnessed a significant expansion of the Medicaid program and the addition of a prescription drug benefit to Medicare (Howard 2006). The 2010 federal health care reform, discussed in chapter 2, further expanded Medicaid and, more generally, the role of the federal government in health care policy. Second, contrary to Pierson's (2000) suggestion, systematic, path-departing change is possible in the absence of "external shocks" such as massive economic crises (Mahoney and Thelen 2009). The enactment of the 1996 welfare reform is an example of this type of comprehensive reform that took place in the absence of "external shock." Even if the 1996 welfare reform typifies retrenchment, it suggests that major policy change is possible in the contemporary welfare state. Overall, recognizing the limits of the concepts of retrenchment and path dependence is necessary to provide a subtler picture of federal welfare-state politics in contemporary American society.

Mechanisms of Policy Change

This critical discussion of Paul Pierson's work points to the ongoing debate about the potential sources and the nature of policy change in contemporary developed societies (e.g., Brown et al. 2010; Campbell 2004; Clemens and Cook 1999; Hacker

2004; Hinrichs and Kangas 2003; Mahoney and Thelen, 2009; Marier 2008; Palier 2002; Steinmo 2010; Thelen 2004; Streeck and Thelen 2005; Weaver 2010).[8] The framework formulated in this book recognizes the limitations of the "punctuated equilibrium model" according to which path-departing change taking place during rare "critical junctures" is followed by long periods of institutional stability characterized by path-dependent change (Mahoney and Thelen 2009; Thelen 2004).[9] In fact, our framework starts from the perspective that path-departing change can emerge gradually outside such junctures.[10] From this angle, the line between incremental and path-departing change is blurred in the sense that seemingly minor changes can have transformative consequences over time (Hacker 2004; Mahoney and Thelen 2009; Streeck and Thelen 2005; Thelen 2004). A proper understanding of contemporary welfare state politics, therefore, needs to be informed by the study of these relatively undramatic but potentially transformative processes of change. This is especially true in the United States, where institutional fragmentation and related obstacles to comprehensive reform make incremental strategies especially attractive to federal policymakers, who can use them to weaken the programs they seek to replace and promote alternatives using subtle, "subterranean" means (Hacker 2004).

Three main forms of incremental yet potentially path-departing changes are discussed in the literature (Hacker 2004; Mahoney and Thelen 2009). First, layering involves "the grafting of new elements onto an otherwise stable institutional framework. Such amendments . . . can alter the overall trajectory of an institution's development" (Thelen 2004, 35).[11] Second, conversion refers to situations when formal institutional rules remain the same but are "interpreted and enacted in new ways" as actors "actively exploit the inherent ambiguities of the institutions" (Mahoney and Thelen 2009, 17). Third, policy drift points to the fact that new economic and social trends can transform the role and the effects of existing social policies in the absence of major reforms. This is true because political inaction on the part of policymakers who refuse to enact reforms designed to update existing programs is a form of political behavior that can ironically lead to significant yet gradual policy transformations in the context of rapid economic and social change (Hacker 2004; Hacker and Pierson 2010).

Importantly, these three incremental mechanisms of potentially transformative policy change do not entirely displace but exist alongside comprehensive legislative revision, which is about swiftly creating, discarding, or explicitly transforming social programs (Hacker 2004).[12] While two of the cases at the center of this book prominently feature layering and other incremental forms of change, our analysis of the 1996 welfare reform (chapter 1) provides a striking example of comprehensive legislative revision.

Concepts such as layering and policy drift are useful to describe how, over time, incremental changes can lead to path-departing reforms. But in themselves, we claim, these concepts explain little, which is why scholars who use them, such as James Mahoney and Kathleen Thelen (2009), have attempted to account for why specific forms of change take place in specific contexts. For these authors, characteristics of the political context, especially the presence or the absence of specific veto points, interact with the features of the targeted institutions (in our case, particular social programs) to help determine which type of change strategy actors mobilize (Mahoney and Thelen 2009, 19), which points directly to the two elements of historical institutionalism at the center of our own framework: the impact of formal political institutions (the "political context") and feedback effects from policy legacies.

Although recognizing the role of formal institutions and policy legacies in shaping the reform strategies of political actors, Mahoney and Thelen (2009) offer a narrow understanding of what motivates these actors to bring about change— or to support the status quo—in the first place. For these two scholars, material interests related to the perceived distributional effects of the targeted institutions are determining factors in actors' behavior. Yet this vision of actors' motivations is too deterministic because it leaves little room to the ideational processes according to which actors make sense of their political and institutional world. In their framework aimed at "explaining institutional change," for example, Mahoney and Thelen (2009) reduce the role of cognitive processes to the "ambiguity" inherent to some institutional legacies and their related distributive consequences.[13] Such an overly limited acknowledgment of the fact that the ideas of actors affect their behavior explains why these two scholars formulate a seemingly arbitrary typology of "types of change agents" that simply describe forms of behavior rather than stressing the deeply rooted assumptions, beliefs, and perceptions of actors, which are far more than a simple reflection of institutional structures and material interests (Béland and Cox 2011). We argue here that because nonideational approaches to policy change do not systematically account for the ideological motivations of "change agents" that make them "change agents" in the first place, such approaches cannot explain why actors choose to pursue specific reform strategies. In other words, these approaches are unable to comprehensively explain specific patterns of policy change because they fail to systematically analyze the beliefs and motivations of actors that give substance to agency. By bringing the role of ideas to the forefront of the analysis of both sharp and incremental change, our framework offers a better way to explain policy change.

Before we move on to discuss the ideational component for our analytical framework, it is crucial to explain why we turn to ideas rather than to other potential causal factors. This is especially true of material factors that are well-known alternatives to ideational factors in the social science and policy literature.[14] As the ideational literature cited in the following section makes clear, although material factors such as financial cycles and economic structures directly impact the politics of policy change, under most circumstances these factors typically matter at least in part as a consequence of the ways actors perceive them. Thus, ideational factors help mediate the political impact of material and environmental factors, which matter largely through the perceptions of actors. The same remark applies to "material interests" because actors must make sense of them before act-ing upon them (Hay 2011). This is especially true in periods of economic uncer-tainty, when what is good for actors becomes blurred at best (Blyth 2002). More generally, because ideas are necessary for actors to make sense of their world as well as their position within it, we should play close attention to ideas when study-ing the behavior, networks, and strategic preferences of political actors involved in policy change (Béland and Cox 2011).

Ideas

The main argument of this book and a key assumption of our integrated frame-work is that bringing ideas (defined as "claims about descriptions of the world, causal relationships, or the normative legitimacy of certain actions"; Parsons 2002, 48) to the forefront of institutional analysis is absolutely necessary to explain spe-cific cases of policy change.[15] Take the examples of conversion, layering, and pol-icy drift. To understand the dominant direction that these processes and strategies take (e.g., producing market friendly or redistributive outcomes), we must pay close attention to the ideas and assumptions of actors who promote them (Béland 2007a). As Mark Blyth (2002) has shown in his study of economic policy in Sweden and the United States, shared policy ideas help actors reduce uncertainty and cre-ate political coalitions that challenge existing institutional and policy frameworks. For instance, it has been argued that ideas help actors make sense of their inter-ests that are not simply derived from their economic and institutional position (Béland and Cox 2011; Blyth 2002; Campbell 2004; Hay 2011; Jenson 1989; King 1973; Schmidt 2011; Steensland 2006, 2008; Stone 1997; Weir 1992). This is cru-cial because coalition building is partly about the construction of interests (Blyth 2002). According to this literature, alongside institutional obstacles and incen-tives, ideas motivate actors to behave in certain ways and forge political alliances with other actors as they give meaning to the world around them and what they see as beneficial for them and their constituencies.

From this perspective, because ideas help explain the behavior, policy deci-sions, and strategic choices of actors, policy change has a strong ideational com-ponent, and, we argue, paying attention to ideas is necessary to account for the direction and meaning of policy change (e.g., liberal, conservative, or "third way"). Our main argument is not that ideas alone always explain change or that ideational shifts always result in concrete policy change but that paying close attention to the ideas of political actors helps explain both continuity and change. Although embedded ideas taking the form of policy paradigms can reinforce the legitimacy of existing institutions, in many cases actors seeking to bring change to existing policy legacies promote new ideas that they then attempt to sell to other actors in order to create a coalition or construct the "need to reform" (Cox 2001) existing policy legacies. This is one of the key ways in which ideas matter for policy change.

Another important role ideas play in policy change is to shape the perception of the issues moving in and out of the agenda. In this context, agenda-setting scholars such as Kingdon (1995) study the assumptions of policymakers about what they perceive as the most important problems of the day.[16] Debates about the efficiency and the quality of programs impact the perception of the policy issues that actors attempt to address (Weir 1992, 18; see also Hall 1993; Heclo 1974; King and Hansen 1999; Rose 2004; Sabatier 1988; Stone 1997). In the United States, the welfare debate that raged during the 1980s and the first half of the 1990s illustrates how ideas can impact the construction of social problems (see chapter 1). In that debate, social problems ranging from teen pregnancy to unemployment and racial inequality became prominent political issues that actors understood in the mirror of existing policy legacies, in particular the Aid to Families with Dependent Children program (AFDC). Ideas play an important role in serving as basic assumptions and beliefs that help actors to make sense of these policy legacies and to design appropriate alternatives aimed at addressing the policy challenges they face (Blyth 2002). The concept of policy paradigm illustrates the impact of such assumptions on policy development (Albrekt Larsen and Goul Andersen 2009; Hall 1993; Merrien 1997; Skogstad 2011). With regard to AFDC, conservatives promoted the idea that cash benefits were damaging to welfare recipients by fostering welfare dependency rather than helpful by alleviating poverty (see chapter 1). As this initially controversial interpretation of the role of AFDC gained ground, it created an environment in which the program was increasingly seen as fundamentally broken and in need of massive repair. Yet, our book does not focus primarily on policy paradigms because they only constitute one type of idea among others (in this case, a set of ideas) in the policy process. This is due to the fact that policy ideas do not always take the shape of a coherent paradigm (Wincott 2011). In fact, policy actors tend to borrow from different sources when they formulate their policy blueprints (Campbell 2004; Carstensen 2011). One original aspect of our study in the context of the growing literature on ideas is that, instead of focusing only on the role of ideas in comprehensive institutional revision, which is associated with the concept of "paradigm shift," we explore the role of ideas in both institutional revision (the 1996 welfare reform) and transformative incremental change (the 2003 Medicare reform and policy drift in private pensions, which are closely related to Social Security).[17]

Beyond policy paradigms, ideas as assumptions can also take the form of strategic deliberations according to which actors develop political tactics aimed at reaching their goals (Béland and Waddan 2010). This means that once actors have a clear idea of what their goals and preferences are, they attempt to formulate coherent political strategies about how to advance their perceived interests.[18] Studying the strategic ideas of politicians is essential because these ideas shed light on the behavior of actors as they attempt to bring about or oppose policy change. Taking the example of the 2003 Medicare reform (see chapter 2), our book shows that the decision to develop health savings accounts as part of this legislation is part of a broader strategy to promote a conservative—individualistic—vision of social policy. Although existing institutional settings played a role in that strategic choice, as we show, it is impossible to explain it without turning to the motivations and strategies of the conservative actors who believe in the political and economic value of personal health savings accounts stemming directly from their ideological belief in the virtues of individualism and "consumer choice" (see chapter 2). This also applies to the development of retirement savings accounts and defined contribution pensions, which have been layered alongside the Social Security program (Hacker 2004). There is strong evidence that conservatives supported this trend conducive to policy drift because they believed that, later on, it would help them make a stronger case for Social Security privatization (Teles 1998).

Finally, ideas serve as ideological frames that help actors make a case for reform (Béland 2005; Campbell, 1998, 2004; Schmidt 2002; Schön and Rein 1994). Ideological frames can help particular actors legitimize or oppose policy change (Bhatia and Coleman 2003; Cox 2001; Schmidt 2002). In the United States, ideological frames are consistently present in social policy debates. For instance, in the 1980s and early 1990s, a popular frame central to the debates on welfare reform was the "perversity thesis" popularized by Charles Murray (1984) that welfare programs, however well intentioned, were not a solution to existing social problems. In fact, according to this framing narrative, welfare programs exacerbated social problems by creating "perverse" incentives that seemed to offer short-term reward to welfare recipients that actually locked those recipients into a damaging spiral of dependency (Somers and Block 2005). As suggested in chapter 1, once Clinton, a Democratic president, acknowledged that "welfare as we know it" was the problem, the "need to reform" (Cox 2001) was irreversibly established and used by conservatives to justify the enactment of a landmark legislation that would effectively end AFDC.

Overall, this book shows how ideas matter in the politics of both sharp and incremental policy change. As argued, in addition to looking at institutional constraints and opportunities, turning to ideas as embedded assumptions and ideological frames is essential to explain the strategies of actors and the choices they make when they try to bring about policy change. Instead of focusing primarily on "paradigms shifts" in time of perceived crisis like so many other scholars, our analysis contributes to the analysis of ideas and policy change by pointing to the relationship between ideational and incremental institutional processes as they relate to actor mobilization in an ideologically divided political environment.[19]

Issue Ownership

Another innovative aspect of our integrated framework is that it bridges the literature on ideas and institutions in policy change with the scholarship on issue ownership (Petrocik 1996; Ross 2007), a concept that refers to the political "parties' recognized capacity or reputation to deal competently with a number of issues and problems . . . . To appeal to voters, policy positions taken by a party have to be credible and therefore have to be minimally consistent with the party's past positions and commitments" (Bélanger 2003, 540).[20] In the United States, the two-party system somewhat simplifies the logic of issue ownership, which typically refers to "the idea that the Democratic and Republican parties each 'own' a set of issues which the public trusts the party as substantially better able to 'handle' than the other party" (Egan 2006, 3). The need for ideational analysis to bring issue ownership to the forefront stems from the fact that the policy ideas and frames put forward by political actors must be credible in order to help these actors construct the "need to reform" (Cox 2001) and convince the public and interest groups to support them. In general, this credibility depends largely on how actors who formulate such ideas are perceived by the general public and key constituencies, and on their perceived relationship with the specific policy issue they seek to address. Thus, some policy ideas and ideological frames are more likely to become influential when it is widely believed that the politicians who put them forward know what they are talking about and, importantly, can be trusted when dealing with a particular issue or program (Shafer and Claggett 1995). In some cases, a specific party may effectively have political "ownership" of an issue because the public trusts that party more than their opponents to address that issue well. For example, in the United States, citizens typically trust Republicans more than Democrats when issues such as fighting terrorism and reinforcing national security are at the fore. In other areas such as Social Security reform, the opposite is true (Ross 2007).

As this book suggests, issue ownership is a central aspect of the politics of ideas surrounding policy reform.[21] Yet, as we argue, where federal welfare state politics is concerned, issue ownership is frequently much more complex than a superficial look may suggest. In particular, our examination of issue ownership is not entirely derived from the analysis of public opinion data, which is not always available to measure the sometimes-subtle changes in issue ownership during key policy moments. In addition to public opinion data, we believe that it is possible to draw on interview data, political discourse, and media commentary to understand how issue ownership evolves over time. From this perspective, our discussion of issue ownership is innovative because it departs from the purely quantitative approach of other scholars using this concept.

Regarding issue ownership, our analysis shows that, whereas Social Security as an issue is largely "owned" by Democrats, health care and welfare reform are far more ambiguous from a partisan perspective. First, as far as health care is concerned, although Democrats have an advantage when the time comes simply to defend Medicare against overt attacks, health care reform at large is a potential minefield for politicians, both Democrat and Republican. This is true because the tasks of expanding coverage and controlling costs—tasks central to the recent health care debate—involve potential trade-offs that are hard to sell to key segments of the population who are afraid to lose what they have (in this case, public or private insurance coverage) in the name of "change." Second, before the enactment of the 1996 legislation, welfare reform involved major political and electoral risks for Democrats. Here, Republicans were quite successful in reframing welfare as a moral problem tied to so-called American values (Stryker and Ward 2009). When then-governor Clinton chose to emphasize a commitment to "end welfare as we know it" during the 1992 presidential campaign, he was deliberately challenging conventional party positioning on the issue of welfare by dissociating himself from the established image of Democrats as "soft" on welfare recipients. Hence, a central political actor divorced himself from his party's position on a key social policy question. This strategy illustrates the complexity of the concept of issue ownership. Keeping this in mind, our analysis illustrates the different factors involved in successfully constructing a "need to reform" particular policies (Cox 2001). It is important to consider the agency of political actors and the role of their ideas in the context of the relationship that those actors are perceived to have with existing programs and policy legacies. Moreover, from an institutionalist standpoint, it is also easier to make a case for reform if such legacies are tied to weaker constituencies, as was the case with welfare recipients in the years preceding the enactment of the 1996 federal legislation. When assessing the strength of a program's constituencies, it is crucial to look beyond the direct beneficiaries of cash or in-kind aid and to consider other groups that may have a vested interest in a program's future. For instance, when policymakers deliberate over reforming Medicare and Medicaid, they take into account the wishes of health care providers. With regard to AFDC, although welfare bureaucrats may have preferred policy inertia to change, there was no equivalent economic interest to doctors and hospitals with a stake in the outcome of reform.

The discussion about issue ownership brings into focus the key role political parties and of public perceptions in the politics of policy change, and highlights the relationship between ideas and institutional processes.[22] On one hand, politicians frame their policy ideas in relationship to their perceived ownership—or lack of ownership—of a specific policy issue. Or at least their proposals are commonly interpreted in the mirror of the apparent relationship between their party and the policy domain and program at stake. On the other hand, the way citizens and key constituencies perceive issue ownership is related to existing policy legacies in the sense that a party may have long identified with a program because officials belonging to the same party created and expanded it in the first place. But this does not mean that members of the other party cannot reframe the issue to their advantage, as Republicans did in the field of welfare reform.

An Integrated Framework

At the broader level, this discussion about issue ownership points to the interaction among actors, ideas, and institutions in politics and policymaking.[23] This points to the need for us to finally put the pieces of the puzzle together to clarify the articulation of the core elements of the integrated framework we use to analyze our three cases. Analytically, this framework is based on the assumption that drawing a clear analytical line between ideational and institutional processes, while recognizing the agency of political actors in a competitive electoral environment marked by issue ownership, helps to explain key policy episodes and sheds light on both stability and change in the federal welfare state (Parsons 2007). Recognizing that a number of institutional forces such as power fragmentation and the relative absence of party discipline that characterize the American polity are likely to constrain the impact of ideas on policymaking (Walsh 2000), we claim that paying close attention to the ideas of political actors is necessary to explain how and when they promote change and, more specifically, what strategies and type of change they favor. In general, change is promoted through their ideas, framing processes, and the way these interact with policy legacies, issue ownership, and changing electoral and economic circumstances, which have an impact on policy development largely through the way actors make sense of them. Leaving room for contingency, our integrated framework recognizes the existence of asymmetrical power relations, which are structured by existing institutions and policy legacies (Skocpol 1992) but also by ideas and cultural categories related to class, gender, and race that are reflected in existing institutional legacies, such as the distinction between the "deserving" poor and the "undeserving" poor central to American welfare programs (Fraser and Gordon 1994; Steensland 2006). As some of the best literature on gender and race suggest (e.g., Bleich 2002; Jenson 1989; Lieberman 2002; Orloff and Palier 2009), these two historically and socially constructed factors have a strong ideational component, something that our analysis directly takes into consideration, especially the discussion of the welfare debate (see chapter 1), which is deeply racialized and gendered (e.g., Orloff 2002; Schram, Soss, and Fording 2003). More generally, throughout this book we pay close attention to both the policy ideas of actors and the institutional frameworks that can empower them or can create obstacles to the implementation of such ideas in a concrete partisan context.

Considering these broad remarks, we can now formulate a set of analytical statements that should help clarify the relationship between the factors central to our integrated framework for the study of policy change. First, institutional factors, especially formal political rules and existing policy legacies, create constraints and opportunities for policy actors. Second, in addition to comprehensive legislative revision, incremental forms of policy change—namely, conversion, layering, and policy drift—can bring about path-departing change outside of episodes known as "critical junctures." Third, institutional factors alone do not determine the strategic choices of actors involved in political battles over policy change. Fourth, alongside institutions, ideational processes directly impact the choices of actors, which means that it is impossible to adequately study the policy process and specific forms of policy change such as conversion, layering, and policy drift without paying close attention to the ideas that motivate policy actors while framing their public discourse. Fifth, issue-ownership effects can either reinforce or weaken the political effectiveness of ideological campaigns and frames central to most policy episodes. Overall, it is the interaction between the features of political and policy institutions (programs), the ideational commitments of policy actors, and their partisan relationship to issues in a concrete political and electoral context that explain not only why path-departing policy change can occur (or not) but also what specific form (sharp or incremental) it is likely to take at a specific moment in time. As is often the case in politics, historical contingency and timing are crucial (Pierson 2004) because it is the changing relationship between our causal factors (ideas, institutions, and issue ownership) over time that explains policy outcomes and patterns of policy change. Because of the historical nature of our analysis, the framework developed here is not about making strict "predictions" concerning future behavior but about specifying the main causal factors and the way they interact over time to produce specific forms of policy change. From this perspective, our framework is likely to help scholars analyze other cases in the world of social policy and beyond.

Although our framework is not about predicting the future, it can help anticipate how actors are likely to behave under specific ideological, institutional, and partisan circumstances. For instance, our framework and the following empirical analysis suggest that, beyond the existence of concrete institutional obstacles to comprehensive reform, actors are likely to promote incremental forms of policy change when they have a strong ideological commitment against existing policy legacies. Because this commitment cannot be reduced to mere "material interests," our framework pushes scholars to pay close attention to the ideas of actors in order to understand the goals and strategies they pursue in concrete institutional and partisan contexts. From this perspective, the ideological motivations of actors largely drive policy change, even when it takes an incremental form. Moreover, while the presence of powerful policy legacies and institutional obstacles may explain why they embrace an incremental strategy such as layering, it is their ideas and perceptions that motivate them to support change in the first place. Conversely, only a close look at the ideas and beliefs of actors can help explain why they oppose change and support the status quo. From this perspective, ideational analysis is necessary to explain both stability and change, be it sharp or incremental. However, as our book suggests, the study of ideas is not only about looking for "paradigm shifts," which are rare and are not the only ideational sources of policy change. Beyond the apparent stability of policy paradigms, major ideological and institutional battles take place. This is especially the case in the context of American politics, where ideological and partisan polarization remains strong (Lakoff 2002) and is even increasing (Hacker and Pierson 2005b). Yet, following our institutionalist framework, it is clear that institutional factors such as the nature of existing policy legacies affect the strategies that actors adopt to pursue their ideological and partisan agenda.

Overall, this integrated approach provides new insight on the three main episodes examined in this book. The 1996 welfare reform was an example of retrenchment that was not driven simply by the new politics of austerity (Pierson 2001) but was a swift and ideologically driven form of legislative revision. With the 2003 Medicare reform, the Bush administration expanded the program to defuse the issue of a prescription drug benefit that was owned by the Democrats, but the law simultaneously incorporated and promoted conservative health policy preferences through layering processes. The result of the 2005 Social Security reform effort was legislative stasis, but it is important to appreciate why conservative advocates pushed their promarket ideas and to understand how the existence of seemingly powerful constituencies tied to the program encouraged them to pursue long-term, incremental strategies that are embedded in core ideological beliefs (Teles 1998). In short, the approach taken in this book helps explain a variety of social policy developments such as retrenchment, expansion, and stasis as well as the three incremental but potentially path-departing forms of policy change discussed earlier—conversion, layering, and policy drift.

Defining Policy Change

At this point of the discussion it is essential to define the "dependent variable" under study (policy change), which is not always well specified in existing social policy research (Clasen and Siegel 2007). Not defining policy change properly can lead to confusion as identified by Jill Quadagno and Debra Street (2006) in their survey of the recent American literature on welfare state change. In fact, there is no consensus about what should be defined as path-departing policy change. For instance, many scholars perceive the 1996 welfare reform as a path-departing reform, but it is possible to stress some forms of institutional and ideological continuity between AFDC and Temporary Assistance to Needy Families (TANF), the program that replaced it (Quadagno and Street 2006). The confusion here stems from the fact that path-departing change is sometimes implicitly understood as a full break from the past, which is extremely rare if not impossible under most circumstances (i.e., change is typically grounded in some form of ideological or institutional continuity). In the case of the 1996 welfare reform, although it is hard to describe the abolition of a major federal social program and the entitlement it offered as a minor change, it is true that the program remained a means-tested benefit largely aimed at single-parent families. But recognizing that some type of continuity is present in most forms of change does not mean that we should not recognize the existence of path-departing change at one level or another. Let's consider the well-known example of the French Revolution. In France, as Alexis de Tocqueville (1955) suggested, there was some continuity between the Ancient Regime and the Revolution through the expansion of the bureaucratic state. Recognizing that Tocqueville has a point does not mean that the Revolution itself was inconsequential, nor that it did not involve profound changes in other areas than state bureaucracy. Returning to the United States, we find that although the New Deal created new social programs and constituted a departure from the past in many aspects of welfare state development, the programs enacted before 1929 impacted future policy decisions, notably in the field of social assistance (Skocpol 1992). Acknowledging that some form of continuity is largely unavoidable in human life should not lead scholars to downplay the potential scope of change that actors can bring about in politics and policy development.

Beyond these general remarks, scholars must explain what they mean by "change" before they try to explain it (e.g., Capano and Howlett 2009; Capano 2009; Kay 2009; Quadagno and Street 2006). In this book we define policy change primarily in institutional terms in the sense that we focus on how social policy rules and institutions change or are reproduced over time. Of course, the policy importance of institutional changes to existing programmatic frameworks varies depending on the impact on the constituencies affected by the reform and in the context of the broader economic, social, and political environment. For example, we consider the imposition of welfare time limits as a key form of policy change because this change in institutional rules is likely to profoundly affect millions of beneficiaries. The change in welfare rules, imposing a five-year lifetime limit on welfare receipt for most recipients, meant that from the time that TANF replaced AFDC, many low-income families could not collect federal cash benefits in the long term as had previously been the case. The aim of the reorganization of welfare was to make these families behave differently. Whether or not that happens, the reform still means that the socioeconomic position of those families changed significantly as a consequence. More generally, as conservatives declared the 1996 reform to be a clear success story, this increased the likelihood that this policy change would have a wider affect on the future of other means-tested social policy entitlements in the United States. Thus, the time limits introduced as part of the 1996 welfare reform represent a categorical example of sharp policy change. But assessing the significance of incremental change can be more difficult. A small change can have wider unintended consequences, or legislative action designed to bring it about might be thwarted through the implementation process. Additionally, by definition transformative incremental change sees change take place over an extended period of time, which raises the issue of time frame addressed below.

Moreover, when assessing change, we should consider both public and private policy institutions and the relationship between them because changes in private social benefits can directly impact public programs, and vice versa (Béland and Hacker 2004; Hacker 2002). By focusing only on public benefits, scholars can lose track of the "big picture" and depict as static a policy landscape that is facing deep transformations, at least when private institutions are systematically taken into account (Hacker 2004). For instance, after the demise of Clinton's health care plan in 1994 there were some limited public policy changes. Conversely, there were significant changes in the wider delivery of health care driven by the movement of capital and the interaction of health care providers and insurers (White 2007a). In turn, these changes impacted on policymakers as they considered further public policy shifts.

Furthermore, we must recognize the complexity of policy legacies and the existence of contradictory trends that can simultaneously push a specific program or policy area in different directions. The case of American health care reform illustrates this remark because recent reforms have favored both extended public coverage for some categories of the population as well as the expansion of private providers and personal savings accounts (see chapter 2). In this book we recognize the complexity of policy change but we also try to make sense of recent trends and to assess the dominant directions they take in each of the policy areas under study. Additionally, although we focus primarily on institutional characteristics to define change, we do take the perceptions of actors into account when we assess the level of change.[24] In the case of the 1996 welfare reform, the fact that the vast majority of actors involved in the welfare reform believed that it represented a profound and even radical shift in social assistance policy is significant to us. Although reducing policy change to the perceptions of the actors involved would be problematic, we do take what they have to say about specific policy cases seriously.

Drawing on the earlier discussion, at the most general level we define path-departing change as a consequential change in policy rules and institutions that, sharply or gradually, alters the dominant course and features of major public or private policy developments. This points to the role of time frames in the analysis of policy change (i.e., it can take many years for the significance of policy change to fully materialize), which is a central issue for students of policy change (Campbell 2004). Although we know that it is sometimes premature to reach definite conclusions about the meaning and long-term impact of specific policy changes, we do make claims about the nature of the changes that have taken place in federal social policy since the beginning of the Clinton years.[25] In fact, we suggest that our three cases correspond to three distinct patterns of policy change, which makes our comparison especially insightful as far as policy change is concerned. Even if we selected these three cases because they represent major and controversial social policy areas that have durably moved to the center of the federal policy agenda at least once since 1993, we see them in hindsight as three different stories about the nature of policy change in the contemporary federal welfare state.

First, because of the factors discussed earlier, we see the 1996 welfare reform as a major institutional turning point and a key example of path-departing—conservative—policy change in American social policy. Second, we understand the 2003 Medicare reform as a major but complex and ambiguous form of policy change in which a significant expansion of the program took place simultaneously with the layering of promarket provisions and health savings accounts that are consistent with conservative policy ideas. Because the 2010 Affordable Care Act (ACA) only reversed some of these provisions, this new Democratic legislation has not dismantled the conservative ideas that have been embedded in Medicare since the

2003 reform. Finally, we describe the 2005 case as a conservative failure to promote the idea of privatization. In other words, the 2005 case is about stasis rather than change, at least as far as public social programs are concerned. However, we note that changes in private pension benefits that form the institutional and ideological backdrop of the privatization debate constitute crucial yet incremental developments that have reshaped the American pension system (Hacker 2004). The field of old-age pensions is thus characterized by a dual path: stability as far as Social Security is concerned and path-departing change in occupational pensions and private savings that directly involve tax incentives and government regulations.

By using our integrated framework to compare these three cases located in distinct policy areas, our book sheds new light on the nature and the political sources of policy change in the federal welfare state. It also helps understand subsequent developments and, in particular, the impact of the 2010 health care reform on Medicare.

Data and Analysis

Our book compares and contrasts three major reform episodes affecting three distinct policy areas: the 1996 welfare reform, the 2003 Medicare reform, and the failed 2005 Social Security privatization campaign. We decided to focus on three policy areas rather than on one because of the need to demonstrate the added value of our framework across political episodes and policy areas. Moreover, although it is relatively common to compare health care and pensions (e.g., Hacker 2002; Klein 2003), bringing welfare reform in is particularly insightful because of the sheer scope of the 1996 welfare reform. In fact, systematically comparing three cases allows us to test the added value of our framework by addressing different empirical puzzles. This is true because what we have here are three cases that are distinct in terms of their policy outcomes and political logics but that operate within the same basic environment (the American polity). As for the choice of these three policy areas, they are among the largest and the most debated within the federal welfare state, which allow us to contribute to the general literature about American social policy instead of focusing only on one program. By doing so, we place ourselves in a much better position to show the analytical insightfulness of our framework. Finally, although our approach is largely deductive, our integrated framework is grounded in empirical observations that we make through the detailed analysis of the three cases, which illustrate—and challenge us to explain— three distinct patterns of policy change. If we can show that ideas are necessary to explain both sharp and incremental policy change across three different cases and policy areas, we make a much stronger empirical case for it than if we focus on one policy area and its unavoidable idiosyncrasies. By comparing in detail the politics of policy change in welfare, Medicare, and Social Security, we demonstrate that our framework can be applied to more than one social policy area.

To explain and compare our three episodes, we will use a "process tracing" (Mahoney 2003) approach that will help us identify relevant institutional and ideational mechanisms while exploring how these mechanisms interact over time to produce change. More concretely, at the empirical level, this book is largely based on the analysis of policy documents, political speeches, and media reports. These data are essential to the study of policy ideas and framing processes that lie at the forefront of political discourse. To grasp less public strategic ideas about controversial issues such as deficit spending, we interviewed more than three dozen policymakers and advocates. We spoke to congressional aides, especially those working with members of Congress actively involved in at least one of the three main policy cases at stake. These interviews are especially crucial because they fed the analysis of the unspoken political strategies that represent a major but low-profile element of the politics of social policy. For example, with regard to the 2003 Medicare Modernization Act (MMA), the interviews provided an opportunity to assess the extent to which conservatives in Congress supported the 2003 MMA either as a result of electoral expediency (i.e., to satisfy the popular demand for a new drug benefit for seniors) or because of the policy layering that took place (i.e., the expanded availability of health savings accounts). Furthermore, we spoke to people working in think tanks, including former White House officials. We also interviewed a number of advocates from both sides of the partisan divide. Overall, we are aware that by their nature such interviews are of varying quality and value, and they do not, by themselves, constitute categorical evidence. This is why we also rely on other types of evidence, such as newspaper articles, political speeches, government documents, and scholarly contributions.

For the sake of clarity and to make the book more readable and accessible to readers who may not be familiar with these three policy areas, each of the following three empirical chapters offers a historical overview of the policy area under consideration. This type of overview is necessary not only to understand how the three programs under consideration work but also to sketch a clear picture of their major institutional and ideational features, without which the cases we study in detail in the last sections of each chapter would be impossible to explain. Because our starting point is historical institutionalism, we pay great attention to broad historical processes, both institutional and ideational. We believe that it is important to study the three cases and policy areas separately and in considerable detail while bringing in comparative remarks about the other two cases in each chapter when relevant. At the end of each chapter and in the book's conclusion we put the pieces of the puzzle together by systematically returning to the analytical issues outlined here. This approach allows the reader to know the cases well and to assess the veracity of our claims about the nature and the causes of change—or relative stasis—in the three policy areas.

Overview of the Three Cases

Since the beginning of the Clinton years, despite some high-profile failures such as the unsuccessful push to privatize Social Security in early 2005, there have been major policy changes in federal social policy. Perhaps the most radical example of social policy change in the United States since the 1960s is the 1996 welfare reform. This reform appeared as the triumph of conservative policy ideas. While there was a general consensus that welfare was ripe for reform and while Clinton promised reform in his 1992 campaign, the final legislation was more conservative (i.e., with a greater emphasis on work requirements rather than education and training, and with the introduction of lifetime limits) than earlier proposals, including the Clinton administration's own plan. As we suggest, policy ideas and framing processes played a crucial role in that case and, alongside the institutional vulnerability of AFDC, they help explain why path-departing change took place in that policy area.

As noted earlier, the 2003 MMA was a complex piece of legislation. Clearly, introducing a new prescription drug benefit entitlement for seniors was an expansion of the health care state (albeit with the significant so-called "donut hole"). But this new benefit was to be administered through the private sector, and the law refused to maximize the potential of Medicare's bargaining position to demand that pharmaceutical companies provide drugs more cheaply. Furthermore, the law expanded the availability of health savings accounts in line with President Bush's vision of the "ownership society." Hence, the 2003 legislation provides a striking example of ideologically driven layering. Critically, the health savings accounts provisions were instrumental in persuading many conservative Republicans in Congress to support the Bush administration's enactment of this controversial legislation even though they were wary of the expense of the new drug benefit (Rosenbaum 2003b). This illustrates the role of ideas in forging and strengthening political coalitions necessary to bring about policy change as conservative congressional Republicans were won over to the legislation largely because health savings accounts reflected their promarket and individualistic ideas. As suggested earlier, the 2010 ACA reversed some of the policy changes enacted seven years earlier. This is why chapter 2 discusses the impact of the 2010 reform on Medicare in relationship to the 2003 MMA.

With regard to Social Security, the Bush administration clearly suffered a huge political setback as its reform proposals made no legislative headway through 2005. As opposed to the two other policy areas, where issue ownership seemed both ambiguous and unstable, Social Security is a field where Democrats have a clear and stable advantage (Ross 2007). The ownership of Social Security helped Democrats unite against President Bush, whose poorly articulated ideas about Social Security privatization came under massive attack and failed to convince the public to support this policy alternative. Yet it is important to note that, despite this crushing defeat, this was the first time that a president explicitly supported Social

Security privatization, a well-known idea that previous Republican presidents (i.e., George H. W. Bush and Ronald Reagan) never publicly embraced. Finally, the absence of major legislative change to the Social Security program since 1983 does not mean that the field of retirement policy as a whole remains stable as profound changes in the nature of private pensions, such as the shift from defined benefit to defined contributions, evidence a clear source of policy drift (Hacker 2004).

These three cases have been studied before on an individual basis but this is the first attempt to systematically compare them to further explore policy change. Although we do draw on existing scholarship about each of our three cases, each empirical chapter is informed by our original analytical perspective and by the interview data that directly informed our analysis. This means that even people who know these cases relatively well should find something new about them, both at the empirical and at the analytical level. For instance, in the chapter on welfare reform, we argue that the waivers implemented in the years preceding the 1996 reform constituted an example of ideologically driven institutional layering that helped pave the way to reform.[26] As for the discussion about the 2003 Medicare reform, it benefits greatly from taking into account the content of the 2010 health insurance legislation, which consolidates some of the changes introduced in 2003 while reversing others. Finally, regarding Social Security, we show that the defeat of President Bush's push for Social Security privatization actually exacerbated institutional dualism within the American pension system. This means that, in part because of our interview data, in part because of our analytical perspective, and in part because of the hindsight provided by recent policy and political developments, our book makes a distinct empirical contribution to the welfare, Medicare, and Social Security literatures. Perhaps more important, beyond our three cases, this book feeds the ongoing scholarly debate about the nature and sources of policy change, notably through the introduction of an integrated framework and, especially, an emphasis on how ideas matter in both sharp and incremental change.

The empirical core of this book takes the form of three empirical chapters devoted to our three case studies in the following order: welfare, Medicare, and Social Security. Although these chapters feature comparative remarks about the three cases, we decided that devoting a stand-alone chapter to each of them under study was the best way to provide the necessary historical, ideological, and institutional background about each case. The conclusion then systematically compares the cases to draw broad analytical lessons and reinforces the contribution of our analytical framework to understanding social policy development. The conclusion finishes with a brief discussion about the relative weight of conservative ideas across our three policy areas and in contemporary American social policy in general.

Notes

1. The full scope of the relevant literature about our three cases is discussed in each of our three empirical chapters.
2. Historical institutionalism is distinct from organizational institutionalism and rational-choice institutionalism: Campbell 2004; Hall and Taylor 1996. For a critical perspective on this typology of institutionalisms, see Hay and Wincott 1998. Over the last two decades, scholars have also meshed historical institutionalism with the power resource approach, which focuses on the role of labor politics and, more generally, partisanship in welfare state development (Huber and Stephens 2001). Although our framework is not centered on labor power, it does recognize the impact of partisanship, notably through the inclusion of issue ownership as a potential causal factor interacting with ideational and institutional processes.
3. For a detailed critical overview of existing approaches to welfare state development, see Béland 2007b, 2010b; Myles and Quadagno 2002.
4. However, as Jacob Hacker and Paul Pierson (2005b) have convincingly shown, in the 1990s and 2000s, Republicans attempted to create something like party discipline in the US Congress. This in turn led to intensified levels of partisanship on both sides of the aisle (Aldrich and Rohde 1997–98, 2001; Fleisher and Bond 2004; Sinclair 2006). Nevertheless, from an institutional standpoint, it is clear that formal party discipline remains absent from federal institutions, as was evidenced by the failure of congressional Republicans to line up behind President Bush's Social Security reform effort in 2005. Throughout this book the concept of "welfare state" simply refers to the aggregation of major social programs that attempt to reduce inequality, poverty, and economic insecurity. For a systematic critical discussion of the concepts of "welfare state" and "social policy," see Béland 2010b.
5. In recent decades, a number of other scholars have systematically explored the role of private benefits in welfare state development (Béland and Gran 2008; Berkowitz and McQuaid 1980; Gilbert and Gilbert 1989; Gottschalk 2000; Howard 1997; Howard and Berkowitz 2008; Klein 2003; Quadagno 1988; Stevens 1988).
6. For a comparative perspective on the politics of austerity in the United States and Canada, see Pal and Weaver 2003.
7. Blame avoidance is explicitly defined in opposition to credit claiming (Weaver 1986). On credit claiming, see Mayhew 1974.
8. A work not discussed in detail here is Paul Pierson's *Politics in Time* (2004), which focuses on continuity and self-reinforcing mechanisms rather than on change.
9. For an explicit example of punctuated equilibrium analysis, see Baumgartner and Jones 1993. For systematic critiques of the concept of path dependence, see Brown 2010 and Kay 2005; for a debate, see Wilsford and Brown 2010.
10. Incrementalism is not a new idea in policy analysis (Lindblom 1959; see also Atkinson 2011; Hayes 2001).
11. On layering, see also Schickler 2001. This overview draws on Béland 2010a.

12. Comprehensive revision is also known as "displacement," according to which "existing rules are replaced by new ones" (Mahoney and Thelen 2009, 16). We should stress that, as we depict it throughout this book, revision typically occurs in a relatively short time frame, which is why it is distinct from incremental (yet potentially transformative) policy change.

13. It is interesting to note that some of the scholars who contributed a chapter to Thelen's edited volumes on institutional change (Mahoney and Thelen 2009; Streeck and Thelen 2005) pay direct attention to ideas (e.g., Palier 2005). With regard to the contributions of these scholars, see Schmidt 2011; Wincott 2011.

14. On material explanations and their relationship to ideational and to institutional explanations, see Parsons 2007.

15. On the relationship between ideas and politics–public policy in general, see Béland 2005; Béland and Cox 2011; Blyth 2002; Campbell 2004; Dobbin 1994; Fischer 2003; Genieys and Smyrl 2008; Gofas and Hay 2010; Goldstein and Keohane 1993; Hall 1993; Hansen and King 2001; Hattam 1993; Jenson 1989; Lakoff 2002; Mehta 2011; Merrien 2001; Padamsee 2009; Peters, Pierre, and King 2005; Schmidt 2002; Somers and Block 2005; Surel 2000; Taylor-Gooby 2005; Weir 1992; Weyland 2008. For institutionalist perspectives on the role of ideas in policy change, see Blyth 2002; Campbell 2004; Lieberman 2002; Schmidt 2011.

16. On agenda setting, see Baumgartner and Jones 1993; Kingdon 1995; on problem definition, see Mehta 2011; Rochefort and Cobb 1994; Stone 1997.

17. The few studies of the role of ideas in incremental policy change do not focus primarily on the United States: Bhatia 2010; Kay 2007; Palier 2002; Wincott 2011. For an exception, see Béland 2007a.

18. On how actors draw strategic lessons from concrete policy episodes, see Béland and Marier 2006.

19. This book does not focus on political ideologies in the strict sense of the term because we do not assume that actors necessarily follow coherent ideational dogmas and values. However, our analysis is compatible with the recent literature on political ideologies, which directly draws on the recent scholarship about ideas and politics: Berman 2006 and Freeden 2003.

20. Issue ownership is closely related to the concept of "party image." On this concept, see Trilling 1976.

21. On issue ownership, see Damore 2004; Petrocik 1996; Ross 2007.

22. For a bold—and controversial—take on the public opinion–social policy nexus, see Brooks and Manza 2007.

23. On this point, see Campbell 2004; Padamsee 2009.

24. However, we refuse to reduce policy change to the perceptions of the actors involved, as Philippe Zittoun (2009) does in a recent article. Doing that would make it impossible to grasp subtle forms of change that are not immediately visible to some actors.

25. We would like to thank John Myles for his insight about this issue.

26. On the role of welfare waivers, see Rogers-Dillon (2004).

Chapter One
Welfare Reform, 1996

I n August 1996 President Bill Clinton signed into law the Personal Responsibility and Work Opportunity Reconciliation Act (PRWORA). This legislation ended the Aid to Families with Dependent Children (AFDC) welfare entitlement program for poor, single-parent families and replaced it with a new conditional benefit named Temporary Assistance to Needy Families (TANF). As suggested by its title, TANF is a time-constrained benefit with most welfare recipients restricted to a five-year lifetime limit on receipt of federal welfare benefits. PRWORA also imposed new work requirements on those receiving TANF that were significantly tougher than existing arrangements. Hence, welfare policy stands in contrast to the other two policy domains discussed in this book. While there have been changes of some significance to the organization of Medicare, and while the relationship between private and public pensions is gradually shifting, neither of the major social insurance programs providing benefits for the elderly and the disabled—Medicare and Social Security—has been overhauled and restructured in one dramatic legislative episode in the manner that welfare has. That is, despite some continuity with the past, the 1996 welfare reform was a path-breaking transformation that directly impacted on the lives of millions of Americans as it restructured the relationship between the state and welfare recipients. It was, in short, a landmark reform in both ideational and institutional terms, and, as evidenced in the following analysis, its distinctly conservative ideological trajectory was reinforced by the 2005 reauthorization of the 1996 law.

It is important to understand the events of 1996 in the wider framework of previous welfare reform efforts, some successfully legislated and some not, at both federal and state levels. In particular, some of the state-led initiatives in the early 1990s acted as an entering wedge—constituting a form of institutional layering—that provided ammunition to those calling for a comprehensive reform at the federal level. Looking at the story of welfare reform over an extended period illustrates the overall shift in ideological perspectives that culminated in the 1996 law. The longer time frame also demonstrates the importance of welfare's policy legacies and the critical nature of legacy interpretation, which is directly related to the complex politics of issue ownership.

The purpose of this chapter is to examine how conservatives were able to develop their ideas about what was wrong with AFDC into such an effective political weapon that, in the mid-1990s, a Democratic president signed into law a set of rules that would have been denounced as an example of right-wing extremism a quarter century earlier. The *1996 Green Book*, then effectively an annual encyclopedia of social policy data, commented that the passage of PRWORA was "the first time that major welfare entitlement benefits have been repealed or substantially altered" (US Congress 1996, 1328). Certainly any comparison of the principles of PRWORA with some of the earlier attempts at welfare reform, notably Republican president Nixon's Family Assistance Plan, shows how far ideas about welfare policy had evolved since the early 1970s (Waddan 1998). Perhaps more precisely, the comparison over time shows how ideas that were seen as being on the fringe of political discourse in the late 1960s had become "mainstream" a generation later. When looking at the emergence and triumph of conservative ideas vis-à-vis welfare policy, it is also crucial to understand the response of liberals, and to ask why the constituencies defending the existing AFDC arrangements proved to be so vulnerable politically.

Before looking at the development of welfare policy in more detail, one immediate point to establish is that, even though PRWORA was signed into law by a Democratic president, it is clear that the legislation was a triumph for conservatives and represented the culmination of a sustained conservative ideological campaign attacking a key pillar of the welfare state. PRWORA was a complex bill that affected eligibility and access to a variety of means-tested benefits and services, especially for immigrants. Its primary objective was clear: to bring an end to the AFDC program that had originally been part of the 1935 Social Security Act. Critical to comprehending why this reform was so significant is the fact that AFDC was a cash benefit that distributed money to poor, largely single-parent families with children—clearly one of the most vulnerable family types in society. In 1996 AFDC benefits were distributed to more than 4.5 million families. Of these, only 302,000 were receiving benefits via the AFDC-UP program available to two-parent families, where the principal wage earner had a recent work history but was then unemployed (US Congress 1998, 402). For all intents and purposes, PRWORA explicitly targeted poor, female-headed households with a primary goal of moving them off welfare and into work. Interestingly, and indicating a slightly different but still conservative priority, PRWORA also promoted the traditional family unit as an ideal type in its opening paragraphs of Title 1, which emphasized the importance of marriage: "Marriage is an essential institution of a successful society which promotes the interests of children."[1] This commitment to marriage promotion remained a secondary feature of the bill, but it did reflect important strands of conservative thought.[2]

Underlying the overall policy initiative was the belief that AFDC had effectively constituted a give-away program that violated traditional American respect for work ethic and individual responsibility. In the eyes of its critics, AFDC had undermined the independence of welfare recipients themselves by trapping them into a cycle of dependency and ultimately self-defeating behavior and had simultaneously bred resentment among taxpayers who were frustrated at having to fund what many perceived as the indolent lifestyles of those on welfare. Whatever the merits of that argument, it was clearly derived from conservative ideas emphasizing the primacy of personal responsibility and individual agency rather than a wider socioeconomic structural context. To some liberal commentators, this analysis harkened back to the New Poor Law of 1830s Britain with Malthusian enthusiasm (Katz 1993; Handler and Hasenfeld 1997; Somers and Block 2005).

The Historical Development of AFDC

First known as Aid to Dependent Children (ADC), AFDC was established as part of the Social Security Act of 1935.[3] Despite being created alongside Social Security, AFDC was never regarded as an equal partner to that program. Unlike the social insurance schemes that were put in place for wage earners to cover pensions and unemployment, AFDC did not depend on recipients having made previous contributions; instead eligibility was based on the criteria of circumstance and need. Thus, AFDC did not have an actuarial relationship between contributions and benefits, meaning that AFDC recipients could not make a claim that they had "earned" their benefit entitlement. As noted in chapter 3, the actuarial logic of the Social Security system was modified and weakened in 1939, but throughout that program's history, the discourse depicting Social Security as a deserved reward for contributions paid through a working life (i.e., payroll tax) has helped sustain its popularity. In turn, the lack of an equivalent sense that AFDC was an earned right meant that its recipients were more liable to be regarded with suspicion than were Social Security beneficiaries (Fraser and Gordon 1992). Furthermore, a key decision made during the legislative process in 1935 placed control of AFDC under the auspices of the Social Security Board rather than the Children's Bureau (Gordon 1994, 267–73). This meant that AFDC was run by "a male dominated agency that consistently built up contributory insurance and downplayed the development of non-contributory public assistance programs" (Skocpol 1992, 535).[4] From the start, therefore, AFDC and Social Security had different distributional logics built into their operation that produced correspondingly different policy legacies and feed-back effects.

But because AFDC was designed to provide income support for poor, single parents with children at a time when the expectation was that mothers would not do paid work but would concentrate their energies on parenting, it might be supposed that the program would treat its recipients sympathetically given their "unfortunate" circumstances. As Edwin Witte expressed it, the aim was "to release from the wage-earning role the parent whose task is to raise children" (quoted in DeParle 2004, 86). Such sympathy and empathy, however, was severely limited in its application. It did not translate into a significant sum of hard cash, even for those who were eligible for benefits. A defining feature of AFDC in its early days was that eligibility was strictly limited to those mothers who were deemed worthy of help. In practice, this meant widows and a few "deserted" mothers. Any claimant could find herself subject to rigorous investigation to check on her appropriate worthiness, with these checks being particularly intrusive when it came to investigating sexual behavior (Gordon 1994, 298). Moreover, for those who were granted benefits, even if the stated intention was to allow these women to play the role of mother rather than worker, the actual benefit levels were often so low that recipients had to supplement their income through undeclared work. One of the features of AFDC's demise was that this initial ambivalence about whether the program should pay out meaningful benefits was replaced by a more categorical hostility to the notion that single mothers be subsidized to stay out of the workforce; but from the start, the reality, if little recognized, was that AFDC recipients were often already working to make ends meet (Edin and Lein 1997).

Another critical feature of AFDC, embedded in the program at its birth, was the degree of discretion that remained with state and local governments. Hence, in a critical fashion, AFDC differed from Social Security and Medicare. That is, while all three were legislated at the federal level, AFDC was the only one of these programs that split funding and regulation between federal and state governments. Thus, while much of the later debate about the AFDC program was conducted in general ideological terms, the importance of state-to-state variation should not be underestimated in terms of either the day-to-day consequences for welfare recipients or the overall political impact of relatively weak federal supervision. The original draft of the 1935 legislation contained relatively broad federal guidelines about eligibility and benefit levels, but these were significantly watered down through the legislative process (Gordon 1994, 273–75). Instrumental in diminishing federal government regulation were members of Congress from the South, who negotiated their own preferences with the Roosevelt administration. Consequently, there were few clear national standards about who was eligible for AFDC and what payment they should receive. Once again, in the words of Witte, "No other federal aid legislation has ever gone to such lengths to deny the federal government supervisory power" (quoted in DeParle 2004, 86). Not surprisingly, especially in the South, these arrangements led to the systematic exclusion of most African American mothers from the welfare rolls (Teles 1996, 24). There were also significant discrepancies in benefit levels. For example, in 1940 the average national monthly AFDC payment was $32.39. In Alabama, however, the monthly average benefit that year was $13.63 (Gordon 1994, 276).

Overall, the early days of AFDC's development provided mixed messages. A program granting relief to poor, single-parent families was established; in theory, it was meant to help mothers and their children survive without recourse to the labor market. Yet there were minimal federal norms in terms of the state-by-state implementation of this program, and there were strong aspects of discrimination in its street-level application. Thus, from the start AFDC provided an ambiguous ideological message that in turn left a somewhat confused policy legacy. By the 1990s the dominant interpretation of that legacy was that AFDC was a failed program because of the very provision of benefits that allegedly demeaned welfare recipients, undermined their independence, and, therefore, trapped them in a self-destructive cycle of welfare dependency. But there was not a clear, linear ideological progression from the 1930s through to the conservative conventional wisdom of the 1990s about the "failure" of AFDC. Indeed, the conservative movement gained its momentum as a result of a backlash against the perceived deviation in welfare policy and liberal thinking of the 1960s and early 1970s. At the end of the 1960s, the conventional wisdom of many liberals was quite different from that which transformed welfare policy in the 1990s. Even as the welfare rolls expanded dramatically throughout the 1960s, many liberals came to believe that AFDC was a failed program because it was discriminatory and provided inadequate benefits.

It is clear, and in stark contrast to the Social Security and Medicare programs, that the policy regime surrounding AFDC was regularly under fire. Up until 1996 the program proved to be robust under fire because the consensus that the program needed repair was not matched by agreement on how to fix it. By the end of the 1960s, following a dramatic expansion of the AFDC caseload, the demand for "welfare reform" was a constant refrain in American politics, even though it was not immediately evident that this would result in the triumph of conservative policy ideas.

The development of welfare policy and politics exemplifies some of the key theoretical propositions of this book about the role of ideas and institutions in policy change. From the late 1960s through to the 1990s there were important, presidentially led efforts at welfare reform that were thwarted at veto points embedded in US political institutions. Importantly, the policy and ideological impetus behind these reform efforts changed over time and, in 1996, a combination of factors proved conducive to the passage of path-breaking reform. Critical political actors in the shape of congressional Republican leaders and a Democratic president saw legislative action as desirable. For the former, PRWORA was an ideological triumph reflecting many of the ideas that conservatives had promoted with increasing stridency for the previous two decades. For President Clinton, who was committed to reform of the existing system but had reservations about the details of PRWORA, strategic as well as policy considerations encouraged the decision to sign rather than veto the bill. In 1992 Governor Clinton had used the issue of welfare to help define his political identity. Specifically, he repudiated the idea that Democrats were "soft" on welfare recipients and in doing so challenged the presiding pattern of issue ownership whereby Republicans criticized Democrats for their overly generous welfare policies. In 1996, with electoral considerations again to the fore, President Clinton was determined to share the credit for welfare reform and not cede issue ownership of welfare back to the GOP. Thus, this is a story that emphasizes the importance of ideas and the manner in which political actors frame policy questions in order to highlight the relevance of their narrative. The road to PRWORA also illustrates the significance of both formal and informal institutional rules and particular policy legacies and the interpretation of those legacies. Clinton's embrace of welfare as an issue in a deliberate effort to challenge prevailing orthodoxies also illustrates that issue ownership can be a complex and changing matter. Finally, while PRWORA was a sharp rather than incremental reform, the chapter will outline how reform advocates were able to point to smaller-scale experiments in welfare reform conducted at the state level as models for change at the federal level.

The 1960s and the Expansion of AFDC

In 1950 the average number of families receiving AFDC monthly was 651,000. By 1960 that figure had risen to 803,000 (US Congress 1998, 402). Moreover, from the end of World War II through 1960, the number of African American families as a proportion of the welfare caseload nearly tripled, now making up to 40 percent (Gilens 1999, 106). Still, up to that point the "welfare expansion was incremental and bureaucratic—almost accidental," resulting largely from the migration of many African Americans to northern cities where discrimination, while still apparent, was less systematic, and resulting from slight increases in the levels of income at which families were eligible to receive benefits (DeParle 2004, 88). During the 1960s the increase in welfare numbers was the product of much more deliberate action, and by 1970 the average number of families receiving AFDC monthly had jumped to just over 1.9 million (US Congress 1998, 402). While some of the increase during the 1960s was a result of more households becoming eligible as a consequence of their circumstances (that is, single parenthood and impoverishment), a significant part of the increase is explained by the fact that many more families whose circumstances had not changed had applied for benefits and many more of these had been deemed qualified for AFDC payments than had previously been the case (Teles 1996, 19–22).

Hence, by the end of the 1960s, eligibility for AFDC had expanded to such an extent that it did effectively constitute an entitlement program for poor, single-parent families. At the start of the 1960s, only about one-third of households applying for AFDC were successful, but by 1971 that number had risen to 90 percent (Katz 1989, 106). Corresponding to the increase in the numbers receiving AFDC, costs to government rose from 1 billion dollars in 1960 to 6.2 billion dollars in 1971 (Weaver 2000, 55).

While this more generous attitude toward welfare applicants was in tune with the mood music of the civil rights revolution of the 1960s and the attack on poverty by presidents Kennedy and Johnson, it is crucial to note that the most significant changes to the rules about eligibility came from unelected branches of government. Although Congress passed an amendment in 1962 that allowed states the option of paying AFDC to families where a father was present if the household had a recent history of employment (AFDC-UP), of more importance were the series of Supreme Court decisions throughout the late 1960s that removed much of the effective discretion that state and local officials had been able to use to determine eligibility for AFDC. Perhaps most notably, the Court overturned state rules that denied AFDC to those who had not fulfilled state residency requirements, or who were alleged to have "substitute fathers," or where midnight raids had found a "man in the house" (Piven and Cloward 1971, 301–11; Teles 1996, 107–17). In one instance, referring to the 1962 amendments, the Court ruled that "federal welfare policy now rests on a basis considerably more sophisticated and enlightened than the 'worthy person' concepts of earlier times" (quoted in Teles 1996, 108). Thus, by the end of the 1960s the rules governing access to AFDC had changed significantly. This was not a consequence of deliberate legislative action but resulted from a process that amounted to significant incremental change effectively brought about by bureaucratic and judicial conversion.[5] That is, while the goals of AFDC were not explicitly challenged by Court rulings, the management of the program in many areas across the United States was changed, and in doing so the impact of welfare policy was altered.

Whatever the merits of these Court rulings, the fact that it was unelected elites that opened the door to AFDC's growth proved to be of long-term political significance as this chimed with later conservative complaints that the champions of welfare were out of touch with the values of most Americans. Furthermore, and in contrast to the political maneuvering surrounding the expansion of Social Security in the early 1970s, there was no scrambling among politicians to claim credit for the expansion of AFDC. Conversely, a movement in Washington, DC, at the turn of the 1970s to enact legislation that would transform welfare policy appears, especially in hindsight, remarkably liberal in nature.

The Politics of a Guaranteed Income

There is an intuitive convergence between the relaxing of conditions for receipt of welfare benefits and the advent of President Lyndon Johnson's "War on Poverty," but the two should not be conflated. For Johnson, the War on Poverty was to be waged by providing services rather than simply giving out cash to help the poor. The language of a hand up rather than a handout was a constant feature of his rhetoric (Davies 1996; Patterson 1994, 142–55). In the 1980s conservative critics lampooned Johnson and the War on Poverty for encouraging a descent into a benefits and dependency culture that allegedly harmed rather than helped swathes of America's poor; yet Johnson's antipoverty strategy was not based on increasing the "dole" but on expanding economic opportunity. However, by the end of the 1960s many policymakers had decided that sharing the country's wealth through a better channeling of jobs and education was an unlikely prospect, and the simplest answer to poverty was to redistribute the existing wealth. Consequently, and in a quite remarkable contrast to the development of ideas and policy initiatives in the 1980s and 1990s, successive administrations throughout the 1970s attempted to implement income-maintenance schemes that would have guaranteed minimum annual incomes to American families to replace the more arbitrary payments that some received through AFDC (Steensland 2008).

While liberal commentators such as John Kenneth Galbraith (1958) and Michael Harrington (1962) are credited with having helped push the issue of poverty to the top of the political agenda in the early 1960s, the work of Oscar Lewis deserves as much attention because he developed the concept of the "culture of poverty" (Lewis 1961, 1966, 1969). Although Lewis's focus was not especially on the United States, his argument that poverty had become a way of life that often perpetuated itself from generation to generation drew attention. The 1964 report of the Council of Economic Advisors (CEA) elaborated on this theme by stating: "Poverty breeds poverty. . . . Lack of motivation, hope, and incentive is a more subtle but no less powerful barrier than a lack of financial means. Thus the cruel legacy of poverty is passed from parents to children" (quoted in Sundquist 1968, 140).

As it was, both Lewis and the CEA intended their analysis to justify activist government policy in order to disrupt the cycle of poverty, but the "culture of poverty" thesis could also equally lend itself to the interpretation that the real problem of poverty was not a lack of income but a failure to conform to society's prevalent norms. This idea became a dominant theme of the conservative-led discourse about welfare dependency in the 1980s, so "the culture of poverty echoed old ideas and prefigured future debates" (Katz 1993, 12). And in the late 1960s some conservatives were already rehearsing the key arguments that were to be more fully developed in the 1980s. For instance, Edward Banfield maintained that government intervention into the problems of the deprived inner city was based on misguided premises and therefore would only make matters worse for the urban poor (Banfield 1968). But throughout the Great Society era liberals assumed that welfare policy would develop in line with their preferences. The forthcoming triumph of conservative ideas and, in particular, the definition of poverty as a problem of dependency rather than as a matter of inadequate income were not yet evident to most commentators on welfare, even as the old New Dealer and architect of the Great Society, Lyndon Johnson, left office to be replaced by a Republican, Richard Nixon.

Indeed, Nixon put forward a welfare reform plan that would have effectively guaranteed a minimum income for American families. In the end, the Family Assistance Plan (FAP) was passed by the House of Representatives but died a legislative death in the Senate Finance Committee at the hands of a combination of liberal and conservative senators. (This odd coalition reflected the general confusion of the American political establishment about how to respond to the novelty of the Nixon proposals.) The ideas underlying the FAP manifested hybrid ideological thinking. The basis of the FAP was a so-called negative income tax (NIT) scheme. The FAP proposed to guarantee an annual income of $1,600 to a family of four, with such a family eligible to continue to receive benefits on a sliding scale up to a total household income of $3,920 per year.[6] The NIT concept in fact had advocates from across the political spectrum. On one hand, Milton Friedman recommended this type of income-maintenance program because it would simplify the welfare system and reduce bureaucracy (Friedman 1962). On the other hand, for the liberal left, the attraction was to guarantee the income of all families (Tobin

1968). One feature of an NIT scheme is that while it features a means test, it does not make judgments per se about why people have a low income, nor does it have consequent criteria of worthiness. Thus, such "schemes concentrate on *outcome* rather than cause" (Barr 1993, 263, emphasis in original).

It should be stressed that the Nixon administration did not want to give the impression that it was offering an unconditional income guarantee. The president was keen to maintain that his plan was in line with conservative values and insisted that taxpayer money would not be paid to the work-shy. For instance, when campaigning for George H. W. Bush in a Texas Senate race in 1970, Nixon declared: "I will put it bluntly: If a man is able to work, if a man is trained for a job, and then he refuses to work, that man should not be paid to loaf by the hardworking taxpayer" (quoted in Moynihan 1973, 530).[7] But Daniel Patrick Moynihan, acting as an advisor to Nixon at the time, maintains that the emphasis on the work requirement was bluster to keep conservative skeptics on side. Moynihan quotes Nixon as saying: "I don't care a damn about the work requirement. . . . This is the price of getting the $1,600" (ibid., 219–20). Certainly, the legislative detail of the FAP suggests that the work requirement was not too serious a qualification on the guaranteed income element of the proposal. Family heads had to register as available for work, but income would only be deducted if the head of household refused a job when offered one (Bowler 1974; Burke and Burke 1974; Mead 1986).

The legitimacy of the principle of a government-guaranteed income was reinforced among liberal elites by the emerging consensus that many poor families could not significantly improve their lot through any effort that they could reasonably be expected to make. Consequently, the best way in which to alleviate their poverty was through an income distribution strategy. The Kerner Commission, established to report on the urban riots of the mid-1960s, recommended that AFDC be extended and that families on the program be guaranteed an annual income (US National Advisory Commission on Civil Disorders 1968). In the summer of 1968, more than one thousand economists signed a public petition advocating the idea (Small 1999, 187). In January 1968 President Johnson created the President's Commission on Income Maintenance Programs. This body, better known as the Heinemann Commission, did not report until after Johnson left office, but its findings were a sharp rebuke to the notion that an individual's efforts would be enough to raise them out of poverty. The report noted, "Unemployment and underemployment are basic facts of American life," adding that "the simple fact is that most Americans remain poor because access to income through work is currently beyond their reach" (US President's Commission 1969, 23). It is worth noting that Johnson remained wedded to his hand-up approach and was unconvinced by the need for a guaranteed income, but many of the leading figures running Great Society programs did gravitate toward the concept (Davies 1996).

Critical to the development of the FAP was Nixon's decision to employ Moynihan to report on the welfare "crisis" in New York City where the welfare rolls had doubled between 1962 and 1966 and did so again by 1972 (DeParle 2004,

89–90). His conclusion was that "it is increasingly clear . . . that the amount of money a low-skilled family head can earn in a city such as New York is not enough to maintain a family at what are now expected standards of living" (Moynihan 1973, 61). Lawrence Mead, a key conservative figure in the later welfare debate, notes the breadth of opinion supporting this perspective: "The policy making behind the proposals showed the consensual patterns characteristic of the Great Society. Guaranteed income drew surprising support from business as well as social workers and welfare advocacy groups" (Mead 1986, 97). Thus, however uncertain the public was about the notion of a guaranteed income (Erskine 1975), a considerable part of elite opinion, especially liberal elite opinion (Davies 1996) was persuaded by the idea.

There was significant opposition to the concept of a minimum income and even more so to the specifics of the FAP. Some conservatives were horrified. When the plan was announced, the American Conservative Union denounced Nixon for being unduly influenced by "liberal ideologues" and reflected, "Moynihan makes no secret of his satisfaction at having convinced a Republican President to recommend a far more liberal welfare program than any Democrat ever dared."[8] California's governor, Ronald Reagan, expressed his opposition, as did Vice President Spiro Agnew within the walls of the White House. According to Moynihan, Agnew warned Nixon: "After months of heated oratory . . . the issue will be Nixon's niggardly ideas against the progressive proposals of Democrats" (Moynihan 1973, 201). If Agnew did issue such a warning, it was prescient inasmuch as many liberal Democrats did respond by dismissing the $1,600 figure as desultory while barely acknowledging the radical nature of the underlying principles. For example, Senator Hubert Humphrey dismissed the FAP as comprising "nothing new, nothing startling" (Fox 1969, 25) when in reality there was much that was new and that should have been startling.

One aspect that liberals complained about was the figure of $1,600 for a family of four with no other income. This was denounced as inadequate and significantly below the contemporary poverty line of $3,721 for such a family (US Census Bureau 1971, 321). However, this denouncement ignored how the mechanics of the NIT scheme worked, allowing a family of four to carry on receiving benefits on a diminishing scale until its income reached $3,920 per year. The FAP also came under attack from a pro-welfare New York–based group. The National Welfare Rights Organization (NWRO) was inspired by the work of two academics, Francis Fox Piven and Richard Cloward, and led by George Wiley, a former associate national director of the Congress for Racial Equality (Steensland 2008, 56–58). In principle, these three people supported the introduction of a guaranteed minimum income, but FAP was not enough to satisfy the NWRO. The NWRO demanded a minimum income of $5,500, and executive director Wiley denounced FAP as discriminatory because it abolished AFDC, a program that disproportionately helped African Americans, while introducing a scheme that would benefit the working poor, who were mainly white. "There is a welfare crisis in this country that welfare clients have precipitated. . . . He [Nixon] has felt he has had to make some kind of response. He has responded by trying to give the benefits to the areas in which he thinks his constituents are" (Fox 1969, 25). Yet this analysis neglects the dramatic change that the plan would have made to the Southern political economy—a region where discrimination against African Americans in both employment and access to AFDC had historically been the greatest. While AFDC payments in the vast majority of states were higher than $1,600, the figure in eight southern states was below $1,600. While the average national AFDC payment in 1970 was $187 a month per family in the United States, in Alabama it was only $60 a month, and in Mississippi it was only $46 a month (US Census Bureau 1971, 291 and 294). In Louisiana one-quarter of the state's population would have qualified as FAP recipients (Heclo 2001, 178).

Furthermore, the FAP stipulated that states paying AFDC benefits that were higher than $1,600 would need to continue to pay out benefits at that higher rate. Certainly, the guarantee of $1,600 was enough to concern Rep. Phil Landrum (D-Ga.) who worried: "There's not going to be anybody left to roll these wheelbarrows and press these shirts" (quoted in Quadagno 1994, 130). The segregationist and veteran congressman William Colmer (D-Miss.) captured the potential impact of the legislation: "Unquestionably, it is the most controversial, it is the most important . . . and disturbing piece of legislation that I have had occasion to consider . . . as a member of this body. I am very much disturbed by this bill . . . about the threat it poses to our system of government, to our way of life" (quoted in Moynihan 1973, 433). In short, the FAP would have significantly reordered the political economy of the South (Myles and Pierson 1997).

Despite the overwhelming opposition of southern Democrats, the FAP passed the House of Representatives by 243 votes to 155 in April 1970.[9] Its prospects in the Senate were helped by the more liberal nature of the Senate at the time but were hindered by that chamber's institutional processes. In particular, the composition of the Senate Finance Committee (SFC), through which the legislation would have to pass, was unpromising terrain since "the committee was conservative, rural and non-northern" (Steensland 2008, 147). At one point, the SFC's chair, Russell Long (D–La.) declared, "Let's junk the whole thing and start over again" (Weaver 1970, 13). The fears of the FAP's supporters were eventually realized when, in November 1970, the SFC voted ten to six against reporting the bill. The administration calculated that it had sixty votes in the Senate that would support the bill (Steensland 2008, 152), but the vote in SFC meant that the administration never got the chance to test this belief. This points to the institutional complexity of the legislative process in the United States and illustrates how a specific veto point can stand in the way of controversial legislative proposals. For two days prior to that SFC committee vote the most liberal member of the SFC, Eugene McCarthy (D-Minn.), had organized hearings at which NWRO representatives denounced the FAP as a tool of the repressive state (Burke and Burke 1974, 161–65). This shows just how the right and some of the left, for quite different but equally damaging reasons, had come to reject the FAP. The Nixon administration did try again in 1971. This time the proposal was known by its bill number, HR 1, and the income guarantee was raised to $2,400 per annum financed by "cashing out" the Food Stamp program. As with the FAP, this bill progressed through the House but made no headway in the Senate.

Thus, when Jimmy Carter took office, AFDC remained largely as it was—an unpopular program with an expanding number of claimants. Carter promised welfare reform in his 1976 campaign, and the Carter plan, known as the Program for Better Jobs and Income (PBJI), followed Nixon's example and put forward a minimum income plan based on a NIT scheme, though with differing initial floors depending on whether a head of household was expected to work. Unlike the FAP, the PBJI also offered income guarantees to individuals and childless couples. More radically, it also promised to create 1.4 million public service jobs and training slots. Discussion of the PBJI never really got past how much it would cost and the plan made minimal legislative headway. The demise of PBJI marked the end of plans for a guaranteed annual income. Subsequent reform efforts were to take a very different direction.

In the aftermath of the failure of the FAP and HR 1, it is interesting to reflect on the comments in the two party platforms for the 1972 elections. These cast quite differing interpretations on what had transpired. First, the Democratic platform ignored the principles involved in a minimum income plan by denouncing Nixon's efforts: "H.R. 1 . . . is not humane and does not meet the social and economic objectives that we believe in. . . . It perpetuates the coercion of forced work requirements" (quoted in *Congressional Quarterly Weekly Report* 1972a, 1727). The Republican platform meanwhile declared: "We flatly oppose programs or policies which embrace the principle of a government-guaranteed income. We reject as unconscionable the idea that all citizens have the right to be supported by the government, regardless of their ability or desire to support themselves and their families" (quoted in *Congressional Quarterly Weekly Report* 1972b, 2160). This would suggest that the GOP was almost in denial about the significance of Nixon's efforts, but it has stood the test of time, at least as a statement of conservative policy intent. It is a testament to how far the welfare debate shifted over the next quarter century that, at the end of the 1990s, the concept of "forced work requirements" was embraced by mainstream political figures from all parties.

In his memoirs Nixon commented that he had hoped to develop "creative and innovative social legislation" (Nixon 1978, 425). In pursuit of this goal, he had expected opposition from conservatives but anticipated "a legislative alliance with Democrats and liberals" (425). Surprised by the liberal opposition, he reflected: "As Moynihan observed, it was as if they [liberals] could not tolerate the notion that a conservative Republican President had done what his liberal predecessors had not been bold enough to do" (427). Here Nixon acknowledges the influence of liberal ideas, yet many liberals rejected his plans thus reflecting their notion that welfare was still an area of social policy where they set the agenda. But, if enacted, a guaranteed minimum income program would have been a path-departing change from AFDC and would have introduced a very different principle to US social policy with a potentially radical distributional consequence.

In hindsight, one of the remarkable features of the debates about the PBJI and particularly the FAP, given how close that plan came to enactment, is that so many commentators, especially on the liberal left side of the argument, either underestimated or ignored the radical nature of what was being proposed. In August 1977, as the details of the PBJI were announced, a *New Republic* editorial commented that a minimum income plan was "not inherently liberal or conservative; it is a managerial tool. Whether it is progressive or not depends on the payment level in any given program. The service strategy has clearly failed" (quoted in Waddan 1997, 96). The assumptions inherent in this statement were that welfare policymaking had moved beyond ideology and that an income-maintenance strategy—that is, comprehensive cash benefits—was the inevitable way forward. Minimum income plans were so different because they categorized the poor simply according to their income level rather than separating out the deserving and undeserving poor for differential treatment. The idea of a strict separation between cash and services strategies weakened political support for FAP and other income-maintenance policies that attempted to move away from the deserving/undeserving poor dichotomy ever-present in American society (Steensland 2008). The significance of this issue was highlighted with the creation of the Earned Income Tax Credit (EITC) in 1975 that refunded low-income families through the tax system (Myles and Pierson 1997). This benefit, which in fact cost more than AFDC by the time of the latter's demise, helped the working poor by reinforcing the dichotomy between the deserving and the undeserving poor instead of moving beyond it as FAP would have done (Steensland 2008). In fact, when President Clinton pushed through a major expansion of the program in 1993, it was justified on the basis of "making work pay." Hence, the ideological question is not restricted to whether low-income families should receive government benefits but also which low-income groups should receive benefits and how those benefits should be distributed. The answers to these questions reflect important ideas and value judgments about the poor typically tied to the deserving/undeserving dichotomy.

The Attack on AFDC

The liberals who had rallied against Nixon presumably did not foresee that, ten years later, a leading conservative critic of Nixon's plans would become president. As governor of California, Ronald Reagan had requested a state waiver from the provisions of HR 1 should it become law. This waiver would have allowed California to have a lower minimum income than set out by federal law and tougher work requirements (Steensland 2008, 168–70). In 1976, in his near-miss campaign for the Republican presidential nomination, Reagan had argued that responsibility for an array of social welfare programs should be transferred from federal to state government to save money and cut federal taxes. In addition, during this campaign Reagan made clear his belief that some Americans received benefits who simply did not deserve them. To make his point, he invoked the image of the "welfare queen" who was a vacationing, Cadillac-driving, and, by implication, African American woman who lived heartily on food stamps (Gilbert 2009, 390).[10] At that stage Reagan's views about how to resolve the welfare "crisis" remained on the fringes of mainstream political discourse, but the essential message, the idea that the government welfare bureaucracy had become bloated and self-perpetuating, was to become increasingly influential as economic conditions deteriorated throughout the late 1970s.

One perceived manifestation of that antigovernment mood was the passage of Proposition 13 in California in 1978 (Martin 2008). This property tax–cutting initiative was a much broader revolt against the Californian political establishment, led at that point by Democratic governor Jerry Brown, than it was an attack against welfare programs. One poll conducted at the time found that 70 percent of respondents agreed with the following statement: "Proposition 13 is the only way to send a message to government that people are fed up with high taxes and too much government spending" (Field 1978, 5). When asked which services they would like to see cut because of the predicted drop in the state's revenues with Proposition 13, 62 percent of Californians answered that welfare and cash assistance payments should be reduced (ibid., 6). In Washington, DC, Proposition 13 was interpreted as part of a mounting backlash against big government (Martin 2008), and within the Department of Health, Education and Welfare (HEW), the last hopes of any reform plan along the lines of the PBJI died.[11]

Thus, when Reagan campaigned on his conservative platform in 1980, the message had a resonance beyond the confines of conservatives in the Republican Party primaries. One vibrant message of the Reagan campaign was that his administration would cut both taxes and general domestic federal government spending with a particular focus on combating welfare abuse (Katznelson 1981). Reagan insisted that, since the 1930s, too much social welfare spending had been directed at people who did not need the help that they were being given and that, even worse, this "help" backfired by undermining the economic independence and personal responsibility of the recipients (Davies 2003, 209). This message was not at all new, but it had been sidelined in policymaking circles for a generation. Yet in the early 1980s the idea that dependency was a cause of poverty gained new momentum and credibility. In part this new credibility reflected a change in the composition of the population living below the poverty level.

Poverty, AFDC, and Policy Drift

The new intellectual vigor and political energy of conservative critics of the welfare system was given considerable impetus because of the changing composition of the population living in poverty and because of the interpretation that was put on this data by an emerging breed of conservative thinkers. The evidence showed that there had been what might be termed "a feminization of poverty" throughout the 1960s and 1970s. In the 1960s, the majority of Americans in households with incomes below the poverty line lived in homes headed by men, but the chances of male-headed households having incomes below the poverty line dropped significantly between 1960 and 1980. In 1960, 17.8 percent of all people younger than 65 living in households headed by men were below the poverty line. By 1980, the incidence of poverty for such people had dropped to 7.9 percent (Palmer 1988, 10). This meant that between 1960 and 1980, the proportion of the poor who were younger than 65 living in male-headed family units dropped from 65 percent to 44.6 percent, whereas the proportion of the poor younger than 65 living in households headed by women increased from 21.2 percent to 42.2 percent (ibid.). Furthermore, by the 1980s, the vast majority of single mothers who headed AFDC households were not widowed but divorced, separated, or had never been married (Bane 1992; Garfinkel and McLanahan 1986). By then the traditional small "c" conservative notion that mothers should concentrate on parenting rather than paid labor looked increasingly outdated as more and more women entered the labor force. Throughout the 1940s and 1950s, AFDC had not been a controversial program, but "a program that stays the same while the society around it is changing can actually amount to a transformed policy" (Heclo 2001, 173). This points to an interesting case of policy drift, according to which societal change triggered a major transformation of the impact of AFDC in the absence of sharp legislative revisions to the program (Hacker 2004). In turn, the politics also shifted. By the 1980s, conservatives argued that AFDC benefits had undermined traditional family structures and encouraged women to have children while remaining single. Conservatives claimed that reducing easy access to benefits was not an example of conservative disdain for the welfare poor but was a mark of how profoundly conservatives understood the interaction of welfare dependency and poverty.

Conservatives and the Battle of Ideas

An early example of how previously marginal conservative thinkers became somewhat more "mainstream" came with the publication of George Gilder's 1981 book, *Wealth and Poverty*. This antiwelfare and antifeminist tract became a *New York Times* bestseller. Gilder's chief theme was the relationship between poverty and family structure: "An analysis of poverty that begins and ends with family structure and marital status would explain far more about the problem than most of the distributions of income, inequality, unemployment, education, IQ, race, sex, home ownership, location, discrimination and all the other items usually multiply regressed and correlated on academic computers" (Gilder 1981, 72). For Gilder, the biggest culprit in explaining family breakdown was access to welfare, which undermined the economic role of the male in a household. That is, over time, a "welfare culture" arose because of the "constant, seductive, erosive pressure on the marriages and work habits of the poor" that came with the receipt of cash benefits (ibid., 122).

A more prominent figure than Gilder—indeed, a key figure—in the early 1980s was Charles Murray. Murray was influential partially because he used social science methods, which had previously been dominated by liberal thinkers, to "prove" the validity of his analysis. In his seminal book, *Losing Ground*, Murray maintained that higher rates of illegitimacy and the increased welfare rolls reflected "rational responses to changes in the rules of the game of surviving and getting ahead" (Murray 1984, 155). Reflecting on various means-tested benefits, Murray went on to say that the changes in eligibility rules had combined to alter peoples' behavior and lifestyle choices. That is, eligibility regulations "affect men as well as women, calculations about marriage and children as well as calculations about jobs and welfare. . . . It is the total effect of well-intentioned changes in the incentive structure, not any one specific change, that is key to comprehending what happened" (ibid., 164). Murray was also adamant that there were jobs available for the welfare poor, and that not working reflected an individual choice. Thus, "poverty in America is seldom the result of uncontrollable events involving the economic system. . . . The old wisdom—that anyone who is willing to work hard can make a decent living—has much more truth to it than has recently been acknowledged" (Murray 1987, 5).

As well as questioning the work ethics of the welfare poor, Murray also maintained that the incentive structures of AFDC and other benefits had contributed to rising rates of illegitimacy. In turn, he argued that the breakdown in traditional family structures not only reinforced income poverty but was also a cause of a wider moral poverty. The potential explosiveness of this theme, particularly when intertwined with issues of race, had previously been illustrated in the mid-1960s with the publication of the so-called Moynihan report (US Department of Labor 1965). Moynihan, who at that time was assistant secretary of labor in the Johnson administration, authored an examination of the relationship between African American family structure and the rise in numbers of African American families receiving AFDC between the 1940s and the 1960s. At many points the report's tone was ambivalent; it was thus possible to read it as either an indictment of self-inflicted family disruption or a lament about the economic conditions of the poor parts of the inner city that made ordinary life impossible. Whatever Moynihan intended, by the 1980s Murray and other conservatives were asking similar questions about the relationship between family instability and welfare use and coming to the emphatic conclusion that the latter was a cause of the former. One liberal commentary lamented that conservatives had taken "Moynihan's pronouncements of the 1960s" and "resuscitated [them] ... with a new and resounding legitimacy" (Ginsburg 1989, 66).

Murray's conclusion was that it was impossible to unravel the existing welfare arrangements in order to undo the perverse incentives that were built into the system. Consequently, he proposed his radical "thought experiment" that involved "scrapping the entire federal welfare and income support structure for working-aged persons" (Murray 1984, 227). Simply put, his argument was that such dramatic action would improve the lives of the working-aged poor by forcing them to take responsibility for their actions. If the state no longer provided benefits to poor, single parents, then fewer women would become single parents and fewer would live in poverty. Thus, conservatives increasingly focused on the behavior of the poor rather than their lack of income and economic opportunity. It was in this context that Murray's work was so important. Nearly all commentators, whether friend or foe, agree on the importance of Murray's controversial ideas and use them to explain the renewed conservative intellectual vigor on the subject of welfare. He was by no means the first conservative writer to bemoan the dangers of welfare (Anderson 1978; Banfield 1968; Gilder 1981), but his work came at an opportune time as it provided intellectual ballast to the rhetoric of President Reagan and his administration.

Yet Murray's immediate influence had waned by the mid-1990s when PRWORA was being developed and his proposal simply to cut aid with no replacement was not carried through. Hence, while Murray's was a critical contribution to the battle of ideas that provided considerable shock to all and awe to some, perhaps equally important was a second wave of conservative thought that called for radical reform of the welfare system but not for the removal of all support mechanisms for the welfare poor. In this context an academic and commentator on welfare policy, Lawrence Mead (1986, 1987, 1988, 1992), became an increasingly influential voice.

Mead's overriding concern was that welfare recipients engage with the world of paid work. He argued that there were jobs available but that the welfare poor had not grasped these opportunities. Mead (1986, 1992) acknowledged that many of these available jobs were menial and low paid, but he insisted that work of any sort was the prerequisite for a long-term escape from poverty. Stressing the contrast in political legitimacy between social insurance and means-tested welfare programs, Mead noted, "High work levels for the general population sustain the citizenship rationale for the social insurance welfare state, but low work levels for the poor put that case in question for welfare and other antipoverty programs" (Mead 1997a, 206). Contrary to Murray, Mead did not call for the withdrawal of the state. In fact, Mead called for a "new paternalism" and supported interventionist strategies to integrate the welfare poor into the workforce (Mead 1997b). Mead acknowledged that most of the nonworking, able-bodied poor expressed a desire to work, but he argued that after time spent living on benefits, many welfare recipients needed a jolt to push them to conform with their own expectations. Thus, he recommended strong work requirements backed up by a strict sanctions regime for noncompliance. Mead differed from Murray and other conservatives, such as Robert Rector, in that he was willing to see government play a significant role in helping people adjust from life on welfare to life in work. "Before 1960, poverty levels were much higher than now, but most poor adults were employed, and this tended over time to integrate them. Today, there is less poverty, but the separation of the poor from the economy makes integration more doubtful. Therefore, social programs must promote work, and even enforce it, assuming the function that the workplace did before" (Mead 1997b, 229). As we will see, the final reforms of 1996 did bear considerable resemblance to the model advocated by Mead.

Another statement of broadly conservative sentiments that in many ways looked forward to future reforms came in 1987 with the publication of *A Community of Self-Reliance: The New Consensus on Family and Welfare*. This book is notable because it is not the work of a dedicated conservative but the product of twenty welfare policy experts from a variety of backgrounds. The group, known as the Working Seminar on Family and American Welfare Policy, described itself as "composed of scholars and practitioners from several institutions, many backgrounds, and a broad range of points of view" (Berstein et al. 1987, 14). The group did include Murray and Mead but also people with more liberal credentials such as Alice Rivlin and Robert Reischauer. The final report echoed some of the key themes of the growing conservative discourse. Notably, it agreed with the view that poverty had a deeper meaning than an inadequate household income. "Money income alone does not define poverty. The connotations of the word poverty suggest something beyond low-income. . . . The most disturbing element among a fraction of the contemporary poor is an inability to seize opportunity even when it is available. . . . Their need is less for job training than meaning and order in their lives" (ibid., 11).

The report went on to call for strict work requirements backed up by sanctions as well as a limit on the time that people could receive cash benefits. Furthermore, it called for more authority to be devolved down to the states allowing them to experiment more with their welfare arrangements. The seminar shied away from Murray's brand of antigovernment fundamentalism and echoed Mead in its recommendation that government, at its various levels, should work to help welfare recipients move from benefits to the labor force. As Ron Haskins, a key behind-the-scenes player throughout the 1990s and leading Republican staff member to the House Ways and Means Resources Subcommittee, points out the seminar's "recommendations uncannily anticipated several major provisions of the 1996 reform legislation" (Haskins 2006, 13).[12] The seminar was perhaps exaggerating the point when using the word "consensus" in its title, but the liberal response to this emerging conservative critique of welfare policy was muted.

The Uncertain Liberal Response

Not surprisingly, many liberals had responded with dismay to the rise of the conservative ideas promoted by Gilder and Murray. Some questioned Murray's methodology and therefore disputed his conclusions (Danziger and Gattschalk 1985); others expressed frustration at the emergence of a "blame the victim" discourse

(Katz 1986, 1989); and some defended the War on Poverty's track record and argued that the policy legacies of the 1960s should have been built on rather than ridiculed and retrenched (Schwarz 1983). Some liberal scholars have even argued that Murray's work was a "direct recycling of Malthus" and, more specifically, disputed his claim that state activism has a "perverse" impact on human behavior (Somers and Block 2005, 278). Furthermore, just as Malthus gathered an array of acolytes, so Murray's work paved the way for other conservatives "who were even more explicit in recycling the perversity framework from the early nineteenth century" (ibid.).[13]

In the 1980s and early 1990s, facing this increasingly dominant conservative welfare discourse, liberals were on the defensive and sounded an uncertain trumpet. Prominent sociologist William Julius Wilson (1987a, 1987b) reflected on the general hesitancy and discomfort of many liberals in dealing with the evidence of family breakdown in the inner city. According to Wilson (1987b), the primary causes of increases in the welfare rolls were the economic conditions that often prevailed in inner-city areas. These conditions, he maintained, made it difficult for the poor, and particularly poor, black men, to escape poverty through work. In turn, this made the prospect of traditional nuclear family life less appealing for inner-city women (Wilson 1987b). Wilson's own arguments received considerable acclaim, but, as he recognized, conservatives dominated the political discourse about welfare policy. Too often liberals had "not only been puzzled by the rise of inner-city social dislocations, they . . . also lacked a convincing rebuttal to the forceful arguments by conservative scholars who attribute these problems to the social values of the poor minorities" (Wilson 1987a, 14). Wilson reflected that this was to some extent a consequence of how discussions about inner-city life had been put off limits within liberal circles by the damning reaction of some leading African American academics to the Moynihan report (Wilson 1997, 172).

Furthermore, some liberal voices, while continuing to rebut the analysis of conservatives such as Murray, were beginning to engage in debates about the merits of time limits on welfare receipt. One influential book illustrating this liberal rethink on welfare policy was published in 1988. David Ellwood's *Poor Support* was an important book in its own right, but the significance of Ellwood's ideas was further emphasized when he later joined the Clinton administration as a leading advisor on welfare matters. From a liberal perspective, *Poor Support* broke existing taboos by recommending time limits for the receipt of AFDC. Ellwood also called for this time limit to be accompanied by a series of support services to help people move from welfare to work, including, if necessary, a government-guaranteed job for those willing to work but unable to find a job in the private market, but it was the suggestion of time limits coming from a recognizably moderate liberal voice that made this analysis so eye-catching (Ellwood 1988). Ellwood, when part of the Clinton White House, helped to devise the administration's own welfare bill that was unveiled in 1994 under the title Work and Responsibility Act (WRA). As is discussed in the following section, the WRA drew fire from both liberals and conservatives before it was superseded by PRWORA. It is perhaps a mark of how far PRWORA represented a shift to the ideological right that Ellwood resigned and publicly opposed that final bill (Ellwood 1996).

Policy Change in the Reagan Era

It is an irony that the first legislation to end a large federal benefit entitlement program was signed by a Democratic president, particularly after AFDC had largely survived the Reagan era. Yet, while Reagan's presidency did not witness the culmination of conservative critiques, there were some important portents of what was to come in policy terms in evidence throughout the 1980s.

The most direct attempt to roll back AFDC during the 1980s came in 1981 with the passage of the Omnibus Budget Reconciliation Act (OBRA). OBRA was enacted despite continuing Democratic control of the House of Representatives. This legislative success for the administration reflected how, in the early months of the Reagan presidency, "defenders of the welfare state were on the run" as Reagan's triumph and apparent popularity seemed to give legitimacy to the conservative argument that the economic problems of the late 1970s were the result of the excesses of "tax and spend" liberalism (Davies 2003, 211). As it was, OBRA reduced both the income levels that families could earn and the asset amounts they could own and remain eligible for AFDC. These changes reduced the AFDC rolls by about four hundred thousand recipients and cut benefits for nearly another three hundred thousand (ibid.). The administration also called for states to introduce new work requirements, but this was watered down in the Senate Finance Committee and the House's Ways and Means Committee so that states were allowed to introduce new workfare measures but not required to do so (Weaver 2000, 68). While this did not constitute displacement of the existing AFDC rules, it was a case of policy layering that clearly indicated that welfare recipients were now viewed with suspicion rather than with sympathy.

In another provision pushed by the Reagan White House, OBRA undid one of the incentives of the 1967 amendments to AFDC that had been designed to encourage welfare recipients into the workforce by allowing them to keep some of their earnings and remain eligible for benefits. The 1967 law had required states to disregard the first $30 of a family's monthly earnings and then one-third of earnings over that when calculating benefit levels. OBRA stipulated that these disregards could only last for four months. This measure was a clear rejection of the incentive structures built into the Nixon and Carter administrations' NIT plans. The changes made in the OBRA package not only enacted cutbacks to AFDC eligibility and benefit levels but also meant that the government provided less support to those attempting to transition between welfare and work. For Reagan-style conservatives, federal government efforts to supplement the incomes of low-paid workers were not interpreted as justifiable aid to the deserving poor but as dangerous policies that might spread the contagion of dependency to the working population (Davies 2003, 212–13). Interestingly, however, this was one area where, politically at least, liberals prevailed as the EITC for working poor families was expanded in the 1980s and 1990s (Myles and Pierson 1997). Yet it is worth reemphasizing that the EITC is based on a principle quite different from Nixon's proposed FAP. The latter was an income guarantee that would have been based simply on need, whereas the EITC explicitly reinforces the division between the working and nonworking poor (Steensland 2008). Moreover, one consequence of the OBRA reforms was that it reduced the likelihood of AFDC recipients working, at least in the formal economy, meaning that just as more women generally were entering the labor market, AFDC mothers were reducing their levels of work. In turn, that trend further weakened the coalition continuing to support the AFDC program (Weaver 2000, 68).

Incremental Change and Conservative Ideas

After these initial cuts, the Reagan administration found it increasingly difficult to advance explicitly its conservative social policy agenda, but the president's rhetoric continued to emphasize the dangers of welfare dependency. His 1986 State of the Union address referred to the "spider's web of dependency" and declared, "we must revise or replace programs enacted in the name of compassion that degrade the moral worth of work, encourage family breakups, and drive entire communities into a bleak and heartless dependency" (Reagan 1986). Two years later, in his 1988 State of the Union address, Reagan argued that the effect of government spending on welfare programs since the 1960s had "too often . . . only made poverty harder to escape. Federal welfare programs have created a massive social problem. With the best of intentions, government created a poverty trap that wreaks havoc on the very support system the poor need most to lift themselves out of poverty— the family. Dependency has become the one enduring heirloom, passed from one generation to the next, of too many fragmented families" (Reagan 1988). Hence, the failure to build on the 1981 reforms did not stop Reagan from continuing the ideational attack on welfare. In fact, it is possible to see the 1986 State of the Union address as the point at which the momentum gathered for another effort at welfare reform. In addition to denouncing dependency in that speech, President Reagan also called for a new study on welfare reform. Reports and studies in themselves can mean little but Reagan's speech reignited media attention about welfare reform and legislative efforts were renewed (Haskins 1991, 617).

Importantly, by the late 1980s, the terms of the debate had shifted not only among policy entrepreneurs and intellectuals but in Congress as well. Reflecting how ideas previously seen as distinctly conservative had become mainstream, all sides emphasized, or at least conceded, the importance of work, and there was agreement that more needed to be done to force absent fathers to face up to some financial responsibility for their children. In addition, there was a greater willingness to allow states to experiment with their own programs (Weaver 2000, 71). In this context, the National Governors Association (NGA) became an important voice pushing for reform, with Governor Clinton of Arkansas at the forefront of the NGA's lobbying.[14] Nevertheless, there remained significant disagreements about the specifics of reform, and these were reflected in the battle for control of the reform agenda within Congress. House Democrats were keen to formulate a bill that had as little Republican input as possible, but Senators Pat Moynihan and Lloyd Bentsen were more willing to compromise with their GOP counterparts. The bills that emerged from the two chambers of Congress were therefore quite different, but the conference committee negotiated enough compromises to secure comfortable final passage. Thus, the final bill included a provision favored by House liberals that AFDC-UP be made a mandatory rather than an optional program for the states, whereas a Senate amendment sponsored by Robert Dole (R-Kan.) recommended that one parent in these families work for at least sixteen hours a week in community work experience programs was incorporated. Elsewhere the bill stipulated that welfare leavers would remain eligible for Medicaid for twelve months after leaving the rolls, while conservatives were cheered by requirements that the states enroll 20 percent of their welfare clients in the Jobs Opportunities and Basic Skills training program (JOBS) by 1995. As enacted in 1988, this Family Support Act (FSA) was estimated to cost just 3 billion dollars over five years, with a billion of that reserved for the new JOBS program.

As it turned out, the FSA was a staging post rather than the final destination for welfare reform and, according to Weaver, it "was full of compromises between liberals and conservatives" (Weaver 2000, 76). Weaver's judgment, however, understates the important manner in which conservative ideas had encroached into the welfare policymaking mainstream. In comparison to the later PRWORA, the FSA did contain a mix of conflicting principles, and there was enough diversity in the final form of the legislation that it passed Congress with remarkable levels of bipartisan support; yet the FSA was not ideologically neutral. The bill did expand access to AFDC-UP in a manner consistent with liberal ideas, but it also—and in retrospect, decisively—thrust the principle of workfare more squarely onto the policy agenda.

Furthermore, the conservative elements of the FSA were to prove more enduring than the liberal ones. While the FSA was a legislative compromise, "the conservative side of the act was more notable" (Mead 1992, 177). In particular Mead notes that the debates about the FSA "witnessed the full flowering of dependency themes" (ibid., 198). From a different political perspective, Desmond King argued that the FSA illustrated the "political power of advocates of liberal market-oriented policies." The FSA assumed "a distinction between deserving and undeserving recipients" and then reinforced that "stigmatizing distinction" (King 1995, 197). Moreover, the passage of the FSA illustrated "the weak electoral and political power of program participants. The success of New Right ideas in influencing politicians formulating these programs demonstrates their political power and the weakness of those governed by them" (ibid., 198). Notably, in 1988 there was no equivalent to the NWRO protests on Capitol Hill that had helped sink the FAP during the Nixon era.

Overall, the FSA is perhaps best understood as an incremental step that was part of an ongoing ideological trend. The work requirements in the FSA, however diluted and in practice ineffective, were an important foundation that embedded the principle of workfare into the future building blocks of welfare reform. Overall, while Democrats insisted on incorporating some of their pre-ferred aspects in the FSA, they also conceded some key conservative principles. Critically, reflecting the ideas assertively pushed by conservatives throughout the 1980s, the debate about welfare recipients increasingly focused on their depen-dency rather than on their poverty.

The Welfare "Crisis" and Issue Ownership

For all the effort that went into legislating the FSA, the new policy structures were barely put in place before they were overtaken by events. The numbers of AFDC recipients had in fact held relatively steady throughout the 1980s, but there was a further surge in the welfare rolls just as the FSA hit the statute books. From 1980 to 1988, the number of AFDC recipients rose from 10.6 million to 10.9 million. By 1990 there were nearly 11.5 million AFDC recipients, and by 1992 the number had jumped sharply to more than 13.6 million (US Congress 1994, 325). Whatever its merits as a policy, the FSA had not resolved the issue of welfare at either the street or the political level. This undermined those welfare policy experts who had hoped that, after the passage of the FSA, energies would be concentrated on implementation rather than on a continuing battle over the fundamentals of pol-icy (Bane 1992).

President George H. W. Bush was not as strident in his rhetoric as his prede-cessor, but in his inaugural address he lamented the "addictions" of welfare and single motherhood, adding that "public money" was not the way to resolve these "problems" (Bush 1989). Through his presidency, there was no serious attempt at further reforming the welfare system, but when Governor Clinton emerged onto the national political scene in 1992, one of Clinton's major themes was the need to once again return to welfare reform.

As indicated by his involvement in the development of the FSA, Clinton had a genuine interest in welfare policy and a deep knowledge of the issues. In 1992 Clinton brought the welfare policy domain to the fore of the presidential cam-paign not only because it was an area where he could legitimately demonstrate his expertise but also because, in denouncing the existing welfare system, he was able to show that he was not an old-fashioned liberal (Béland, Vergniolle de Chantal, and Waddan 2002; Béland and Waddan 2006). To properly understand Clinton's motives, it is important to reflect on how the shift in the terms of the welfare debate since the 1970s had recast the issue ownership of welfare policy.

AFDC had always struggled for popular legitimacy, and there was little political credit to be distributed as a consequence of the expansion of the welfare rolls throughout the 1960s. As welfare rolls increased, political elites nevertheless proposed guaranteed income schemes, even though such schemes did not command clear popular support. Prior to the FAP proposals, polls showed clear opposition to the idea of a guaranteed income. As FAP was debated in the public arena, there was a rise in support for the principle of an income guarantee as long as this was tied to strong, enforced work requirements (Erskine 1975). Certainly, in retrospect, it seems surprising to reflect on how close the United States came to enacting a guaranteed income scheme for all families at the end of the 1960s (Myles and Pierson 1997).

In his memoirs Nixon described the FAP as "an idea ahead of its time" (Nixon 1978, 427), but in hindsight it looks more like an anomaly because a Republican president tried to preempt what turned out to be a faltering liberal consensus (Béland and Waddan 2006). By the 1990s the ideological and partisan dimensions of welfare politics were much more clearly defined. This was an area of social policy where liberal sentiments were out of touch with wider public feeling (Shkalr 1991; Feldman and Zaller 1992). Summarizing poll findings, Weaver, Shapiro, and Jacobs concluded: "Welfare has come to denote dependence. . . . Majorities of the public are concerned that welfare benefits may be too high and that welfare encourages long-term dependence, and that too many welfare recipients do not want to work. . . . 'Welfare,' in short, is perceived as being at odds with the widely shared American values of individualism and the work ethic" (1995, 607). Furthermore, there was disengagement between much of the community of research experts— many of them clustered in liberal-leaning think tanks—and public opinion. When reflecting on a poll showing that 89 percent of respondents agreed that there should be a two-year limit on welfare receipt followed by work, and that 76 percent thought that welfare mothers who had another child should not receive increased benefit payments, Isabel Sawhill, who served as an associate director in the Office of Management and Budget during Clinton's first term, acknowledged that

> research gives insufficient emphasis to the role of public morality in shaping the current welfare debate. It ignores the public's desire to align welfare rules with their own values. The public is not lacking in compassion but it does believe that poor people should play by the same rules as the middle class. When you don't work, you don't get paid. And when you have another baby you don't get a raise. The public may even be willing to risk doing some harm to children in order to instill more of this kind of discipline into the system. (Sawhill 1995, 8)

If liberal researchers recoiled from these popular sentiments, the sustained ideological attack on welfare from conservatives, given political form by Reagan and an intellectual rationale by Murray, was continued into the early 1990s by a band of congressional Republicans and writers such as Robert Rector from the Heritage Foundation (Rector 1992, 1996). According to these voices, AFDC had led to social breakdown among an "underclass" of Americans as welfare dependency fostered increasingly dysfunctional personal behavior. Even if terms such as "underclass" and "undeserving" were not precisely defined, their very use was a powerful ideological weapon in framing the welfare policy debate (Mann 1994), particularly since these conservative ideas were in tune with—and helped shape (Somers and Block 2005)—public opinion. An NBC/*Wall Street Journal* poll in June 1994 found 59 percent of respondents agreeing with the statement that "the breakdown of the traditional family unit" was a "major reason" for the increase in welfare rolls. A *Times Mirror* poll from March of the same year saw 75 percent agreeing with the idea that welfare "changes things for the worse by making able-bodied people too dependent on government aid."[15] Some liberals were concerned that these attitudes reflected racial stereotyping as well as a simple dislike of welfare. Studies by the scholar Martin Gilens gave evidence to support these concerns. Prior to the mid-1960s, news stories about poverty and welfare focused on the white population, but after that time media coverage of welfare focused on African Americans (Gilens 1996, 1999). Gilens concluded, "The symbolic power of welfare as a political issue stems in large measure from its racial undertones" (1996, 602). Yet whatever the possible hidden agenda behind hostility to welfare, the political and, increasingly, policy momentum were gathering behind the conservative tide. At the federal level it had historically been Democrats who saw themselves as the welfare policy experts. By the 1990s, however, welfare, unlike the big-ticket social policy items of Social Security and Medicare, was a Republican issue, illustrating the relative instability of issue ownership in the field of welfare reform.

It was into this environment that governor and Democratic presidential candidate Clinton stepped in, embracing welfare policy as one of his core issues. For candidate Clinton, the shifting patterns of welfare politics and policy offered a political opportunity to reinforce his rebranding of the Democratic Party. In 1992 Clinton did not simply elaborate on welfare in a policy-wonk style. Welfare became a critical part of his political identity and his effort to develop an effective preemptive strategy (Skowronek 1997) by defining himself as a "New Democrat." Backed by the Democratic Leadership Council, candidate Clinton quickly developed the overarching themes of "opportunity" and "responsibility" (Cook 1992) as part of an effort to redefine the Democratic Party at the presidential level in the aftermath of three defeats throughout the 1980s (Hale 1995; Baer 2000). It was in the arena of welfare policy that candidate Clinton was able to illustrate that he was a "different type of Democrat." What better way to distinguish New Democrats from old ones than by attacking a program closely associated with the perceived "excesses" of Great Society liberalism? In addition, Clinton's long-standing and genuine interest in welfare policy, demonstrated by his enthusiastic involvement in drawing up the FSA, gave legitimacy to his dissatisfaction with the traditional Democratic defense of the existing AFDC system. Thus, welfare reform and the need to move more welfare recipients into work became one of his consistent stump speech pitches from the start of his presidential bid. It was on October 23, 1991, that he first used a line that was to become one of the hallmarks of his campaign: "In a Clinton administration we're going to put an end to welfare as we know it" (quoted in DeParle 2004, 4). After that, Clinton's efforts to turn welfare into a wedge issue that worked to the Democrats' advantage rested on the resonance carried by that repeated sound bite. As the campaign drew to a close, Democratic pollster Celina Lake called this phrase "pure heroin" (DeParle 2004, 4 and 345n).

The Clinton Welfare Plan

In reality, Clinton's campaign promises about "ending welfare as we know it" were open to both interpretation and misinterpretation. In their 1992 campaign book, candidates Clinton and Gore elaborated on the message. "It's time to honor and reward people who work hard and play by the rules. That means ending welfare as we know it—not by punishing the poor or preaching to them, but by empowering Americans to take care of their children and improve their lives. No one who works full-time and has children at home should be poor anymore. No one who can work should stay on welfare forever" (Clinton and Gore 1992, 164). Here, ending welfare was placed in the context of making work pay amid the wider Clinton campaign themes of marrying "opportunity," "responsibility," and the "new covenant." This raised the possibility that liberals could do a trade with conservatives whereby the former would concede the need to move more welfare recipients into work while the latter would acknowledge the need for investment in antipoverty programs (Soss and Schram 2007, 111–13).[16] Therefore, much of the devil of what "ending welfare as we know it" actually meant was likely to lie in the legislative detail.

Once in office, however, the Clinton administration's legislative agenda was crowded out by the budget proposals, NAFTA, and health care reform. A welfare reform task force was established, but progress was slow. There were delays in naming its membership and, thereafter, indecisive leadership, open division, and leaks hampered the task force's effort. For all that, the administration did eventually put forward a reform bill in June 1994. When President Clinton signed the Republican-crafted PRWORA in August 1996, his administration's own effort at legislating reform had largely been forgotten. But the 1994 Work and Responsibility Act (WRA) does merit some consideration because it witnessed a Democratic administration place new obligations and time limits on welfare recipients.

The political selling point of the WRA was its proposal to limit AFDC receipt to two years. After that welfare beneficiaries would need to participate in community work schemes to carry on receiving cash support. School-aged mothers would be required to attend school. Noncompliance would result in termination of the whole family's benefits. In addition, new single mothers would have to name the father of their child in order to qualify for benefits. The legislation proposed that states should decide whether to impose a so-called family cap that would limit or deny extra benefits to families who gave birth to another child while already on welfare. These plans appeared radical in principle, but the implementation schedule undermined the significance of the headline proposals. The administration's emphasis on deficit reduction meant that the WRA had to be budget neutral, but the education, training and child-care expenditures predicted meant that new revenues would be needed. It was a political nonstarter to suggest that extra revenues come from increased taxes, so the administration needed to find savings elsewhere in discretionary social welfare budgets; but this meant juggling with small pots of money and inevitably restricting the WRA's scope. In the end, the White House came up with $9.3 billion of funding over five years largely by tightening welfare eligibility for legal immigrants and restricting aid to states for emergency welfare programs, but this sum was far from sufficient to pay for the transition of the AFDC population to work. Indeed, the reality was that only 170,000 of the adult AFDC caseload of more than 5 million were expected to be in government-subsidized employment by 1999 (Weaver 2000, 243).

Despite the limited scale of the plan, there had been a series of internal disagreements among those drafting the proposals. Of particular note were the disputes between David Ellwood, who had been drafted as a special advisor on welfare policy, and Bruce Reed, who had been an early advisor to the Clinton campaign and was a senior domestic policy aide. Ellwood had made his reputation as a liberal who was prepared to countenance welfare time limits and work obligations (Ellwood 1988), but he did not embrace the "ending welfare" rhetoric. His concept of time limits applied to unconditional cash welfare, not to government help for those who were willing to play by the rules but were unable to find private-sector employment. Reed, on the other hand, had been instrumental in promoting the "ending welfare" catchphrase and felt that fulfilling that promise meant divining an absolute time limit. This resulted in a critical disagreement, as the reform plan was being drafted, about how long AFDC recipients could remain in government-sponsored work schemes.[7] On the one side of the debate stood Ellwood and like-minded advisors, who were determined that as long as recipients made a sincere work effort, they should be allowed to remain in a government work scheme for as long as necessary. Banded against these forces were those led by Reed, who wanted a time frame for when government help would be terminated. The final compromise was that people could remain on government work schemes but that they would need to be reassigned every twelve months with their cases thoroughly reviewed after a two-year period (Waddan 2002, 121). Perhaps one surprising aspect of the overall process was Clinton's relative disengagement from it, reflected in his ambiguity over whether he did or did not favor an absolute time limit (DeParle 2004, 120–21).

As it was, the WRA came up against an array of institutional barriers and made no legislative progress. It divided Democrats. New Democrats applauded it as an example of tough but fair social policy reform, but liberals were not rec-onciled to the concept of time limits. When the House started hearings on the bill, Californian liberal Bob Matsui derided Ellwood when the latter gave testi-mony. Matsui was worried that discussing welfare in election season would lead to any legislation leaning further in a conservative direction (ibid., 122). Republicans lamented that the bill did not go far enough or fast enough in its implementation of work requirements. Newt Gingrich commented: "The President is brilliant at describing a Ferrari, but his staff continues to deliver a Yugo" (Marcus and Balz 1994, A18). What Matsui did not know was how soon the drafting of welfare legis-lation would be in the hands of Gingrich and a Republican Congress.

State Experimentation as Institutional Layering

Before analyzing the process that finally led to the enactment of PRWORA, it is important to understand how developments at the state level throughout the 1990s, taking the form of genuine institutional layering (i.e., waivers), had enabled con-servatives to claim that their ideas were supported by an array of evidence gathered from welfare experiments at the state level. Congress had in fact granted limited authority to the states to test alternative arrangements to AFDC in 1962, but the dis-cretionary authority was constrained and few states took advantage of the chance to apply for these waivers. Toward the end of his presidency President Reagan was keen to promote the idea that states act as policy laboratories and pressed the Department of Health and Human Services (HHS) to take a more sympathetic view to waiver applications. In his 1988 State of the Union address he declared,

> It is time—this may be the most radical thing I've said in seven years in this office—it's time for Washington to show a little humility. There are a thou-sand sparks of genius in 50 states and a thousand communities around the nation. It is time to nurture them and see which ones can catch fire and become guiding lights. States have begun to show us the way. They have demonstrated that successful welfare programs can be built around more effective child support enforcement practices and innovative programs requiring welfare recipients to work or prepare for work. Let us give the states even more flexibility and encourage more reforms. (Reagan 1988)

But even at this point, relatively few states took advantage of waivers in order to try expansive reforms (Weaver 2000, 132). The real revolution came when another former governor, Bill Clinton, arrived in the White House. In a speech to the NGA shortly after taking office, President Clinton promised to streamline the waiver process and added that the administration would look favorably at waiver requests even when they were not in line with the White House's preferences. Encouraged to seek discretionary powers by the federal government, and with welfare being an increasingly important theme in state politics, a bandwagon effect was stimulated among the nation's governors. By the time of the passage of PRWORA, more than half the states were using waiver provisions to implement statewide changes to the AFDC regulations. These experiments varied quite significantly in terms of whether they chose to emphasize "carrot" or "stick," or a combination of the two, and they did provide some new evidence about how reform of the AFDC regulations governing incentives and sanctions might affect the behavior of welfare recipients.

There had always been significant variation in benefit levels between states. For example, in 1995, families on AFDC received an average income amounting to 41 percent of the poverty line, but this varied from 16.2 percent of the poverty threshold in Louisiana and 16.5 percent in Alabama and Texas to just more than 60 percent in California and Connecticut and 88.9 percent in Alaska (Zedlewski and Giannarelli 1997, 6). These disparities reflected AFDC's patchy historical development rather than the systematic testing of how benefit levels impacted recipient behavior. The modifications that states introduced in the early 1990s changed much more than simply benefit levels. On the "carrot" side, waivers were granted that allowed states to improve incentives to enter the workforce such as increasing income disregards and expanding the eligibility of welfare leavers to continue to access Medicaid. Equally, the stick was evidenced as states introduced considerably more stringent welfare-to-work rules accompanied by tougher sanctions regimes for noncompliance, and some also experimented with family caps whereby families would not receive extra payments if a mother had another child while already receiving AFDC.

One condition of the waivers granted by HHS was that the effects of the reforms had to be monitored. Furthermore, in addition to the states' own efforts to monitor, the changes were analyzed by a series of independent think tanks such as the Manpower Demonstration Research Corporation. This resulted in a number of studies (see, for example, Gueron 1996; Parrot 1998) about welfare-to-work programs that were "crucial in convincing people that such programs could have positive effects on earnings and labor supply and negative effects on spending" (Blank 2002, 6). In reality the results from across the nation were mixed and inconclusive about the likely impact of national reform, and it was possible for onlookers to learn quite different lessons from the data that was made available. For liberals, the message was that significant movement of welfare recipients into work would be a slow process and that changes were best introduced incrementally. Yet from a conservative perspective, the evidence appeared to show that reform could have an impact but that change needed to be dramatic, and that welfare recipients needed to be made aware that they had no choice but to adapt to a new set of rules (Weaver 2000, 160).

Of particular importance were the programs that emphasized moving welfare recipients into any sort of entry-level job as quickly as possible. This contrasted with the liberal wisdom that education and training were the prerequisites of a successful transformation from welfare to work. The results that gained the most publicity were the ones that seemed to offer the most encouragement to the conservative argument. In particular, the data gleaned from a waiver program in Riverside, California, chimed with conservative sentiment that the best cure for welfare dependency was immediate work. Six counties in the state implemented new guidelines under the title of Greater Avenues to Independence (GAIN). In five counties the emphasis of GAIN was on education and training as a pathway to the labor market. In Riverside County the message to welfare recipients was to get a job, any job, as quickly as possible. The results suggested that this latter approach was more successful in both moving people into work and in raising household incomes. Again, the evidence was ambiguous because the increase in income was limited and many families remained eligible for welfare despite working (Riccio, Friedlander, and Freedman 1994; Gueron 1996). The dominant narrative, though, was that a "work first" approach was a more effective tool for combating dependency than putting off a day of reckoning through education and training. In policy terms, this "lesson" was a triumph for conservatives inasmuch as it fitted with their argument that the primary ingredient missing from the lives of welfare recipients was the discipline of work, whereas liberals preferred to see the problem as a prior lack of opportunity.

Another major aspect of the waiver programs was to persuade the governors of the virtues of devolving welfare authority from federal to state government. The Clinton administration had kept its word to grant many waivers, even radical ones, but there had been times when requests were turned down, provoking frustration among state authorities (Rabinovitz 1995). In turn, this encouraged some Republican governors to make partisan points and contest the ownership of welfare reform by attacking the White House for not acting quickly enough. One state continually in the vanguard of efforts to make radical changes to AFDC was Wisconsin. In September 1995 Kevin Keane, a spokesperson for the state's Republican governor, Tommy Thompson, praised the welfare bill then being discussed in Congress. Keane approved the proposal to devolve AFDC into a block grant program: "No longer would we have to go to Washington and kiss somebody's ring" (quoted in Johnson 1995). The war of words between Thompson and the Clinton administration emerged again in the spring of 1996. In April Governor Thompson signed into state law a plan for a dramatic restructuring of welfare that would have ended the AFDC entitlement. As the plan diverged from existing federal rules, the state government needed a waiver to implement its ideas. At this point Thompson declared, "The only person standing in the way of welfare's demise in Wisconsin is Bill Clinton, the man who promised America he would devote his presidency to ending welfare" (quoted in Pear 1996a). In response, the president at first appeared to endorse the state's efforts. In his weekly radio address on May 18, 1996, Clinton said of the Wisconsin proposals: "Wisconsin submitted to me for approval the outlines of a sweeping welfare reform plan, one of the boldest yet attempted in America, and I'm encouraged by what I've seen so far" (ibid.).

A month later, the administration let it be known that there were details of the Wisconsin plan about which it was uncertain (Pear 1996b). To the administration's critics, this delay and obfuscation was typical.

In July 1996 Clinton and Republican presidential nominee Bob Dole clashed, again contesting issue ownership, when addressing the NGA's annual conference. Clinton praised those governors who had experimented with welfare policy, and he asserted that his administration had granted "more than twice as many waivers as the previous two administrations combined." But Dole told the governors that they were still too restricted: "Our states deserve freedom, not just waivers. You must be given power—power, not just permission. Our problems are too urgent for inertia" (quoted in Clymer 1996).

This pressure from Republican leaders to engage in ever-more radical experimentation was despite the inconclusive evidence gleaned from the programs already operating under waivers. The momentum was difficult to resist because "the public favored change . . . and policymakers had made commitments to produce it" (Weaver 2000, 162). Some figures, such as Senator Moynihan, protested that time limits and devolution of authority to the states would hurt vulnerable children (Moynihan 1995), but while there was little from the states' various experiments that supported the idea that strict time limits were a necessary part of any reform package, by 1996, this had become a sine qua non of the conservative mantra on welfare.

This selective interpretation of the research evidence suggests that, even if the overall data gleaned from the various state experiments was inconclusive about the impact of reform measures, the political construction and use of the evidence in the national reform debate was more clear-cut. A genuine form of institutional layering, the pilot projects were perceived as legitimizing conservative ideas about how welfare could be reformed. Indeed, it was not just that the ambivalence of the findings of the state experiences was neglected because the results were used to endorse the conservative position. The very fact that the experiments took place illustrated that welfare systems could be significantly redesigned. Pilot programs at the state level gave life to the concepts under discussion. Moreover, the experiments themselves "change the bureaucratic structures of the institutions being targeted for reform. In the mid-1990s, pilot programs made time-limited welfare a reality and took away the argument that it could not be done" (Rogers-Dillon 2004, 7).

Because a disproportionate amount of attention was devoted to a select number of states where workfare was deemed a success, conservatives were enabled to proclaim that restructuring welfare was not only a good idea but was also institutionally viable. Wisconsin's welfare changes, for example, loudly championed by Gov. Tommy Thompson, drew considerable notice and were used to promote the message that imposing time limits on welfare receipt was neither a random nor harsh measure but an effective tool to change the behavior of welfare recipients (Rogers-Dillon 2004, 142). In fact, Wisconsin's political configuration was particularly conducive to bold welfare experimentation in the late 1980s and early 1990s, and it was far from certain that the same conditions could be replicated nationally, but the Wisconsin example was promoted as a model for reform. Mead notes: "Without Wisconsin's example, PRWORA would have been less radical" (Mead 2004, 6). Overall, institutional layering through welfare waivers helped conservatives legitimize the adoption of their workfare model nationwide. From this perspective, institutional layering taking the form of welfare waivers meshed with the politics of conservative ideas and the discursive "construction of the need to reform" (Cox 2001).

The Road to PRWORA: Reconciling Ideas and Institutions

Newt Gingrich had been dismayed in 1992 as Clinton usurped Republican ownership of welfare as a political issue, but the legislative inaction on welfare that followed gave the Republicans the chance to reclaim possession of this potentially critical political turf. Thus, one of the central planks of the Gingrich-inspired Contract with America that many congressional Republicans candidates campaigned on in the 1994 midterm elections was welfare reform. In November 1994 there was an appearance of Republican unity that contrasted with the divided ranks of Democrats on how welfare needed to be reformed, although that unity had not emerged painlessly. Reflecting different priorities in conservative thought, there had been arguments within conservative circles on what the primary goal of reform should be. All shared the sense that there needed to be greater pressure on adult welfare recipients to move into work, but some placed even more emphasis on the objective of reducing illegitimacy rates. In turn, the debate was further confused by arguments about whether withdrawing aid to prospective mothers might result in an increase in abortions—a prospect that was anathema to social conservatives. In addition to these disagreements, differing institutional perspectives had fueled further tensions. First, the relative discipline that Gingrich had exerted with respect to House Republicans was not matched in the Senate. Second, Republican governors, while embracing the idea of devolving some power over welfare policy down to states, were less happy if that authority was accompanied by cuts in federal transfers and requirements that would effectively constitute an unfunded mandate (Weaver 2000, 254–56).

Republican divisions had in fact been illustrated through 1994. In November 1993 the party's leadership had introduced its own welfare reform bill. This bill, known as HR 3500, appeared to show GOP unity with 160 out of 176 House members acting as cosponsors. This apparent consensus unraveled throughout the following months as HR 3500 came under fire for being too moderate and mainstream. Ron Haskins, one of the key architects of HR 3500, explained how this conservative bill was attacked from the right in a fashion that was typical of the way in which conservative actors such as the Heritage Foundation worked to push their agenda. First, conservative lobbyists and think tanks criticized the proposal for being too moderate and not constituting "real reform." Second, those forces joined with several members of Congress to produce a bill that did "deliver" on "real reform." From that point onward, all other efforts to produce reform legislation would be measured against the blueprint of the "real reform" bill. Finally, supporters of "real reform" would hit the airwaves, write op-ed columns, and lobby members of Congress in order to "reduce support for the moderate bill and rally support for the conservative bill" (Haskins 2006, 69).

A particular cause of concern for social conservatives was their feeling that HR 3500 did not propose to sanction illegitimacy with sufficient vigor. Social conservatives in Congress were urged on by voices from outside the legislature. In particular, Robert Rector at the Heritage Foundation insisted that the provisions of HR 3500 neglected this critical realm of welfare policy.[18] James Talent, a social conservative and member of the House from Missouri, argued that women under age twenty-one who had babies outside marriage should be ineligible for AFDC and food stamps, and their children should be permanently ineligible for these benefits. In the end, a compromise was reached so that a bill titled the Personal Responsibility Act (PRA) was included in the Contract with America. This bill featured both strong work requirements and provisions designed to discourage illegitimate births. The latter were not as tough as those advocated by Talent but did exclude from AFDC any children whose paternity was not established as well as children born to a mother under age eighteen. The PRA also called for a five-year lifetime limit on AFDC receipt and demanded that any single parent work at least thirty-five hours per week in order to continue receiving AFDC after two years on the program. The negotiations that led to the PRA were bitter, and all factions felt that the result was less than optimal (Weaver 2000, 264–65), but the proposal allowed Republicans to highlight their "toughness" in contrast to Clinton and congressional Democrats who had failed to deliver on the president's 1992 campaign promise.

Despite Republican control of Congress following the 1994 elections and an apparent plan in the shape of the PRA, the path to final welfare reform legislation was not smooth. An early complication for the congressional Republican leadership was to reach agreement with Republican governors. While the former were happy to devolve some authority to the states over the details of welfare programs, this authority (as laid out in the PRA) came with considerable strings attached. The plan left the possibility of states having to find the funds to implement welfare-to-work schemes, and to provide aid to those families who hit time limits and immigrants whose access to benefits would be restricted by the bill. Unsurprisingly, the governors preferred fewer strings and more money. Moreover, many Democratic governors were vociferously opposed, meaning that the NGA could not act as a co-coordinating body for the states in the manner it had as the FSA was deliberated. In turn, this gave a greater voice to a limited number of Republican governors, such as Tommy Thompson of Wisconsin and John Engler of Michigan, who claimed extra credibility on welfare issues due to the policy experiments already under way in their states (Weaver 2000, 267).

The means of reconciling the PRA with the wishes of the governors came in the shape of block grants. Block grants had been mentioned in the Contract with America but had been inserted more as a symbolic gesture than as a serious policy option (DeParle 2004, 124; Haskins 2006, 83). Nonetheless, once Republicans controlled Congress, the idea gained credibility because it seemed to offer both ideological and practical benefits. In principle, it fit with the conservative theme of delegating spending power and, hence, responsibilities for program design to the states rather than keeping it with the federal government. If states were given a sum of money to spend on alternatives to AFDC, within parameters set by Republicans in Congress, then that would categorically end any sense that welfare was a federal entitlement program. States would be left to decide whether the primary goal of their welfare programs would be to emphasize work or simply to get people off the welfare rolls by tightening eligibility requirements. Moreover, block grants appealed to Gingrich and the Republican leadership in Congress because they offered the possibility of effective cost control, at least from the federal government's perspective. That is, once states had been allocated their funds, there would be no more continuing demands on the federal purse. Furthermore, the Republican governors were largely amenable to the idea of block grants that would not increase over time, even in line with inflation. This arose from the publicity garnered by schemes such as those running in Wisconsin that suggested cutting the welfare rolls was possible. The Democratic governors, led by Howard Dean from Vermont, would not give block grants the imprimatur of bipartisanship, but this mattered little to Gingrich who enthusiastically pushed ahead.

The smooth development of the legislative package should not be exaggerated. Previous efforts at welfare reform had shown how easy it was for potential new laws to be derailed at the numerous institutional veto points, and as House Republicans led the way through 1995, it appeared as if once again various diversions would prevent the reform package from arriving at its destination. For example, for a brief period as the new Republican majorities in Congress were settling in, there was a public spat over the prospect of putting into orphanages the children of welfare mothers who failed to find work. In this instance, Gingrich backed down as Democrats gained popular traction by attacking this as an absurd and cruel idea (Weaver 2000, 274–76). This last point illustrates the danger of ideologically overreaching. Nevertheless, Gingrich effectively tacked to the right, leaving the Clinton administration's WRA proposals far behind. Thus, the House plan proposed a five-year absolute time limit and called for a fixed-sum block grant. It also included a family cap and excluded teenage mothers from receiving cash benefits until they reached the age of eighteen. And, unlike the WRA, the plan was devised to save money.

In contrast to the ideological ebullience of conservatives, liberals felt under siege. Liberal defensiveness was exacerbated by reinterpretation of the data about welfare recipients and their use of welfare. In the mid-1980s, David Ellwood and Mary Jo Bane first published research suggesting that 65 percent of AFDC recipients would be on the welfare rolls for eight years or more (Bane and Ellwood 1983). In 1994, as the researchers worked on welfare policy in the Clinton White House, they updated their findings in a manner that posed a critical challenge to the established notion that most people on welfare would be on the rolls for two years or less. Bane and Ellwood distinguished between methods of quantifying the longevity of welfare receipt. Rather than averaging out the time that each recipient spent on welfare after aggregating the total number of welfare spells over a period of time, Bane and Ellwood emphasized methods that looked at welfare recipients at a point in time. This different way of interpreting the data produced startling results. The traditional method of looking at welfare spells over a period of time showed that only 14 percent of mothers beginning a spell on welfare would remain on welfare for ten years or more. Counting the percentage of mothers on welfare at any point in time showed that 48 percent of these women would be in the midst of a spell lasting ten years or more (Bane and Ellwood 1994, 31). Moreover, they calculated that if recipients rather than spells were counted (that is, one recipient could move on and off the welfare rolls), then 56.6 percent of AFDC recipients at any point in time would likely be enrolled on the program for ten years or more in total (ibid., 39). Hence, the authors concluded, "Long term use of welfare is a very real and potentially quite costly phenomenon" (ibid., 40). Congressional Republicans enthusiastically, if selectively, brandished this data produced by these two liberals (Haskins 2006, 7). In addition, the overall increase in female participation in the labor force undermined the original premise behind AFDC that mothers should nurture their young rather than earn a wage. In 1960 less than 20 percent of mothers with a child aged younger than six did paid work outside the home. By 1991 58 percent of mothers of such children were actively participating in the labor market, as indeed were 54 percent of mothers of children aged younger than three (Kamarck 1992). This huge change in American society made it harder to justify the idea that some mothers should receive financial help from the government and not have to make a real work effort.[19]

As it was, many congressional Democrats ran from previously held positions (DeParle 2004, 130). While some Democrats did attack the Republican plans, depicting them as likely to lead to increased hunger and poverty, others took the ideologically counterintuitive step of attacking the developing welfare reform plan for not doing enough to promote work. The institutional dynamics left the Democratic leadership in the House in a particular tactical dilemma. House Republicans were clearly the most aggressively conservative grouping on welfare reform in Congress, and Speaker Gingrich was proving adept at keeping his caucus in line despite the absence of formal party discipline. The tougher the welfare bill that Gingrich could push through the House with clear majority support, the more likely any final bill would be to tack to the right because House Republicans would have more power to argue their case with their generally less-conservative Senate counterparts. House Minority Leader Dick Gephardt was therefore anxious to rally his party behind some alternative to the GOP in order to stop the more conservative Democrats from adding to the overall majority behind Gingrich. In the end, Democrats rallied behind a bill put together by Nathan Deal of Georgia (Pear 1995).[20] Deal's bill did not propose to make AFDC a block grant, and it called for guaranteed childcare, but in other ways it was as conservative as the Republican bill. It proposed a four-year absolute time limit and left states with the option to introduce a family cap and to exclude teenage mothers from cash assistance. By any previous Democratic standard, this was "an extraordinarily conservative measure" (Weaver 2000, 288). The Deal bill was endorsed by the White House but was defeated on the floor of the House. To some extent, it did serve its purpose because only nine Democrats supported the final Republican bill that passed on a vote of 234–199. Equally, it showed how far the momentum of the welfare debate had shifted to the right, and it illustrated that President Clinton would engage with this emerging conservative blueprint.

In contrast, developments in the Senate were always likely to be slower and more moderate. A complicating factor was the presidential ambition of Senate Majority Leader Bob Dole of Kansas. Looking forward to any future nomination campaign, Dole was aware of the need to appease conservatives who would be a disproportionate voice in the Republican primaries. Simultaneously, he wanted to demonstrate that he could be an effective leader in the Senate. With regard to the former, Dole's concern was not to be outflanked on the right by Senator Phil Gramm of Texas, who was another likely contender for the GOP nomination and who championed a tough line on welfare reform. If he was to provide effective leadership on welfare, Dole needed to deal with the reality that the Senate's political center of gravity had not shifted as decisively to the right as was the case with the House. Furthermore, given the Senate's fragmented institutional rules and structures, Dole did not have the tools to impose discipline on his colleagues as Gingrich had managed to do when internal debate among House Republicans had threatened to disrupt the reform effort.

As it was, the basic principles of hard time limits and block grants had quickly become established as the sine qua non of reform. In this respect, it is worth emphasizing how far the debate had moved on even from Clinton's 1994 reform proposal. The WRA had its time limit, but it guaranteed continued help for anyone making a good faith effort to work but who could not find regular employment in the private sector. In short, the WRA acknowledged that the government would act as an employer—and thus a source of income—of last resort. In contrast, a hard time limit imposed a final deadline at which point welfare recipients would have to sink or swim by their own efforts. In this context, Dole was left to negotiate between social conservatives and moderate Republicans while also trying to keep the governors happy. Given the dynamics of Senate procedure, it was also important to bring along some Democrats. The social conservatives, led by Gramm, were adamant that any bill should be framed so that states would have to opt out of provisions excluding teenage mothers from welfare and imposing family caps on benefit receipt, but these proposals alienated more moderate Republicans as well as Democrats. In the end, Dole navigated a bill through in September 1995 by allowing a series of votes on the Senate floor after agreeing with party colleagues that they would not use procedural means to kill the bill at that stage (Weaver 2000, 311). These votes in fact saw social conservatives defeated as the proposal for a mandatory family cap was replaced with a state option and an attempt to exclude teenage mothers from receiving federal monies was voted down. More moderates were brought on board by amendments promising more money for childcare and extra funds to states suffering economic downturns. Importantly, Clinton endorsed this bill, and its final passage was comfortable with an 87–12 margin.

This Senate bill was more moderate than the House bill, but the fact that so few Senate Democrats had voted against it and that the president had endorsed it demonstrated how fundamentally the welfare debate had shifted to the right. This Senate vote was a critical moment (Weaver 2000, 313). In crude terms, it was now clear that any final compromise bill negotiated between the two chambers would be at least as conservative as the Senate bill and in all likelihood would be further to the right than that bill. Critically, and reflecting the profound differences from the administration's WRA bill, hard time limits and an end to the entitlement status of AFDC were now part of the majority conventional wisdom on how to reform welfare. At this point, in September 1995, it was still unclear whether this triumph of conservative ideas would result in a decisive legislative output. It remained to be seen how far to the right of the September Senate bill any House–Senate conference proposal would end up. Would this be legislation that the president would sign? Indeed, did the congressional Republican majorities want to provide the president with a bill he would sign? Or would they prefer to tease him with bills they knew he would veto in order to emphatically claim ownership of "welfare reform" and give themselves and their party's 1996 presidential candidate an issue to run on in the 1996 election campaign?

A Landmark Reform, Eventually

In the end it took eleven months and two presidential vetoes to move from the September 1995 Senate bill to the White House signing ceremony for PRWORA in August 1996. The first veto came as part of the even bigger fight over the budget, which opinion polls showed Clinton winning. That is, through 1995, the Democratic president and Republican Congress had been at war over the latter's efforts to produce a balanced budget plan (Drew 1997). Clinton did in fact shift his ground considerably throughout the course of the year (Pierson 1998, 165) but he remained steadfast in his opposition to deep cuts to the Medicare program. On that matter, and clearly with important ramifications for the story told elsewhere in this book, the public largely sided with the president. In mid-November 1995 Clinton vetoed a budget resolution, which resulted in a six-day government shutdown. Then, in December, he was presented with the overall reconciliation bill that included a welfare reform package, but that reform was only a secondary part of the bigger budget story. In social policy terms, there was much greater reward for the president in opposing Republican plans to cut Medicare than in agreeing to cut welfare. The subsequent shutdown lasted three weeks and affected about 250,000 workers. Opinion polls showed that, by margins of nearly two to one, the public blamed Congress rather than the president for the stalemate and subsequent disruption (Waddan 2002, 57). Overall, this was a decisive setback for the "conservative revolution" in social policy. But welfare reform was not to be denied. Nevertheless, there was another veto to come. In January 1996 Congress sent a new bill to the White House. Regardless of the detail of its provisions about AFDC, this bill invoked a presidential veto because of clauses relating to the food stamp and school lunch programs. There then followed something of a hiatus, and there was a real possibility that welfare would be left to become a political campaign football. However, the institutional dynamics changed again, first because an intervention from the nation's governors revitalized the flagging spirits of those pushing for welfare reform and then, in early summer, because the electoral calculations made by the key political actors in Washington changed in a fashion that encouraged legislative action rather than political posturing.

First, the governors acted in unison when asking for reform along the lines of the January bill but with more federal funds for childcare and more flexibility for the states. It was hardly surprising that the governors made demands along these lines, but it was significant that even Democrats were on board this time. Critically, Howard Dean had been replaced as chair of the NGA by Tommy Thompson—which meant that leadership of the organization had passed from one of the strongest opponents of greater state control of welfare policy to one of its strongest advocates. Furthermore, it was evident by 1996 that the AFDC rolls were declining and that if states were to receive an allocated sum in lieu of AFDC federal funding, this would not necessarily mean a decline in the overall monies coming from federal government. This evidence encouraged the governors to accept the idea that block grant levels would be frozen.

Second, by the spring of 1996, the Republican presidential nomination race was settled in Dole's favor, and he resigned from Senate in mid-May to concentrate on his bid for the White House. Meanwhile, congressional Republicans had their minds focused on polls suggesting that they could lose their majorities in the November elections. Thus, there appeared to be a greater need for legislative accomplishment on which to campaign and to which, should they lose control of Congress, they could point to as a concrete legacy (Weaver 2000, 326). This combination of factors encouraged conservatives in Congress to search for a legislative agreement that the president would either sign or veto at his political peril. Primarily this meant designing a stand-alone welfare bill that removed the political cover for a veto.

The result was PRWORA, which ended the AFDC entitlement and replaced it with TANF. It also devolved authority to the states through block grants. As it turned out, the governors benefited from this because, even though grant levels were frozen through 2002, they were set at levels that coincided with the peak numbers on AFDC rolls, so states received more federal money over the period for TANF than they would have received under the old funding formula for AFDC. Yet the states were required to maintain spending at 80 percent of previous levels to remain eligible for the full grant. As well, states had to impose a five-year absolute time limit, and the bill demanded that welfare recipients be engaged in work activity as defined by the state to remain eligible for TANF after two years. In reality, given the circumstances of the vast majority of families receiving AFDC, these new rules meant that poor, single mothers with children under age eighteen were presumed to be self-sufficient after a short period of government assistance. These rules applied to all single mothers, whatever their domestic circumstances, no matter their prior work experience, and however limited their educational qualifications. PRWORA did allow that states could exempt 20 percent of their caseload from the five-year time limit.[21] States could also carry on giving assistance beyond five years at their own expense. Although the legislation did not detail the punitive action to be taken against families where the household head did not comply with these regulations, the clear implication was that states would apply financial sanction against such families even if this meant that the children in those families would suffer along with the adults. Some conservatives were frustrated that family caps were only included as a state option, and social conservatives would have preferred stronger sanctions against illegitimacy, but these disappointments were secondary when set against the dramatic nature of the changes that were enacted.

The debate within the White House over whether the president should sign or veto PRWORA was a bitter one. As Republicans finalized their plans, Clinton called a meeting on August 1 to debate how the administration should respond. Important voices from people deeply unhappy with the principles underlying PRWORA urged a third veto. Taking that position were the secretary of Health and Human Services, Donna Shalala, the president's chief of staff Leon Panetta, and most of the policy advisors. Championing the bill were the political advisors and Bruce Reed. Hillary Clinton also favored signing the bill—even though this set her against many of her friends (Clinton 2003, 369–70).[22] One calculation overhanging the debate was an electoral one. According to Dick Morris, then acting as an advisor to the president, a veto could cost Clinton the forthcoming election: "I told him flatly that a welfare veto would cost him the election. Mark Penn had designed a polling model that indicated that a welfare veto by itself would transform a fifteen-point win into a three-point loss" (Morris 1997, 300). George Stephanopoulos, in his account of his time as an advisor to Clinton, argues that Clinton's "heart urged a veto, while his head calculated the risk" (Stephanopoulos 1999, 421).

When it became clear that the president would sign the Republican bill, there was little will left for a fight among congressional Democrats because most saw little value in being seen to stand to the left of the president on welfare. Hence, the final votes in Congress were formalities. In the House, PRWORA passed by 328 votes to 101, and in Senate by 78 votes to 21. The senior Democrats in each chamber, Gephardt and David Bonior in the House and Tom Daschle in Senate, did vote against it, but overall House Democrats split exactly evenly at 98 votes each while in the Senate, 25 Democrats were in favor with 21 against. There were some who protested. In the aftermath of the Senate vote, Moynihan lamented: "This bill is not welfare reform, but welfare repeal. It is the first step in dismantling the social contract that has been in place in the United States since at least the 1930s." He predicted that PRWORA was just the start of a conservative rollback of the welfare state: "Do not doubt that Social Security itself—which is to say, insured retirement benefits—will be next" (quoted in Pear 1996c). In contrast, New York's other senator, Republican Alfonse D'Amato, remarked, "To those who are critical of the reform, let me say that no bill is perfect. But to continue business as usual, as if all is well, would have been a kind of conspiracy, a conspiracy to continue to keep our people on that narcotic. Absolutely not acceptable" (quoted in Pear 1996c). Reflecting election-year politics, of the Democratic senators up for reelection, only Paul Wellstone from Minnesota voted against the bill, and, indicating popular approval of the measure, various opinion polls showed clear support for the reform (Weaver 2000, 338).

In his memoirs, Bill Clinton lays claim to a higher motive than simple electoral math. Indeed, he reflects that welfare reform was high among the list of achievements of his presidency: "Signing the welfare reform bill was one of the most important decisions of my presidency. . . . America needed legislation that changed the emphasis of assistance to the poor from dependence on welfare checks to independence through work" (Clinton 2004, 721). Certainly it is the case that Clinton's embrace of welfare reform in 1992 was not simply or even primarily opportunistic. His record as governor of Arkansas illustrates that he was motivated by strongly held ideas about the problems resulting from the AFDC program. However, as evidenced earlier, it is hard to deny the fact that the legislation in signed into law in 1996 departed in crucial ways from the reform blueprint that Clinton had advocated four years earlier.

Aftermath and Reauthorization

By the end of the Clinton presidency, champions of PRWORA were not just claiming an ephemeral political and ideological victory but were insisting that the 1996 welfare reform constituted an undebatable policy success. As evidence, they pointed to the drop in welfare rolls from 4.415 million families in August 1996 to 2.453 million families in September 1999, a fall of 44 percent (Administration for Children and Families 2000). More significant for some reform advocates was the increase in labor market participation by welfare recipients. Statistically, never-married mothers were the least likely category of all women to do formal paid work, yet there was a 50 percent rise in the number of never-married mothers who moved from welfare to work between 1993 and 1999 (Haskins, Sawhill, and Weaver 2001). Researchers at liberal think tanks continued to worry that household income for those welfare recipients who left the rolls was inadequate (Parrot 1998) and that the economic prosperity of the late 1990s made it easier for the labor market to absorb welfare recipients, but the more prevalent view was expressed by Jean Rogers, a senior administrator for the Wisconsin welfare-to-work program, who insisted that the discipline imposed by work requirements gave welfare recipients a route to self-respect and provided a parental role model for children (Rogers 1999).

Some remaining Democratic divisions over the nature of the reform were revealed in the 2000 campaign for the presidential nomination when Vice President Al Gore attacked his principal opponent, New Jersey senator Bill Bradley, for his vote against PRWORA in 1996 (Clymer 2000). More significantly, during George W. Bush's campaign in 2000 and the early stages of his presidency, Bush used welfare reform as an example of what he meant by compassionate conservatism (Bruni 2001). Once in the White House, President Bush had to negotiate with Congress because PRWORA was scheduled for reauthorization in 2002. The debate over reauthorization and the importance of the changes that were finally made have been relatively neglected in the scholarly literature. This is unfortunate because some of the patterns witnessed in the mid-1990s returned. That is, institutional veto points again delayed reform as a battle to establish issue ownership and keenly held ideas influenced the moves and strategies of key political actors.

As it turned out, the task of reauthorizing PRWORA was not fully completed until that legislation was incorporated into the Deficit Reduction Act of 2005 (DRA). In the meantime, President Bush signed a series of extensions of the initial legislation. The delay did not reflect a fight over the major principles embraced by lawmakers in 1996 but rather disagreements over how to amend the reform model. The reauthorization debate did not provoke a liberal backlash against work requirements and time limits, thus undermining those Democrats who had favored welfare reform in the 1990s on the basis that ending AFDC would move the debate away from dependency and toward the problems of poverty (Soss and Schram 2007). In fact, the arguments through 2002 were about whether to impose stricter requirements on welfare recipients and whether to require the states to increase the proportion of their welfare caseload engaged in work activity. In February 2002 the administration published its proposal titled "Working Toward Independence." Largely following the administration's wishes, the House of Representatives passed a bill in May 2002 that required welfare recipients to engage with forty hours of work activity a week rather than thirty, and that required states to have 70 percent of their TANF caseload in work or job preparation rather than 50 percent as stipulated by the 1996 law. Although the debate over these proposals did not see a repeat of the rhetoric employed by reform advocates and opponents in the 1990s, the vote was still highly partisan, with only fourteen Democrats and four Republicans breaking ranks and voting for and against the bill, respectively.

Tommy Thompson, who had moved from Wisconsin to Washington to become secretary of Health and Human Services, praised the vote as a "bold and courageous vote to take the next step of welfare reform" (Pear 2002).

The Senate did not pass an equivalent bill because, once again, the Senate Finance Committee proved a graveyard for welfare reform. However, the Senate's deliberations did illustrate the continuing fractures in the liberal coalition when New York senator Hillary Clinton joined with centrist Democratic senators to push for the work requirement to be increased to thirty-seven hours a week. She and her allies argued that their proposal contained increased childcare funding that would make it possible for single parents to work those hours. But liberal advocacy groups cast doubt on the latter claim (Hernandez 2002). Senator Clinton was also rebuked by a *New York Times* editorial for siding with President Bush in calling for "punitive new work requirements" and for "making a mistake in thinking she can appease both sides on this issue."[23] In her reply to the newspaper, Clinton argued that she was in the "moderate, sensible center" (Clinton 2002; see also Clinton and Lieberman 2002). Whatever the merits of this argument, one consequence of the intervention by Senator Clinton and centrist Democrats was to entrench Republicans in their insistence that a forty-hour work requirement for TANF enrollees was necessary to make sure that their party was not politically outflanked by the Democrats.[24] Once again, as had been the case throughout the first term of Bill Clinton's presidency, this illustrates how policy positions can be driven by political competition for issue ownership.

Ironically, the idea of explicitly increasing work requirements had been dropped from the DRA by 2005. However, another strain of conservative thought did see some reward for its agenda setting efforts. The 1996 reform ended up concentrating on the welfare-to-work aspects of the conservative agenda rather than the profamily elements. The latter were evident in the final version of PRWORA but had become more marginal as the legislative process evolved. But the Bush administration was always keen to revitalize the "moral agenda" and breathe new legislative life into supporting traditional family units and discouraging unmarried motherhood (Haskins and Sawhill 2009, 214). Wade Horn, appointed to the post of assistant secretary for Children and Families, was a particularly influential proponent of programs to promote marriage. Reflecting that influence, the bill that passed by the House in May 2002 contained $300 million for programs to promote "healthy marriage" through advertising, counseling, and high school courses. Additional money was allocated to efforts to encourage "responsible" fatherhood and abstinence (Bumiller 2002). By the time of the passage of the DRA of 2005, these plans had been scaled down, but $100 million was put aside for marriage promotion efforts, and some funds were available for supporting fatherhood.[25]

A further important, if complex, change was made to the 1996 legislation. The 2002 efforts to increase both the number of hours that individual welfare recipients needed to work and the percentage of recipients that states needed to enroll on work programs were not included in the DRA. Yet the apparently technical and incremental change effectively meant that states were going to have to find ways to get more families into work participation schemes or remove them from TANF rolls. In its original form, PRWORA took fiscal year (FY) 1995 as its baseline year when calculating how well states had done in reducing their welfare caseload. If caseloads fell, then states benefited from a so-called caseload reduction credit that in turn eased the work participation requirement stipulating that states needed to have 50 percent of TANF families engaged in thirty hours of work per week. The DRA changed the baseline year to FY 2005. The impact of this switch amounted to much more than a technical adjustment. Welfare rolls had been at their peak in FY 1995 but were much lower in 2005. Thus, states were likely to have a much more difficult job in complying with work participation require-ments when the caseload reduction credit was based on 2005 numbers rather than 1995. A Department of Health and Human Services press release explained this change in a revealing phrase: "The caseload reduction credit, which had *inadvertently undermined TANF's work requirements*, was recalibrated, replacing the FY 1995 base year with a base year of 2005" (US Department of Health and Human Services 2006, emphasis added). This suggests that there was a conscious effort to reverse what might be described as a case of policy drift in order to keep welfare reform in line with conservative ideas.

Overall, the reauthorization process reinforced the patterns seen in the 1990s because the new legislation was a "classical example of policy consolidation" (Daguerre 2008, 369). Conservative Republicans favored tougher work require-ments and a family values agenda. Moreover, they were not prepared to cede ground to Democrats on these issues, either in policy or in political terms. Thus, while in control of Washington's governing institutions, the Bush administra-tion and congressional Republicans acted on their ideas in a manner designed to heighten differences between themselves and their Democratic opponents.

Welfare in the Obama Era

In 2006, ten years after the passage of PRWORA, the authors of that law applauded the results of their work. One of the leading figures in the development of the legislation on the Republican side in the House, Rep. E. Clay Shaw of Florida, claimed, "We have been vindicated by the results. . . . Welfare reform was one of the most successful policy changes in our nation's history" (quoted in Pear and Eckholm 2006). Former president Bill Clinton maintained that, in cooperation with the Republicans, he had fulfilled his campaign 1992 pledge to the benefit of many former welfare recipients: "The last 10 years have shown that we did in fact end welfare as we knew it, creating a new beginning for many Americans" (Clinton 2006). The then-secretary of Health and Human Services celebrated the success of PRWORA and called for further reinforcement of its principles: "Welfare reform has been an unqualified success, but now it is time to 'reboot the system' and strengthen work requirements while putting a renewed focus on marriage" (Leavitt 2006). The evidence was perhaps more nuanced than acknowledged by such accounts. While welfare rolls had fallen and more single mothers were engaged with the labor force, there had also been an increase in the number of poor single parents, neither working nor collecting cash benefits, and thus left with no clear source of income. The incentives created by PRWORA and reinforced by the 2005 DRA meant that state rules often denied TANF assistance to potentially eligible families. In 1995 AFDC served 84 percent of eligible families whereas, in 2005, only 40 percent of eligible families were getting help through the TANF program (Pavetti and Rosenbaum 2010, 3). Nevertheless, welfare reform was widely perceived as success story, and there was no impetus to roll back the changes, even as the economy fell into recession through 2008, leaving people more vulnerable to unemployment and poverty.

In 2008 former senator John Edwards did briefly inject some discussion of antipoverty policy into the campaign for the Democratic presidential nomination, but there was little talk through the campaign about TANF and welfare benefits in general. In April 2008 Hillary Clinton did raise the prospect of creating a cabinet-rank position dedicated to combating poverty, but she divorced the antipoverty strategy from cash assistance programs such as TANF. Speaking of the old welfare regime, she said, "It should not be considered an anti-poverty program. It did not work" (quoted in Goodman 2008). Any chance that liberal Democrats might protest against her role in pressing for passage of PRWORA a dozen years earlier was diminished by then-Senator Obama's general approval of what he termed "an imperfect reform." He commented: "Before welfare reform, you had, in the minds of most Americans, a stark separation between the deserving poor and the undeserving welfare poor. . . . What welfare reform did was desegregate those two groups. Now, everybody was poor, and everybody had to work" (quoted in Goodman 2008). Thus, even when the Democratic candidates were pitching an appeal to the party's primary voters, there was no desire to revisit the issue of welfare. Even among liberal commentators who felt that PRWORA had harmed vulnerable people, there was an acknowledgment that there were advantages to defusing arguments around welfare. Paul Krugman, for example, argued that Barack Obama's candidacy reflected the decline of racial divisions in American politics that owed much to the 1996 welfare reform. Abolishing AFDC had "created a great deal of hardship. But the 'bums on welfare' played a role in political discourse vastly disproportionate to the actual expense of A.F.D.C. and welfare reform took that issue off the table" (Krugman 2008).[26]

Even the severe economic recession that began in 2008 prompted only limited calls for more generous TANF benefits. Indeed, although eligibility for food stamps and unemployment benefits was extended in response to extra demands made on the government safety net following the financial crisis and subsequent downturn, the evidence shows that there was only a limited and uneven increase in TANF use with significant variation from state to state (Lower-Basch 2010).

The 2009 American Recovery and Reinvestment Act (ARRA) did include $5 billion for a TANF emergency contingency fund that states could apply for if they had to cover more families or if they wished to provide one-off benefits to some families or subsidize jobs for the jobless (Pavetti 2009). Some conservatives attacked the ARRA provisions for giving more money to states as their TANF caseload grew, a move that contradicted the principle of a capped block grant embedded in the 1996 law (Bradley and Rector 2010). Through 2010, there was controversy because, according to some accounts, thirty-seven states had accessed the available emergency funding to subsidize up to 250,000 jobs, but Republicans in the Senate refused to agree to an extension of the fund, which had already been passed by the House, by the deadline of the end of September 2010 (Schott and Pavetti 2010, 2). This was despite evidence that some states, seeking to cut their spending, had reduced access to services, such as subsidized childcare, which had been instrumental in giving single parents the chance to enter the labor force (Goodman 2010). Reflecting how TANF had little impact as an antipoverty device in a time of economic stress, the program's caseload rose by only 13 percent between December 2007 and December 2009, during which time the unemployment rate doubled (Pavetti, Trisi, and Schott 2011). Overall, while some of the federal social policy activities did expand in response to the recession, there was little challenge in either ideational terms or through incremental institutional adjustment to the welfare policy settlement of the mid-1990s.

Conclusion

When President Clinton signed PRWORA in the summer of 1996, it marked the successful denouement of a concerted conservative campaign to restructure the relationship between welfare recipients and the state. The new law imposed significant new conditions on the former if they wished to claim aid from the latter. Indeed, PRWORA was based on the premise that government had only a temporary obligation to assist the welfare population. Even more dramatically, PRWORA held that the children of adults who were deemed to be behaving irresponsibly would suffer the repercussions of that parental behavior along with the adults. The stipulation that the head of household must engage with the world of work effectively made work a prerequisite of citizenship for the welfare poor. These principles were further reinforced in 2005. As we will see in the following chapters, the dramatic restructuring of welfare stands in contrast to the limited success of conservative policy entrepreneurs and legislators in reconfiguring Medicare and to the failure to privatize Social Security. The success of conservatives in the welfare policy domain was due to a mix of institutional, partisan, and ideological factors. More precisely, the nature of welfare policy legacies, the transformation of welfare as a partisan issue, and the growing weight of conservative ideas helped pave the way to reform.

First, regarding policy legacies, AFDC itself lacked both popular and political support. Critically, whatever the fiscal problems associated with Social Security and Medicare, these programs worked for their beneficiaries in a way that AFDC did not. Moreover, while Social Security and Medicare beneficiaries represent a powerful political constituency, welfare recipients lacked a strong political presence. At the end of the 1960s, the NWRO gave an organized voice to welfare claimants and liberal think tanks consistently argued for a more generous welfare system, but even these groups did not defend the AFDC program per se. Thus, when conservatives claimed in the 1990s that welfare was damaging to welfare recipients, there was little organized protest from welfare families themselves to dispute that perspective. One former Clinton administration official in the Office of Management and Budget noted that even some welfare recipients would complain that other AFDC beneficiaries were not making sufficient effort to get off the welfare rolls.[27] Moreover, the use of welfare waivers constituted a form of policy layering that over time further weakened AFDC's institutional and ideological foundations. One aspect of the use of waivers was to undercut objections to reform from welfare bureaucracies that administered AFDC. This illustrates how few other parties, apart from welfare recipients, had a perceived interest in continuing the AFDC program. This contrasted with another major means-tested program, Medicaid. In this case, health care providers have a stake in maintaining expenditure levels.

Second, and reflecting the ever-ambiguous political legitimacy of AFDC, conservatives—in partisan terms, the Republicans—had taken ownership of the welfare issue by the time of reform. In the 1930s and the 1960s, New Deal liberalism emphasized broad economic structures when addressing the problem of poverty. This approach played to the Democratic Party's strengths, and welfare was "a positive term that signified a broad spectrum of public benefits" (Soss and Schram 2007, 112). However, by the 1980s the focus had switched to an "individual unit of analysis" and conservative advocates framed the debate about dependency as one primarily of agency (King 2005, 72; O'Connor 2001). In short, liberals "owned" the issue of poverty alleviation but conservatives laid claim to the issue of ending "dependency." In policy terms, once dependency supplanted poverty on the federal policy agenda, the reform agenda changed in favor of Republicans and their conservative allies. The evolution of welfare politics, therefore, stresses the role of issue ownership in the politics of social policy. As this chapter has outlined, there were hugely significant differences in both the practical understanding of what was possible as well as the underlying interpretation of the "welfare problem" in the various reform plans advanced from the 1960s onward. President Johnson did not explicitly set out a welfare reform plan, but his emphasis was on the problem of poverty. President Nixon did more directly identify "welfare" as a problem, and his rhetoric emphasized the value of work as a cure not just for poverty but for dependency as well. Yet his rhetoric sounded harsher toward welfare recipients than his actual proposals ever implied. Carter's abortive attempt at reform was similar in principle to Nixon's. President Reagan moved the debate significantly to the right by defining the problem of welfare as one of dependency while relegating the question of poverty to secondary status. Later Governor Clinton, in a skillful preemptive political move (Skowronek 1997), successfully "stole" the issue of welfare back from the Republicans in the 1992 presidential campaign to reinforce his New Democrat identity. In office, Clinton then developed a complex, multitiered, welfare reform proposal that attempted to craft a "third way" message. But Republicans were not going to cede what had become one of their core issues during the Reagan era, and they pushed a much bolder reform agenda when they regained control of Congress in the aftermath of the 1994 midterms.

Third, underpinning the shift in issue ownership to the Republicans and central to the argument of this book was the increasing influence of conservative ideas in American politics and society. That is, the policy intellectuals and political figures promoting conservative ideas had an increasing impact as they developed a narrative about the "need to reform" (Cox 2001) welfare that legitimized a workfare agenda. The coherence of conservative attitudes toward welfare reform should not be oversimplified. Different agendas were at play as different factions variously emphasized the importance of work, the primacy of marriage and the nuclear family, and cost cutting to downsize the aggregate welfare state. But there was enough overlap between these causes that common ground could be found. Moreover, conservative advocates aggressively promoting their ideas were able to reframe the issue at stake from being about poverty to being about dependency. That is, when poverty was the primary concern, the "central issue was the proper material entitlements of the poorest part of society." By the mid-1990s, dependency was the primary concern and the "central issue was instead the incentive structures being created, and hence the sort of citizens being produced" (Shafer 2003, 226). Importantly, this ideational shift in turn changed the dynamics of the debate about how to help the least well-off in society. It became more difficult for liberals to dismiss conservatives and their ideas about how to treat welfare recipients as mean-spirited and punitive. Instead, conservatives were not just ideologically satisfied; they were also politically comfortable when able to argue their case that "true compassion lay in saving people from a demoralizing and dysfunctional federal program of welfare dependency" (Heclo 2001, 182).

Nevertheless, it is vital to remember that efforts at welfare reform had been thwarted a number of times before the successful legislative outcome in 1996. This brings us to a fourth part of the explanation for the successful conservative reform of AFDC. The earlier failure to achieve substantive reform is partly related to the fragmented nature of federal political institutions and the comparative indiscipline of the party system in the United States, which tend to complicate reform (Steinmo and Watts 1995). As was illustrated by the demise of the Family Assistance Plan in the Senate Finance Committee, major reform proposals, even with broad support in the executive and legislative branches, can be thwarted at quite specific points in the legislative process. Yet, when a relatively disciplined congressional Republican party combined with a Democratic president who had himself promised reform and was anxious not to be seen as reneging on this promise, the legislative dam was breached. This in turn reflects the relatively vulnerable policy legacies put in place by AFDC over its lifetime. It is instructive to reflect that the various reform plans, whatever their important differences, were always borne out of a critique of the existing welfare policy legacies. That is, even as it survived one demolition attempt after another, AFDC's institutional foundations lacked robust support. The problem for reformers was that, despite the minimal backing for the status quo, there was inadequate consensus on what change should look like. Thus, prior to 1996, there was always sufficient opposition to defeat reform proposals in the context of fragmented and veto-ridden federal institutions.

Opposition to reform was not always coordinated; indeed, as exemplified during the battles over the FAP, it sometimes came from ideologically disparate sources, but it was organized enough to block reform. AFDC, therefore, was always likely to prove vulnerable if reformers could generate significant momentum behind a particular reform plan. A critical boost to the reform movement came with the extended use of waivers across the states throughout the late 1980s and early to mid-1990s. This effective process of policy layering provided institutional grounds for conservatives to claim that their ideas worked in practice as well as in principle. Moreover, the fact that workfare was implemented at state level served to "prove" that such programs could be applied and implemented (Rogers-Dillon 2004). As it was, PRWORA still illustrated some differing priorities between conservative factions. Crucially, however, conservatives did come together and were able to exploit the political moment to bring about radical, path-departing policy change through legislative revision.

Notes

1. Personal Responsibility and Work Opportunity Reconciliation Act of 1996, H.R. 3734, 104th Congress. (1996). www.gpo.gov/fdsys/pkg/BILLS-104hr3734enr/pdf/BILLS-104hr3734enr.pdf.
2. On the possible contradictions between encouraging mothers to work and traditional notions of family life, see Beer (1999, 18–19).
3. The words "Families with" (ADC thus becoming AFDC) were introduced in 1962. For the sake of consistency, we use AFDC throughout.
4. For an extensive discussion of the "mother's pensions" movements and the brief emergence of aspects of a "maternalist welfare state" prior to the 1935 Social Security Act, see Skocpol (1992) and Gordon (1994). Gordon argues that with the New Deal and the more formal organization of welfare state structures came a decline in women's influence: "The crux of events in 1935, from a gendered perspective, was that as the welfare system grew in size and importance, men took it over." This contrasted with earlier moves to establish welfare programs when "women had dominated the welfare field" (Gordon 1994, 264).

5. For a different take on this issue see Thelen (2003) and Weir (1992).
6. The figure of $1,600 per year for a family of four is based on the model of a two-parent, two-child household. Each adult would receive $500 and each child, $300. Families of different sizes would be paid accordingly.
7. Nixon was defending Bush's vote in favor of FAP when Bush was a member of the House of Representatives. Bush was under fire from Democratic candidate Lloyd Bentsen for that vote.
8. *The New York Times*, January 11, 1970, 46.
9. The FAP was contained in H.R. 16311. Southern Democrats voted by 85 to 17 against the bill.
10. A fuller history of the origins of the image of the "welfare queen" is given by Handler and Hasenfeld (2007, 158–62).
11. The authors thank Henry Aaron, who was assistant secretary for Planning and Evaluation at the Department of Health Education and Welfare from 1977 through 1978 for this insight.
12. Haskins was a central player through much of the welfare debate. He worked as staff director for House Ways and Means Committee Subcommittee and then worked in the George W. Bush White House as a welfare policy advisor.
13. Somers and Block cite Himmelfarb (1984) and Olasky (1992) as examples of this trend.
14. Governor Clinton "lobbied furiously" for the passage of a welfare bill and "virtually acted as a legislator himself, sitting in as House members drafted the bill" (DeParle 2004, 100).
15. These polls were reported in *American Enterprise*, January–February 1995, 108–9.
16. Some Democrats (Kaus 1995) expressed the view that ending welfare would not only detoxify the issue for the Democratic Party but would also create the political space to shift the debate on poverty in a liberal direction. Soss and Schram (2007), however, found little evidence that the 1996 welfare reform changed mass preferences. One former advisor to President Clinton on welfare expressed frustration that conservatives such as Mead, who were prepared to spend public funds on helping welfare recipients into work, were not committed to ensuring that those who did move from welfare to work were adequately paid for that work. Interview conducted by Alex Waddan with former White House official (Boston, March 1999).
17. Interview conducted by Alex Waddan with former Clinton White House official (Boston, March 1999).
18. Interview with Alex Waddan (Washington, DC, March 1999).
19. Many AFDC mothers did work, but much of this was done in the black market economy (Edin and Lein 1997).
20. Deal switched parties later in 1995.
21. This was a political number rather than one based on social science research. Interview conducted by Alex Waddan with former Republican staff aide (Washington, DC, March 1999).

22. See Edelman (1997) for a strong attack on PRWORA from someone with close ties to Hillary Clinton. Accounts of this meeting were also given in interviews conducted by Alex Waddan with a former advisor to Hillary Clinton (Boston; Washington, DC, March 1999).

23. *The New York Times*, May 15, 2002.

24. A senior welfare advisor to the White House at this time noted that Senator Clinton's intervention disrupted the effort to deal with complex issues about how best to get single mothers into lasting employment. Interview conducted by Alex Waddan with former senior White House advisor (Washington, DC, September 2009).

25. In addition to the money contained in the DRA, some marriage education initiatives had been set up in 2002. For more details on the "healthy marriage" grants, see Haskins and Sawhill (2009, 257–62).

26. As has been noted, however, Soss and Schram (2007) cast doubt on the notion that PRWORA resulted in changes in public attitudes toward welfare itself.

27. Interview with Alex Waddan (Washington, DC, September 2009).

Chapter Two
Medicare Reform, 2003

After Social Security, Medicare is the second-most expensive public social policy program in the United States. In 2006 Social Security paid out $548.5 billion in benefits, amounting to 20.65 percent of federal expenditures, whereas Medicare spending was $329.9 billion, accounting for 12.4 percent of federal expenditures (US Census Bureau 2009a). Like Social Security, Medicare is highly popular and primarily serves the country's seniors, although it also covers the disabled. In 2007 there were 36,155,452 Medicare beneficiaries, amounting to 12 percent of the population (Kaiser Family Foundation 2009). This gives Medicare a large base of beneficiaries, making it a program that prospective reformers need to treat with considerable caution. Nevertheless, the program's rules and regulations have been subject to political interference, and Medicare has been significantly revised since its foundation. Confusingly, as will be evidenced in this chapter, the changes have not had a consistent ideological bias. In fact, the bitterly contested 2003 Medicare Modernization Act (MMA) contained contradictory ideological impulses within itself. The headline aspect of that piece of legislation was a new prescription drug benefit for the nation's seniors, which expanded the program's mandate. Simultaneously, the law introduced, through a process of policy layering (Jaenicke and Waddan 2006a), elements much more to the liking of conservative-minded political actors, which were designed to illustrate the credibility of conservative ideas for future reform.[1]

The MMA and its consequences and implications are discussed later in this chapter, as is the furor about the changes to Medicare included in the 2010 comprehensive health care reform legislation. The broader point to understand is that Medicare, after a period of relative consensus following its creation, increasingly became a focus for political and ideological debate (Oberlander 2003). This was especially the case after the Republican capture of Congress in the midterm elections of 1994. Medicare had been subject to major reform between its foundation in 1965 and the mid-1990s as policymakers sought to contain the program's spiraling costs, but the changes enacted during that period had not generated outright partisan division. From 1995 onward, reform debates took on a more explicitly ideological form when Republicans more vigorously advanced conservative ideas about how competition rather than regulation would best remedy the program's perceived problems (Morgan 2010). Liberal policy analyst Bruce Vladeck, who had served as the administrator of the Health Care Financing Administration from 1993 to 1997, dramatically expressed the perceived political stakes. Writing at a time of Republican political ascendancy, Vladeck commented, "The struggle for the soul of Medicare is the struggle for the future of American society" (2004, 415). Medicare had become a focal point for the wider partisan and ideological battle about the appropriate roles of government and market in American society: "Medicare has become the front line in the two-decade old effort to roll back the last seventy years of social policy" (ibid., 411). For liberal analysts such as Vladeck, Medicare's underlying principles provided a model illustrating the benefits of social insurance programs. Yet, reflecting a deep ideological cleavage, conservatives see Medicare as an example of a fiscally out-of-control big-government program with spiraling expenses, making it a model of exactly how *not* to organize social benefits (Cannon and Tanner 2007).

Assessing the extent of concrete policy change resulting from this ideological battle is not straightforward. It is fair to say, though, that Medicare falls somewhere in between the other two policy areas discussed in this book. On one hand, the program has persisted in a clearly recognizable form since being established in 1965. It has not been, therefore, subject to a comprehensive legislative overhaul in a manner similar to the one that saw AFDC terminated by PRWORA. On the other hand, the changes that have been made to Medicare have been more structurally noteworthy than the revisions made to Social Security.

A complicating factor when assessing the development of Medicare is the manner in which the program is part of a much broader debate about the provision of health care in the United States. This is true because, although Medicare is a stand-alone program providing publicly funded health care to the country's seniors and disabled, the never-ending arguments about the delivery of health care services to the nation's wider population necessarily impact the status of Medicare. Furthermore, the entanglement of Medicare in the wider debate about the United States's health care arrangements increases the number and variety of political actors determined to have their say in Medicare policy development. Health insurers, employers, hospitals, doctors, other health professionals, and the government (both at the federal and at the state level) all have a vested interest in how the health care system operates. Politicians are also obviously sensitive to public opinion and here the picture is again complicated. Because different segments of the population have different degrees of access to health care, it is likely that distinct constituencies will have quite divergent views on whether there is a crisis in American health care and, if there is a crisis, what that crisis is about.

These factors make for an especially complex exploration of the key themes of this book when tracing the impact of ideas, institutions, and issue ownership on Medicare because there are apparently contradictory patterns to be explained. These intricacies were demonstrated during the 2003 debate over the MMA and the arguments over the health care reform enacted in 2010 as, in these cases, some of the prevailing assumptions about the politics of Medicare were challenged. In both instances Republicans argued that they were advancing the interests of the program against the Democrats. Yet the latter party had created Medicare and has assumed issue ownership of the program. This conventional perspective was

highlighted through the budget wars of 1995, when Bill Clinton rallied his presidency by claiming that he was defending Medicare against Republican cutbacks.
But in 2003 the Bush administration and congressional Republicans expanded the
Medicare program by adding a new prescription drug benefit for seniors. As will
be discussed below, this new benefit was accompanied by significant elements of
policy layering that integrated conservative ideas about how to increase private
elements within this federal program. In 2010 Republicans attacked the Obama
administration for its plan to reduce future growth of Medicare spending as part
of the wider health care reform. At times the rhetoric became stark with references
to so-called "death panels." This, ironically, came as the administration included
in the health care bill plans to fill the gaps that the 2003 MMA had left for some
seniors in terms of accessing prescription drug coverage.

One aspect of the debate through 2010 did illustrate a key long-term legacy
of health care policy development in the United States. When creating Medicare,
the United States provided public health care for an age-specific section of the
population, which is unique in the industrialized world. One unintended consequence of serving the needs of America's seniors in this manner was the potential
to put Medicare's beneficiaries at odds with working-age people, especially the
uninsured. That is, from a narrow perspective, seniors, while relatively well provided for themselves, did not necessarily have a perceived interest in comprehensive health care reform designed to cover the millions of uninsured. This created
a possible scenario in which seniors might oppose a comprehensive reform plan
that benefited younger Americans while restricting Medicare provisions. In 2010
the beneficiaries of an existing program tied to liberalism had a seemingly rational reason to obstruct further liberal-minded social policy reform in the health
care arena. But Medicare's liberal founders did not anticipate that potential pre-
dicament as they championed their cause throughout the 1950s and early 1960s.
Indeed, reflecting the complicated ideological picture, in some ways the existence
of Medicare is indicative of a compromised political settlement between reformers pushing comprehensive government involvement in health care provision and
those anxious to keep government out of the health care market, especially where
the working population is concerned.

The Historical Development of Health Insurance

Public health insurance began to emerge in Europe in the late nineteenth and early
twentieth centuries.[2] During the 1910s, inspired by these European examples, the
American Association for Labor Legislation (AALL) launched a campaign across
the United States championing public health insurance (Skocpol 1992). However,
before the New Deal, the institutional logic of American federalism complicated
the efforts of reformers who sought to promote the adoption of public health
insurance schemes in the United States (Hacker and Pierson 2002).[3] Due to the

constraints of federalism, AALL's campaign took place at state level, but that policy decentralization empowered those business interests, including private insurance companies, which opposed state intervention in the field of health and social policy. In the end, AALL's campaign in favor of public health insurance failed miserably, and by 1920 the issue had largely moved off the policy agenda. Ironically, a major consequence of the campaign was to unite the medical profession and other opponents of public health insurance (Béland and Hacker 2004, 48).

During the 1930s, other industrial countries enacted public health insurance programs to reduce economic insecurity stemming from limited private insurance coverage (e.g. Richards 1994). In the United States, however, while the New Deal favored the enactment of major social programs such as old-age insurance and unemployment insurance, there was not a similar bold legislative effort to introduce a public health scheme. Although health insurance received consideration during the New Deal, the Roosevelt administration decided not to incorporate health insurance into the 1935 Social Security Act (Béland 2007c). Three major factors help explain this decision. First, members of the Roosevelt administration feared that the inclusion of national health insurance as part of the Social Security Act could trigger the mobilization of the American Medical Association (AMA). For them, postponing the debate regarding public health insurance seemed necessary to guarantee the enactment of the provisions central to the 1935 Social Security Act (Witte 1962, 184–85). Second, access to health care was not one of the most prominent sources of social policy concern during the Great Depression because in 1935 unemployment and old-age insecurity were widely perceived as the most pressing social policy issues (Berkowitz 2000). Third, and perhaps for that reason, no large-scale social movement emerged during the 1930s to promote the development of public health insurance. This situation contrasts with the one prevailing in the field of old-age insurance, where organizations such as those promoting the Townsend Plan emerged to legitimize the enactment and the expansion of old-age pension programs (Amenta 2006).

Attempts to enact public health insurance in the late 1930s failed, and the following decade witnessed a gradual expansion of private health benefits (Hacker 2002; Klein 2003). This rapid growth of private health insurance reduced the perceived need for national health insurance. By the time President Harry Truman began his push for national health insurance in the late 1940s, the initial enthusiasm of labor officials for this policy option had faded as an increasing number of workers had access to private coverage including through collective bargaining (Béland 2007c; Gordon 1997). Congressional supporters of public health care regularly introduced bills in pursuit of their goal, but there was never a coalition sufficient to drive such a proposal through the legislative process, and opposition from doctors and private providers coupled with strong antistatist and racially motivated Southern mobilization guaranteed strong opposition (Boychuk 2008; Quadagno 2005).

Despite the lack of legislative action, the postwar period witnessed continuing political argument about the relative merits of public and private benefits as a means of providing health care. Critically this debate was framed in "either/or" terms with public and private provision seen as being in competition with each other. This contrasted with the situation regarding old-age pensions, where it seemed that Social Security and the private pension system complemented one another. This was true partly because the expansion of private benefits in the field of old-age pensions emerged *after* the enactment of a major federal program that provided public old-age insurance (Béland and Hacker 2004).

Establishing Public Insurance for the Elderly

In contrast to developments in the United States, the postwar era heralded the advent of universal health insurance in Canada and a number of European countries.[4] Different countries employed different systems, but critically the state, either as a regulator or a direct provider, acted as a guarantor that all, or virtually all, citizens had affordable access to health care services. In the United States, however, the private sector had become entrenched as a dominant player in health care provision. Thus, "private plans emerged as the core source of health security" (Hacker 2002, 232). But the private sector did not provide care for all. One consequence of these developments was that many reformers who supported public provision scaled back their ambitions. Instead of calling for universal public health insurance, these reformers emphasized the needs of those excluded from private coverage. This retreat did not sit well with all advocates of national health insurance. President Truman "initially bridled at the suggestion" (Hacker 2002, 235), but the fate of his own health proposals illustrated the strength of the political forces that were opposed to a national health insurance scheme. In a manner presaging the events of 1993–94, public support for Truman's own national health insurance plan was initially considerable but diminished as the opposition found its voice. In one Gallup poll in spring of 1949, 50 percent of those with an opinion supported the plan. But following highly charged attacks by the AMA and congressional Republicans alleging that Truman's plans paved the way toward socialism, that level of support "dipped abruptly" (Page and Shapiro 1992, 130).

By 1952 congressional Democrats and administration officials sympathetic to public insurance had radically shifted strategy. Instead of continuing to push for a comprehensive federal health insurance program, the emphasis was on the needs of seniors. Even this limited aim remained unfulfilled throughout the 1950s, but impetus was gathering in favor of providing public health care for America's seniors by 1960. Democratic presidential candidate John F. Kennedy publicly endorsed a health program for seniors in a speech to mark the twenty-fifth anniversary of the passage of the Social Security Act (Berkowitz 1991, 168). At this stage even opponents of Medicare felt compelled to offer alternative proposals. Not surprisingly the different plans had quite distinct, normative implications about how government should intervene in the health care market. First, long-standing champions of a Medicare scheme effectively restated ideas formulated at the start of the 1950s; they called for hospital care for Social Security recipients financed through the federal social insurance system. This approach emphasized how it would cover the costs of large hospital bills, including surgical bills, although not doctors' fees. Furthermore, because the program would be paid for through social insurance contributions (i.e., payroll tax), it would not subject recipients to a means test. In contrast, a bill sponsored by Sen. Robert Kerr (D-Okla.) and Rep. Wilbur Mills (D-Ark.) proposed that seniors be means tested. This would allow a more generous package of support, including not only hospital fees but also doctors' fees, to be targeted for the needy, financed through general taxation but with costs and administration shared between the federal government and the states. The Kerr-Mills package provided a vehicle for conservative-minded interests (which, by 1960, included the leadership of the AMA), who recognized that they could no longer simply oppose providing any medical help to the aged.

While liberals sided with the Medicare proposals, there were some contrary ideational features to these alternatives. Liberals wished to help "all social security beneficiaries among the aged, proposing *limited* hospital-surgery for them, to be paid for by *regressive* social security taxes: the more conservative welfare advocates proposing *broader* benefits for a small class among the aged—the destitute— and arguing that *progressive* federal tax revenues should be used, with the administrative organization in the hands of state and local officials" (Marmor 2000, 27, emphasis in original). As it was, the Kerr-Mills proposal was enacted in 1960, but this did not stop the issue of health care provision for seniors from entering the presidential campaign. Democratic presidential candidate Kennedy attacked Republicans for opposing a Senate amendment that had advanced a Medicare-style measure. He compared Republicans opposed to Medicare with those who had earlier opposed the introduction of Social Security. "Ninety percent of the Republicans voted against the social security in the mid thirties and 95 percent in 1960 voted against the medical care for the aged tied to social security" (Kennedy, quoted in Sundquist 1968, 307). Vice president and Republican presidential candidate Richard Nixon emphasized his opposition to anything more in the way of government intervention than had already been legislated. "The American people . . . do not want, they must not have, a compulsory health insurance plan forced down their throats, and we will not allow it" (Nixon, quoted in Sundquist 1968, 308). In this context, Kennedy's victory in the presidential race was critical to Medicare reformers, even though—as with much of his policy agenda— getting legislative action proved to be extremely problematic. Wilbur Mills, who held the position of chair of the House Ways and Means Committee, was a critical player in the legislative process (Berkowitz 1995). Any Medicare plan would have to pass through Ways and Means, and Mills's previous opposition did not auger well. Yet the case for further action persisted because the feedback from the Kerr-Mills program was largely about how unsatisfactory its implementation had been (Berkowitz 1991, 169–71).

The 1964 federal elections critically changed the distribution of power between liberals and conservatives in Congress, making the passage of some form of Medicare bill inevitable (Binder 1999). President Johnson "named the issue his top priority legislative measure" (Sundquist 1968, 317). Opponents responded by advancing their own proposals. Even the AMA came up with an idea termed "Eldercare" that essentially offered more of the Kerr-Mills model, calling for states to subsidize insurance for needy seniors. Congressional Republicans, through John Byrnes of Wisconsin, the ranking GOP member of Ways and Means, put forward a plan that called for a broader program of benefits than Medicare, notably advocating that doctors fees and drug costs be included in a voluntary program whereby seniors could buy federally subsidized insurance.

The next development confounded expectations as Mills turned from obstructionist to apparent health care expansionist when he manufactured the so-called three-layer cake. The three-layer cake combined the administration's Medicare bill and Byrnes' proposal and adopted elements of the AMA's proposals to create a more expansive Medicare program covering more costs and more of the older population than had previously been proposed. The result was a Medicare program that had had two main components: hospital insurance (Part A) and medical insurance (Part B). Reflecting the balance between the administration's original Medicare proposal and the Byrne's package, Plan A was made compulsory according to the Social Security model while Plan B was optional. Mills also engineered the creation of what was to become Medicaid: a program offering basic health coverage to social assistance beneficiaries, with costs shared between federal and state governments (Marmor 2000, 47–53). In July 1965 the House passed the final Medicare package by a vote of 307 to 116. Senate followed with a 70 to 24 majority in favor. Not everyone was impressed. Republican senator Karl Mundt of South Dakota described the impending legislation as "another step towards destroying the independence and self-reliance in America which is the last best hope of individual freedom for all mankind" (quoted in Twight 1997). As for President Johnson, he symbolically signed the bill in Independence, Missouri, with former President Truman as a witness. Johnson declared triumphantly: "No longer will older Americans be denied the healing miracle of modern medicine" (Sundquist 1968, 321).

What is important for the wider themes of this book is to understand the ideological and institutional legacies that were established at this point. How deeply were they embedded and what were the consequences, both foreseen and unforeseen, that resulted from the decisions made at this point? Moreover, which features of this new public health care regime, established in a period of welfare state expansion, were likely to be resilient, and which proved vulnerable to challenge in a time of fiscal austerity and program retrenchment? In partisan terms, what patterns of issue ownership were established?

The Scope of Government Health Care

Part A of Medicare, more fully known as Hospitalization Insurance, fulfilled the ambitions of the Medicare schemes in circulation throughout the 1950s and early 1960s. Part A provided 60 days of inpatient hospital care after payment of a forty-dollar deductible. A further 30 days were covered subject to a daily coinsurance charge. In addition, Part A provided for up to 100 days of nursing home care and 100 days of home health visits. A lifetime limit of 190 days inpatient psychiatric care was also provided (Oberlander 2003, 32–33). Part A was funded by a specific payroll tax on employees and employers set at 0.35 percent.

The payment of doctors' fees was a significant expansion on the original goals of Medicare proponents. Medicare Part B, Supplementary Medical Insurance, paid for 80 percent of doctors' fees, including office visits, surgery, and consultation. In combination with the 20 percent coinsurance payment, a fifty-dollar deductible was applied to these services. Part B also covered 50 percent of the cost of outpatient mental health treatment. It also covered x-rays and ambulance services. Unlike Part A, where the payroll tax was compulsory, enrolling in Part B was voluntary. Those who chose to enroll initially paid three dollars per month. This premium was designed to cover half of the costs involved with the rest of the funds coming from general revenues. Both hospitals and doctors were to be paid retrospectively; hospitals were to be reimbursed for their "reasonable costs" and physicians for their "reasonable charges" (Oberlander 2003, 33).

Once President Johnson signed the Medicare legislation in July 1965, the Social Security Administration (SSA), which was to oversee the new program, prepared the ground for implementation. In particular it focused on enrolling seniors onto Part B of the program so they would qualify for medical as well as hospital insurance. Reflecting the SSA's vigorous efforts, 93 percent of eligible seniors had signed up for Part B by the end of the first year of Medicare's operation (Marmor 2000, 87). Hence, the popular as well as political legitimacy of Medicare was quickly established.

A primary reason why Medicare proponents had focused on a scheme based on Social Security's eligibility principles had been to avoid setting up a "welfare medicine" program. And in the context of the story told in chapters 1 and 3, the anxiety of pro-Medicare reformers throughout the 1950s and early 1960s to avoid the potential stigma attached to "welfare" programs seems quite understandable. The 1935 Social Security Act had created a two-tier welfare state in the United States. The federally administered and funded Social Security pension scheme was viewed as an earned social insurance benefit and was duly awarded a popular legitimacy and political strength. Administered and funded by a mix of federal and state measures, AFDC was less well regarded and unsurprisingly had less political support (Fraser and Gordon 1992). The brief experience of the Kerr-Mills program, which was implemented unevenly across the states (Sundquist 1968, 319), reinforced the perception that programs organized on a means-tested, decentralized basis made for both bad policy and weak politics.[5]

Thus, the long-term viability of the Kerr-Mills-style Medicaid program might have appeared dubious at first. Two aspects of the Kerr-Mills program were embodied in Medicaid and were critical to that program's future development (Grogan and Patashnik 2005, 270). First, while not restricted to seniors, Medicaid was available only to the "medically indigent." Second, the new Medicaid program, unlike Medicare, offered a comprehensive package of benefits to those who qualified as eligible. Over the next decades, Medicaid was the subject of many political fights over funding, and the program has never attained the same level of support as Medicare, but it is also clear in hindsight that any policymakers in 1965 who expected that Medicaid's status as a residual program would mean that it would remain a marginal program were wrong (Brown and Sparer 2003). Federal spending for Medicaid was about $176 billion in 2004. The mix of federal to state spending does vary between states, but on average the federal government paid for 57 percent of funding (CBO 2005b, 28–29). It is insightful to contrast this level of spending with total (federal and state) AFDC expenditures of $23.4 billion in 1994, when AFDC numbers were at their peak (US Congress 1996, 386).

Importantly, and in contrast to AFDC, Medicaid generated powerful supportive constituencies. First, one significant constituency for Medicaid is older Americans who would be left "medically indigent" after exhausting Medicare's benefits. According to the Congressional Budget Office (CBO), Medicaid covered 57 million people in 2004. Of these about 75 percent were poor children, their parents, and low-income pregnant women, and an additional 15 percent were disabled persons. Yet seniors, comprising only 9 percent of the Medicaid caseload, accounted for 25 percent of its payments (CBO 2005b).[6] Second, as indicated by the total Medicaid spending, the program has become an important income stream for health care providers, constituting a "Medicaid medical industrial complex" (Olson 2010, 181). The reimbursement rates paid by Medicaid frustrate some of those providers, but they remain powerful advocates who have a stake in opposing program retrenchment.

Thus, Medicaid has not only proven to be a resilient program but also, particularly from the late 1980s onward, it grew beyond its initial "welfare medicine" mandate (Brown and Sparer 2003; Howard 2006). For example, starting in the late 1980s, Medicaid expanded to cover more children and some adult workers living in poverty.[7] In 1997 President Clinton and Republican leaders in Congress compromised to create the State Children's Health Insurance Program (SCHIP, now CHIP), which provided cover to children in low-income families that did not already qualify for Medicaid. The potential of Medicaid to offer health coverage to even more Americans (Brown 2005) was then fulfilled as part of the 2010 health care reform. As will be discussed below, this ran counter to the expectations of the founders of Medicare and Medicaid, who anticipated that Medicare would provide the role model for a universal health insurance program (Marmor 2000, 95–96; Oberlander 2003, 33).

The Limits of Government Health Care

The presence of Truman at the Medicare signing ceremony served as an illustration of what had not been achieved in 1965. Medicare and Medicaid, while serving many millions of Americans, did not guarantee universal public insurance for health care services. In comparison to countries with government-organized universal health insurance schemes, the public health care state in the United States was "residual" rather than "institutional" in the sense that it simply complemented existing private schemes created for the working population.[8]

Medicare's mandate was expanded as part of the Social Security amendments of 1972. At that point the disabled were also included in the program, and so were people suffering from end-stage renal disease. The addition of the disabled to the numbers covered by Medicare had been a goal of the original Medicare proponents but had been opposed by the AMA, which preferred that Medicaid be used by the disabled who were financially needy (Quadagno 2005, 106). These amendments increased the number of Medicare beneficiaries by about 10 percent (Moon 2006, 55).

However, with the benefit of hindsight and prior to the reform of 2010, it is possible to see the creation of Medicare and Medicaid in 1965 as barriers to wider reform, if reform is seen in terms of an expansion of the health care state for the whole population. That is, the existence of the Medicare and Medicaid programs worked to reinforce an implicit division of labor between government and private insurance in terms of providing health insurance for the American population: the former would cover more vulnerable citizens such as seniors, the disabled, and the poor while the latter would remain the main source of health security for the rest of the population (Marmor 2000; Oberlander 2003; Ruggie 1996, 147–50). Paradoxically, the effort to cover vulnerable citizens may have reduced the apparent need for universal public health insurance to cover the entire population. The government would provide health insurance for those Americans who were unable to provide for themselves while the private insurance industry would provide access to health care for working families. Unsurprisingly, this arrangement was also attractive to the insurance industry because it allowed them to offer insurance packages to the section of the population likely to be healthiest, hence less likely to make costly claims: "although reformers believed that Medicare would establish the philosophical precedent and institutional means for broader public coverage, Medicare's immediate effect was to strengthen the private system and bolster the case against broader action" (Hacker 2002, 250).

Thus, from the 1970s through the 1990s, campaigns to enact a national health insurance scheme failed in part because of the unintended institutional dynamics put in place by the political and policy settlement of 1965. That is, the vested interests of the insurance companies, which were becoming increasingly powerful players in the private health care arena in the 1960s, were reinforced by the manner in which Medicare and Medicaid had segmented the population into those who would turn to the public sector for help and those who continued to rely on the marketplace. Furthermore, the enduring role of tax-subsidized, employer-based health insurance benefits reinforced the private insurance market and strengthened its opposition to the advent of public national health insurance.[9]

The result of these developments, as shown by comparative data, is that the United States spends a higher percentage of its gross domestic product (GDP) on health care than any other nation but is the only economically advanced country that does not provide virtual or full universal health coverage. In 2005 the United States spent 15.7 percent of GDP on health care compared to 11.1 percent in France, 10.7 percent in Germany, and 8.2 percent in the United Kingdom. Using the Organisation for Economic Co-operation and Development's (OECD) definition of purchasing power parity, this meant that the United States spent $6,558 per capita against $3,303 in France, $3,348 in Germany, and $2,693 in the United Kingdom (OECD 2009). These numbers, which effectively place the United States as an outlier in terms of health care spending, reflect a tremendous increase in health care costs since the early 1960s. In 1960 overall health care spending in the United States accounted for 5.2 percent of GDP. This had risen to 7.1 percent by 1970, and 9.0 in 1990. By 2000 that figure had climbed to 13.6 percent (ibid.). Nevertheless, in spite of all this expenditure, significant numbers of Americans do not have adequate health insurance. In 2005, despite more than one in seven dollars in the American economy being spent in the health care sector, 15.3 percent of the population—nearly 45 million people—remained uninsured (US Census Bureau 2009b), with many millions of others underinsured. Yet because of Medicare very few seniors face the prospect of being uninsured. In fact, seniors have by far the lowest incidence of uninsurance of any age group in the United States. In 2010, just 2 percent of Americans age sixty-five and over were uninsured. This compared to an uninsurance rate of 18.4 percent for people aged under sixty-five (US Census Bureau 2011a). Despite this "success," Medicare did not become a model for a national health insurance scheme. Indeed, not only did Medicare fail to act as an entering wedge for widespread government-funded health care, it also failed for many years even to expand its own benefits.

Creating Contrary Policy Legacies

While the creation of Medicare did mean that seniors were accorded a special, deserving status, there were gaps in coverage in the original legislation that remained over the long term. For example, after the initial deductible, free hospital care remained limited to sixty days.[10] And neither the deductible nor the cost of post-sixty-day coinsurance can be described as negligible. In 2009 the deductible payment for each hospital benefit period stood at $1,068 while the daily coinsurance payment for days sixty-one to ninety was $267 a day. In addition, the Part B monthly premium for individuals with an income below $85,000 per annum was $96.40 (Nonnemaker 2009).

The failure to expand on the original Medicare benefits disappointed pro-Medicare advocates who had expected Medicare to expand in terms of both the number of beneficiaries and the generosity of its benefits (Oberlander 2003, 47). Importantly, however, feedback effects reflecting how a variety of private schemes filled the gaps in the original legislation influenced Medicare's development. These supplemental packages meant that the majority of Medicare beneficiaries were protected from the full costs involved in deductibles and copayments. In 2000, roughly 90 percent of program beneficiaries had additional coverage to help defray the cost of the gaps in Medicare coverage.[11] About 32 percent of beneficiaries had employer-sponsored supplemental health insurance. An additional 27 percent had extra cover through a so-called Medigap insurance policy. These private insurance packages generally cover the cost of deductibles and coinsurance. Beneficiaries do have to pay for these policies out of their own pockets but then have protection against catastrophic costs in any given year. An additional 17 percent of Medicare beneficiaries were enrolled in a managed care plan within Medicare that would likely cover some or all of the cost-sharing requirements. In 2000 about 12 percent of Medicare beneficiaries were also eligible for Medicaid benefits. Hence, through a variety of means, most but not all Medicare beneficiaries have at least some of the cost-sharing requirements imposed by the Medicare program's deductibles and coinsurance paid for at the point of use. In turn, this has relieved pressure to reform Medicare itself to get rid of the cost-sharing burden on beneficiaries. This was especially the case because those Medicare beneficiaries with the best private supplementary schemes were likely to be those with the highest incomes and levels of education, meaning that the most "politically active class of the elderly . . . is the class least dependent on public Medicare benefits" (Oberlander 2003, 50). In short, the group of beneficiaries most able to agitate effectively for change to Medicare's rules had the weakest incentive to do so.

Yet, if payments for Part B Medicare and any supplementary coverage for Part A are included, many seniors still had significant out-of-pocket costs to cover all of their health care needs. In 2004 out-of-pocket spending came to 22.6 percent of average income for elderly Medicare beneficiaries who were not hospitalized. For seniors with incomes at or below the poverty level, this figure was 41.3 percent of income (Moon 2006, 22–23).[12]

A second factor powerfully agitating against further helping seniors with their health care expenses was the high rate of medical inflation. The explosion of health care costs from the mid-1960s onward was not confined to Medicare, but thoughts that this program might emulate Social Security's expansion were quickly undermined as Medicare's costs exceeded initial estimates and expectations. In 1970 Medicare accounted for 3.5 percent of the federal budget. That figure had reached 5.8 percent by 1980, rising to 8.6 percent in 1990 and 12.1 percent in 2000 (Moon 2006, 38). Importantly, while Social Security expanded during the era of welfare state growth and through the peak years of New Deal liberalism, Medicare matured as that era came to a close and fiscal austerity emerged as a key policy goal. This illustrates the role of timing and sequence in policy development emphasized by historical institutionalist scholars (e.g., Pierson 2004).

To properly understand the factors driving this inflation, it is necessary to go back to the decisions made in 1965 and to reflect on the legacies of compromises made by Medicare proponents to lessen opposition to their political project. One ironic consequence of the 1965 legislation was the manner in which one prominent group of apparent losers in the legislative drama of that year, American physicians, did quite well under the new program. The law stipulated that "nothing in this title shall be construed to authorize any federal official or employee to exercise any supervision or control over the practice of medicine" (quoted in Hacker 2002, 247). Hence, costs and fees were to be paid at rates that were "reasonable and customary." In effect, this allowed providers to charge what they deemed appropriate. Perhaps unsurprisingly, hospital and physician fees rose "markedly" in the immediate years after implementation, making "American physicians among Medicare's most prominent beneficiaries" (Marmor 2000, 84). Thus, while the creation of Medicare did represent a victory for advocates of greater state intervention in the health care system, the concessions made to medical providers reflected how that health care system had evolved in a manner that saw the state consistently privilege those providers (Moran 2000). In short, Medicare's "architects (at the height of their political power) knowingly caved in to the demands of health care providers" (Jacobs 2005, 46). It makes for an interesting counterfactual to ask whether Medicare's advocates were in such a strong position in 1965 that they could have pushed for more cost controls on hospitals and doctors to be contained in the legislation, but they did not, and Medicare proved in its early years to be a government program that generously rewarded many of the very interests that had most vigorously campaigned against its formation (Jacobs 2005, 45).

A further feature of Medicare's original funding arrangements was the distinction made between how Part A and Part B were to be financed. Part A was modeled on Social Security with a dedicated payroll tax on both employee and employer paid into a trust fund. Part B was supposed to be partially funded by a monthly premium, with the rest of the government's contribution coming from general revenues. As it turned out, both these mechanisms were based on a slightly misguided logic. First, the Social Security model, while understandably politically attractive to liberal-minded policymakers wishing to piggyback on the popularity of an existing program, had a fiscal logic that applied to the calculation of future pension payments in a manner that did not pertain to paying for hospital care. Hospitalization costs are inherently unpredictable given the "unknown" factors such as expensive advances in medical technology. Also, whereas Social Security payments are fixed and the annual aggregate payouts are approximately calculable, Medicare pays out according to the level of hospital and doctor use by seniors, which is much less predictable. Furthermore, the fact that Medicare did not initially establish fees schedules that hospitals and doctors were to charge for procedures meant that there was significant variation in the costs that again made it difficult to draw up clear actuarial models (Marmor 2000, 96–97).

Second, with regard to Part B, it was intended that the initial three-dollar per month premium that beneficiaries would pay to subscribe to Part B would pay for 50 percent of the costs of Part B. That expectation proved unrealistic and by 1981 the premium, then at eleven dollars, covered only 25 percent of those costs (Moon 2006, 190–91). The net consequence of these funding decisions was that "the federal government poured virtually unlimited public resources into financing care for the aged and the poor, turning health care into a profitable enterprise for physicians, hospitals and insurance companies" (Quadagno 2005, 108).

But Medicare Part A is similar to Social Security because of the existence of a trust fund that allows for specific examination of the long-term actuarial viability of (that part of) the program. In turn, the repeated warnings from the Medicare Board of Trustees about the projected funding gaps in the Part A trust fund made it more difficult to argue for Medicare expansion. This example illustrates the contrary nature of trust fund politics. The trust fund itself helps lend a sense of distinct identity to a program, and the element of hypothecation that comes with an identifiable payroll tax reinforces the appearance that beneficiaries are getting something that they have paid for even though that impression is not, strictly speaking, an accurate understanding of how the program actually works. Yet the transparency of the balance between a trust fund's income and its payouts means that a program funded in this way is vulnerable to the idea that it is running out of money (Patashnik 2000). This latter institutional aspect of a trust fund creates a political and ideological dynamic whereby Medicare (and Social Security) can be deemed close to "bankruptcy" in a fashion that does not apply as much to programs funded out of general revenues (Pierson 1992).

Overall, Medicare quickly established two robust but contrary policy feedback loops. The program was popular because it provided for the health care needs of an economically vulnerable but "worthy" section of the population, but it was so expensive that it prohibited policymakers from seeking to gain credit with Medicare beneficiaries by expanding the program's benefits. Thus, policymakers responded by trying to maintain existing benefits while attempting to contain costs. Throughout the 1970s, a series of efforts were made to slow the rise in Medicare inflation, but these proved ineffectual (Marmor 2000, 99–106). In the 1980s, there were concerted moves to rein in Medicare's costs that involved changes to payment mechanisms to providers.

The Contradictions of Cost Control in the 1980s

As documented throughout this book, the Reagan presidency gave concrete form to the revival of conservative social policy ideas. As illustrated by the examination of welfare and Social Security in chapters 1 and 3 of this book, the administration's track record in advancing its ideological objectives in social policy was mixed. The history of Medicare throughout the 1980s provides a different narrative, one that is inconclusive, with neither advocates of conservative policy ideas nor defenders of the existing institutions of Medicare fully triumphant. There were significant changes to how Medicare was financed throughout the 1980s, but these changes were not the subject of heated ideological debate. The changes enacted were very visible to health care providers, who responded by adapting their health treatment patterns. As a consequence, Medicare beneficiaries were affected by the deals reached between Congress and the Reagan and Bush administrations, but the language of those deals suggested that the amendments were more administrative than patient-care directed. The decade closed, however, with the extraordinary episode of the enactment and repeal of the Medicare Catastrophic Coverage Act (MCCA).

As described earlier, the 1965 Medicare legislation effectively confirmed the autonomy of health care professionals, which meant that government intervention in the hospital-doctor-patient relationship was limited even as the program was funding the former two actors to treat the third. This arrangement, with minimal government interference in price-setting for health care provision, would seem to have an ideological appeal to free market conservatives in the Reagan White House. Yet the inflationary dynamic that this system of unconditional funding helped foster clashed with another priority of the Reagan administration, which was to reduce domestic spending. As detailed in chapter 3, this impulse to cut back government social expenditure faced major obstacles when it came to Social Security, but the administration and Congress negotiated changes regarding Medicare that provided new checks on payments to hospitals and doctors and simultaneously extended the hand of government regulation over these institutions.

Underlying the legislative detail, the fundamental change in payment methodology was a shift from retrospective to prospective payments. Retrospective payments were based on the charges or fees that hospitals or doctors asked for their services after they had treated a patient; with prospective payments, charges and fees would be paid according to an amount settled in advance depending on the medical procedure being undertaken. Inasmuch as the prospective payment system (PPS) involved government agreement on charges and fees that could be demanded by and reimbursed to health care providers, this was a significant extension of the administrative role of government. There were, though, compensatory features that appealed to conservatives. First, the PPS system promised to reduce government spending. Second, it also encouraged health care providers to be more efficient. If providers could not keep to the agreed fee, then they would have to absorb the loss themselves. Alternatively, if those providers could do their work for a lesser amount than agreed under the PPS arrangement, then they could keep the difference. Hence, the incorporation of a PPS for hospitals as part of the 1982 Tax Equity and Fiscal Responsibility Act marked a "true watershed" (Tuohy 2003, 77). Further adjustments that satisfied some of the concerns of hospitals were made to the reimbursement schedule as part of the 1983 Social Security amendments. Overall, this reform changed the relationship between Medicare and hospitals significantly but did so in a manner that did not put Medicare beneficiaries on political alert (Moon 2006, 61).

Altering the relationship between Medicare and doctors took longer to accomplish. Doctor's fees were covered under Part B of Medicare and paid for partially by the monthly beneficiary premium but mostly out of general revenues. By the mid-1980s, the pressure to slow the growth of physician fees was strong, particularly as the increase in hospitalization costs eased. In 1986 Congress created the Physician Payment Review Commission (PPRC), which developed a new methodology for reimbursing doctors for their Medicare work (for details, see Moon 2006, 62–65). The underlying goal was to reward office visits and general primary care more generously but to reduce payments for specialist procedures (Hsiao 1988). This system was enacted by Congress and signed into law by President George H. W. Bush as part of the Omnibus Budget Reconciliation Act of 1989.

In hindsight, it is striking how little political controversy these changes aroused at the time. There was consensus that the status quo could not prevail and the reforms were crafted and presented as technical adjustments rather than ones driven by ideology or partisanship. Faced with a rising aggregate fiscal deficit, policymakers in Washington needed to find ways to control expenditure growth in public health care. Thus, the Reagan and Bush administrations and Congress undid the funding principles that had governed Medicare's financing since the program's founding in 1965 with relatively little partisan argument or even interest group opposition (Oberlander 2003, 129–33). Yet these were decisions likely to have a real impact because they changed the incentive structure for health care professionals (Lawlor 2003, 30). This factor in itself has ambiguous ideological implications. On one hand, it suggests that market incentives are an effective mechanism of cost control. On the other, it also indicates that greater government regulation is needed to check the profligacy of Medicare's providers.

The success of these reforms is difficult to assess. Critically, the new measures did not set overall limits for Medicare spending. While Medicare providers had lost the power to determine their own charges and fees, the government would still reimburse hospitals and physicians for all work carried out. In short, the reforms did little to reduce the level of demand for Medicare services made by the program's beneficiaries. Consequently, as medical technologies improved, the aggregate costs of providing health care to seniors were likely to continue growing.

The 1980s ended with one of the most curious legislative cases affecting any major public policy program in recent times, the rise and fall of MCCA, described in the following section.

The Strange Case of the Medicare Catastrophic Coverage Act

The enactment of the MCCA in July 1988 followed by its repeal in November 1989 was bizarre on a number of levels and with much that was politically counterintuitive. The first surprise is that the Reagan administration, guided by its secretary of Health and Human Services, Otis Bowen, initially proposed an expansion of the welfare state. It is less surprising that the Democratically controlled Congress then significantly expanded the administration's plan to offer greater protection to seniors by filling in some of the gaps in Medicare coverage, but President Reagan still chose to sign rather than veto the measure. It then turned out that Congress, the administration, and the American Association of Retired Persons (AARP) had misjudged the mood of the country's seniors—or at least the politically active seniors; rather than welcoming the new benefits, many seniors protested at being asked to pay for them. Legislators responded by backtracking and repealing nearly the entire package. This case suggests that the constituencies stemming from Medicare are more than just the AARP; older voters have become a powerful electoral force as social programs such as Medicare and Social Security have stimulated the political participation of seniors (Campbell 2003).

Bowen's initial plan was to reduce the possibility of seniors being bankrupted by serious illness or disease after they had used up their Medicare entitlements. Bowen recommended that Medicare beneficiaries should be allowed unlimited stays in hospitals and that their annual out-of-pocket expenses should be capped at two thousand dollars. This proposal was unveiled in November 1986 at a mini crisis point for the administration. The Iran–Contra affair was rumbling on and the Democrats had just regained control of the Senate. Moreover, Reagan's reputation with senior voters was particularly poor, so doing something to appeal to that demographic had political logic. Even so, Bowen's plans are hard to reconcile with the conservative social policy ideas embraced by President Reagan. Certainly, some senior figures in the White House did not like what they heard, and it was only Bowen's entrepreneurial skills and his insistence that his plan had the virtue of administrative simplicity that persuaded Reagan to back the scheme (Oberlander 2003, 54–55).

Whatever Bowen's role in promoting catastrophic coverage, congressional Democrats decided to pick up Bowen's ball and run with it, calling for an even more generous package of benefits. Some critics pointed out that the Bowen plan did not provide for long-term care outside hospitals. There was logic to this objection: in 1987 groups representing seniors placed much more emphasis on expanding access for seniors to long-term care outside hospitals than they did on extending the length of hospital stays covered by Medicare because very few Medicare patients actually exhausted their hospital benefits (Oberlander 2003, 60). The problem was that providing such long-term care would be much more expensive. This did not stop Democrat Claude Pepper, chair of the House Rules Committee and acknowledged champion of seniors, from pushing for legislation that provided long-term home care. There was minimal chance of Pepper's proposal being enacted, but the proposal pressured Congress into going beyond the original Bowen plan, and pressured the administration into accepting those congressional expansions (Himelfarb 1995, 25–27). Looking for an alternative way to give the developing legislation a distinctive Democratic identity, thus clarifying Democratic issue ownership of Medicare reform, the Speaker of the House, Jim Wright, proposed subsidizing prescription drug costs for seniors (Rovner 1987a, 1987b). This illustrated a pattern that was to be repeated in 2003 because Democrats were not prepared to cede issue ownership of one of their prized pieces of policy and, hence, their political turf.

The administration threatened a veto of the evolving legislation, but a deal was struck after intense negotiations. As well as taking the limit off hospital stays covered by Medicare and subsidizing prescription drugs, the MCCA also limited Part B out-of-pocket expenses to $1,370 a year and extended the number of days of subsidized care in nursing homes from 100 to 150 days.[13] The final bill was passed overwhelmingly (328 to 72 in the House, and 86 to 11 in Senate) and signed into law by President Reagan on July 1, 1988. In the aftermath, as it became clear that the new benefits package was not as popular as had been presupposed, Thomas Burke, who had been Bowen's chief-of-staff, claimed that he and his boss had "wanted the President to veto this bill" (quoted in Tolchin 1989b). According to Burke, Reagan was still weakened by the Iran–Contra scandal and was pressured into signing the bill by Vice President Bush, then in the middle of his presidential election campaign and did not want to be associated with an administration veto of what he assumed would be a popular measure (Tolchin 1989b).

President Bush was relatively silent fifteen months later as the main planks of the bill were effectively repealed. Yet his position in the summer of 1988 was hardly surprising. The MCCA was unlikely to please antistatist conservatives, but the assumption was that it would appeal to Medicare beneficiaries and to the majority of the public who expressed support for increasing Medicare benefits (Cook and Barrett 1992; Campbell 2003, 105). In the circumstances, credit claiming was a natural political reaction, particularly as a Republican administration veto would reinforce the impression of Medicare as a Democratic issue and would potentially hand the Democrats a wedge issue in forthcoming elections. The question is, why—having overcome the normally formidable institutional obstacles to expanding the state's role in health care delivery—the MCCA was repealed sixteen months after passage with many liberal Democrats as well as Republicans backtracking from their original vote in favor of the bill.

The simple answer is that many Medicare beneficiaries protested, which was most vividly captured when Democratic representative Dan Rostenkowski was forced to abandon his car after he was accosted by a group of elderly protestors in his Chicago congressional district (Tolchin 1989a). So, why were so many seniors angered by benefits directed toward them? Critical here was the funding model of the MCCA. In the era of deficit-driven budgeting, it was perceived as important that a new spending program, especially a social program, should be presented as being budget neutral. That is, the revenue-raising side of the equation as well as the spending side had to be clearly laid out. Because the Reagan administration was not going to sanction either a general tax hike or an increase in the Medicare payroll tax, asking Medicare beneficiaries to pay for the new benefits attracted "a bipartisan consensus" (Oberlander 2003, 61), even though congressional debate rather skirted around the implications of asking wealthier seniors to pay a greater share of the total costs (Himelfarb 1995, 46–50).

The final formula for raising the revenue required all Medicare recipients to pay an extra four dollars per month. On top of that, the 40 percent of beneficiaries with the highest incomes were asked to pay an income-based premium to cover the costs of approximately two-thirds of the cost of the new benefit (CBO 1988, 7). This surcharge was to be 15 percent of federal income tax liability, with a ceiling at $800 for a single person and $1,600 for a couple. This funding formula had contrary ideological implications. For liberals it was redistributive, at least within the Medicare population. For conservatives it chipped away at the universalism of Medicare funding.

What few saw coming was the manner in which the self-funding mechanism would prove so explosive among seniors. One example of the unanticipated consequences of the new law was the manner in which the AARP, which remained loyal to the bill through to the bitter end, found its role as tribune of the elderly challenged by a group called the National Committee to Preserve Social Security and Medicare (NCPSSM). This group protested that the bill did not protect against the potentially catastrophic fiscal consequences facing people needing long-term extra-hospital care, and it objected to the self-funding mechanism. For example, the group distributed fliers that called on seniors to join the effort to "Repeal the Seniors Only Income Tax Increase—costing millions up to $1,600" (Tolchin 1989b). These tactics infuriated supporters of the MCCA because, in 1989, only those couples with annual incomes above seventy thousand dollars would pay that maximum amount (Pratt 1993, 194). California Democrat Fortney "Pete" Stark, chair of the House Ways and Means Committee's subcommittee on health, protested that the NCPSSM was conducting a "fraudulent campaign" that targeted "the most fragile members of our society, who are easily confused, frightened and misled" (quoted in Tolchin 1989b).

Whatever the cause, the MCCA seems to have been little understood by the country's Medicare population, and some of the views expressed in opposition were based on misunderstanding and incomplete knowledge. One survey in spring of 1989 found very low levels of knowledge about the structure of the new program. More than 90 percent of the respondents thought that all beneficiaries would pay more in federal taxes (Rice, Desmond, and Gabel 1990, 79). There was not even widespread knowledge of the new benefits that were provided by the act. For example, fewer than half of the respondents knew that the MCCA included a new prescription drug benefit (ibid., 80). Furthermore, even when respondents were briefed about the details of the bill, there remained more opposition to the MCCA than support. This situation seems to have been at least in part due to the deductibles and coinsurance requirements attached to the drug benefit, and the survey found that few of those with an existing insurance policy planned to drop it (ibid., 83). For those seniors with either an employer-provided insurance policy that covered Medicare's out-of-pocket costs and prescription drug costs, or a Medigap policy that covered some of these expenses, it was unclear what extra value was being provided by the MCCA. This illustrates the importance of the institutional interaction between private and public benefits discussed throughout this book.

In response to the opposition of seniors (Campbell 2003, 110), Congress repealed the measure. The MCCA was still championed in some newspaper editorials (*New York Times*, July 6, 1989; *New York Times*, October 1, 1989), but the public clamor drowned out these elite voices. Amidst the rush to repeal, Henry Waxman, a Californian Democrat who specialized in health care issues, lamented that his colleagues had been "swept up in a herd mentality. They didn't even think about the consequences for a lot of low-income elderly people" (quoted in Rovner 1989, 2637).

In the aftermath of the MCCA's repeal, there was little cause for partisan rejoicing for either Democrats or Republicans. The ideological message was also somewhat mixed. An expansion of the federal welfare state had been rejected by the very people it was meant to benefit, with the revolt centered on the opposition of wealthy seniors who resented having to pay a tax increase. Yet there was no suggestion that there was any support for scaling back Medicare. Putting aside partisan considerations, on balance the episode was probably more damaging to liberal principles than conservative ones, especially as Medicare was a policy domain where liberals would expect to have "issue ownership." Thus, although Democrats can claim credit for Medicare's creation, they remain vulnerable to attacks from those who support the status quo, including some wealthier seniors who are unwilling to pay extra taxes to subsidize program expansion that primarily supports low-income beneficiaries.

Overall, in its first quarter century of existence, Medicare confounded the original expectations of its founders and its critics. The dual feedback effects meant that it was simultaneously too popular to scale back and too costly to expand. So Medicare did not turn out to be a model for wider health care reform, but it did become a bedrock program of the federal welfare state. This did not mean that the politics of Medicare was in some way beyond ideology, but it did mean that ideological preferences were sometimes secondary to immediate practical considerations. The Reagan administration, for example, was ideologically committed to reducing the social and economic role of the federal government. It was also an imperative to control domestic spending. Simply downsizing Medicare would have married these two goals together, but cutting benefits was too politically risky. The decision to introduce mechanisms to reduce payments to medical providers was presented as a technocratic means of controlling Medicare spending. Yet the changes in reimbursement methods to hospitals and then to physicians were an explicit extension of the state's administrative power (Marmor 2000, 113–16). Ironically, therefore, a conservative president colluded with Congress to impose regulatory controls on medical providers that the architects of Medicare, in the liberal heyday of the mid-1960s, had shied from doing. But if the ideological implications of Medicare reform were sometimes disguised during the program's first quarter century of development, as the wider battle over health care politics reignited in the 1990s, so conflict over Medicare intensified in a much more explicitly partisan and ideological manner.

Health Care Politics in the 1990s

Health care politics were pivotal to political developments throughout the Clinton presidency. President Clinton's effort at comprehensive health system reform was first. Then, after the GOP's capture of Congress in the 1994 midterm elections, the congressional Republicans began to target Medicare and Medicaid spending. Following the 1996 elections, Clinton and the Republican Congress agreed to important changes to public health care arrangements as part of the 1997 Balanced Budget Act (BBA). What makes this period so interesting to analyze is the manner in which leading political actors made hugely damaging errors of political judgment as, first, President Clinton and, then, House Speaker Newt Gingrich found that they had bitten off more than they could chew. As it was, the health care wars through Clinton's first term in office, which were critical battles about the future of the federal welfare state, ended in defeat for the forces seeking to change the status quo. Clinton's victory in 1992 looked as if it might herald a major expansion of the government role in health care, but the administration lost control of its capacity to define the debate about reform, and the issue was framed as one of unwarranted big-government interference. Thus, disastrously, the Democrats forfeited issue ownership of health care. In contrast, the 1994 elections suggested that conservatives could pursue their project to downsize the welfare state. As seen in chapter 1, conservative values did triumph in the welfare arena, but when it came to changing Medicare and Medicaid, President Clinton was able to revive more established political alignments, retrieve ownership of health care reform, and, more specifically, define himself as a defender of existing social insurance programs.

There was nothing new in a Democratic presidency committing itself to comprehensive health care reform with the intention of bringing about universal access to health insurance. Previous efforts had failed, but there were good reasons in political terms for Clinton to restate this traditional Democratic promise. First, the issue had taken on an unexpected life of its own with Harris Wofford's surprise win in a special Pennsylvania Senate election in 1991. Wofford was the Democratic candidate running against a popular former governor of the state. Despite being well behind in the polls, Wofford emerged victorious after his campaign placed great stress on health care reform (Hacker 1996, 1997). Second, as a social policy initiative, health care reform provided ideological balance to the emphasis on welfare reform. The latter was an explicit statement of Clinton's New Democrat credentials and was designed to strengthen his claim to be a "different type of Democrat." Health care reform, on the other hand, appealed to liberals who distrusted the New Democrats' embrace of political centrism. Third, health reform offered the opportunity for the administration to stake out a "signature issue" for itself (Skowronek 1997). Elected with only a minority of the popular vote, Clinton's mandate was limited, but if he could push through the comprehensive health reform that had eluded presidents Roosevelt, Truman, Kennedy, and Johnson, then his place in political history was assured.

Yet the Clinton reform effort came to naught and proved to be a political disaster (Starr 1994; Skocpol 1997; Hacker 1997; Johnson and Broder 1997). In policy terms, the administration tried to devise a reform plan that would defuse ideological hostility while insisting on universal coverage. The wraparound term that was used to describe the idea behind the Health Security Act was "managed competition" (Hacker 1996). Walter Zelman, one of the inner-circle experts involved in developing the legislative plan, described the thinking behind managed competition as "a new, higher-level synthesis" designed "to overcome the ideological and political deadlock that has marked the reform debate" (Zelman 1994, 11). That proved to be a forlorn hope.

Republican opposition was steadfast. Conservative fears about how successful health care reform might lead to a renewed credibility for government activism in social policy were revealed in a memorandum distributed to senior Republican figures in early December 1993 by the influential conservative strategist William Kristol. He fretted that reform would: "re-legitimize middle-class dependence for 'security' on government spending and regulation. It will revive the reputation of the party that spends and regulates, the Democrats, as the generous protector of middle-class interests. And it will at the same time strike a punishing blow against Republican claims to defend the middle-class by restraining government" (quoted in Johnson and Broder 1997, 234). In short, no matter how much the White House felt that it had offered a reform package that reflected a distinctively American approach to providing universal health insurance, the president's political opponents were not prepared to negotiate on such a critical matter. Moreover, too many Democrats also abandoned ship. New Democrats were disappointed that Clinton chose to pursue health reform before welfare reform (Kaus 1995), and the fragmentation of congressional Democrats over the Health Security Act was ruinous for the administration's efforts. As onetime Clinton pollster Stanley Greenberg bluntly put it, "The health care defeat was catastrophic for Democrats" (Greenberg 1995, 308). In the end, what began as a bold effort to reshape the health care system in a manner that might have reinforced Democratic advantage in a critical area of social and public policy had quite the opposite partisan effect (Béland, Vergniolle de Chantal, and Waddan 2002).

Having lost control of the wider health care debate, Clinton and the Democrats were able reclaim their political authority in the face of conservative Republican attacks on existing public health care programs. The Health Security Act would have added a prescription drug benefit to Medicare but otherwise would largely have left Medicare alone, which reflects a decision that, after the debacle of the MCCA, Medicare beneficiaries were best left undisturbed (Marmor 2000, 133). But after the Republican capture of Congress in 1994, Medicare—and, to an extent, Medicaid—became central to continuing arguments about the delivery of health care in the United States. Furthermore, unlike the efforts to control Medicare spending in the 1980s, the ensuing attempts to reform Medicare's costs and structure were often highly partisan and ideologically charged. In immediate political terms, this intense partisan struggle worked to the benefit of the Clinton White House as congressional Republicans overestimated the mandate that they had won in the November 1994 elections, and felt a public backlash against their efforts to reform Medicare. On the other hand, while this emerging conservative critique of Medicare was rebuked at the time, the ideas that underpinned its conservative analysis persisted in the longer term and added a new and quite distinct dimension to the debate surrounding the long-term future of Medicare.

Medicare and the Budget Wars, Round 1: Policy Ideas Meet Issue Ownership

After taking over Congress in January 1995, the Republican leaders were keen to implement what they saw as their mandate to downsize the federal welfare state. This was an overtly ideological project (i.e., the conservative crusade against "big government"), but the desire to cut government spending was reinforced by the apparently more neutral rationale of deficit reduction. Underpinning the conservative challenge to Medicare was the argument that the program's built-in incentive structures encouraged beneficiaries to use the program whether they needed health care or not. Conservative-minded health economists maintained that beneficiaries quite rationally exploited the generosity of the existing Medicare system. For example, a Heritage Foundation report published in September 1995 reflected: "Today, the deductible for Part B services is only $100. This figure not only has nothing to do with economic reality, but it is also an incentive to increase demands on the system" (Liu and Moffit 1995, 3). The public choice economic principles underlying this argument—that Medicare beneficiaries would change their behavior to reflect their genuine health needs more reasonably if the incentive structures of the program were altered—became a staple of conservative discourse on Medicare reform from the mid-1990s onward.

The ultimate goal of many conservative analysts, therefore, became to shift Medicare from being a defined-benefit program to a defined-contribution program. Thus, if Medicare beneficiaries were given a specific credit to buy their own health care plan, possibly in the form of a voucher, then, according to conservatives, they would more carefully choose the type of plan that they needed rather than being able to rely on a benefit that covered all types of care regardless of whether it was appropriate to their individual circumstances. In other words, conservatives preferred that Medicare beneficiaries were given a certain amount of money to shop around for their own insurance rather than automatically provided with an insurance package that had some initial costs (in the form of copayments and deductibles) but that effectively allowed beneficiaries to consume a variety of health care services without worrying about whether those services were at all cost effective. Hence, the conservative prescription for cost control in Medicare would be to make seniors think specifically about their own needs and buy health services accordingly. In short, seniors needed to be given an incentive to use health care on an individualized value-for-money basis. To many liberals, such ideas were an anathema because reform along these lines would individualize Medicare and reduce the social solidarity inherent to the existing arrangements. The similarities between this debate and the one on Social Security privatization discussed in the next chapter are quite clear, and the opposition between conservative individualism and liberal solidarity is striking in both cases.

Whatever the ideological implications of Republican ideas, the party's leadership initially tried to frame the debate in pragmatic terms. Consequently, Republican leaders emphasized the impending shortfall in Medicare funds and talked of the need to "slow the rate of growth" of Medicare in order to save and preserve the program (Drew 1997, 204–7). Thus, checking government health expenditures became a key part of the Republican strategy to balance the budget by 2002. That seven-year time frame had no pressing logic but was given some apparent legitimacy with respect to Medicare by the 1995 Board of Trustees report that forecast that the Medicare Part A trust fund would start running a deficit from 2002. Calling their proposal the Medicare Preservation Act of 1995, the congressional Republican leaders demanded a $270 billion reduction in projected Medicare spending over the next seven years. In addition, projected Medicaid spending was to be reduced by $163 billion and was also to be fundamentally restructured with some of the existing entitlement elements of that program removed (for details of the potential impact of the Medicaid proposals, see Weaver 1996, 65–72).

For Gingrich, this was a critical part of the conservative agenda, but he miscalculated presidential resolve. Gingrich anticipated that Clinton would flinch from vetoing his plans (Johnson and Broder 1997, 580), but "protecting" Medicare gave Clinton a chance to link "the proposed Republican Medicare cuts to their proposed tax cuts, presenting this . . . as an attempt by the GOP to transfer money from the poor to the rich" (Zelizer 2007, 127). The budget battle reached its culmination in November and December of 1995, when presidential vetoes of a stopgap funding measure and then of a full budget package passed by Republicans in Congress resulted in government shutdowns for six and twenty-one days, respectively. When issuing the second veto, flourishing the same pen that President Johnson had used to sign Medicare and Medicaid into law, Clinton declared: "Today I am vetoing the biggest Medicare and Medicaid cuts in history." He added "With this veto, the extreme Republican effort to balance the budget through wrongheaded cuts and misplaced priorities is over" (quoted in Hager 1995, 3721). Presidential advisor

Dick Morris quotes Clinton as saying that the Republicans' long-term strategy was to encourage "creaming off all the younger, richer, healthier elderly into private health insurance pools. . . . When they have only the sick and old and the poor in traditional Medicare and everybody else is in private insurance . . . Medicare will be a welfare program" (Morris 1997, 173).

In this budget battle the political and policy stakes were extraordinarily high with few holds barred in the struggle to win over public opinion. Polls illustrated how popular opinion swung behind the Democrats over the issue of Medicare reform through 1995. In February 1995, when asked which party would do the better job of dealing with Medicare, 33 percent named the Democrats and 22 percent the GOP, with 45 percent replying neither, unsure, or both were the same. In December 1995, while the number nominating the Republicans had stayed stable at 24 percent, the number supporting the Democrats had jumped to 44 percent, with only 32 percent now in the other categories (Mebane 2000, 6). Furthermore, polls asking whether the congressional Republican Party or the president could be trusted more on Medicare consistently showed that more people trusted the president than the Republicans in Congress (ibid., 7). The Democratic cause was helped by Gingrich's tendency to use language that undermined Republicans' efforts to portray themselves as primarily motivated by fiscal responsibility. The Democratic National Committee, for example, made a television ad featuring Gingrich saying to a Blue Cross/Blue Shield conference on October 24, 1995: "We don't get rid of it in Round 1, because we don't think that's politically smart. We don't think that's the right way to go through a transition. But we believe that it's going to wither on the vine." The ad then went on to say that Gingrich was specifically referring to Medicare and that President Clinton would thus veto the GOP's budget plans. Republicans objected and argued that Gingrich had in fact been speaking about the Health Care Financing Administration (HCFA) (Toner 1995). The quotation was used again in an AFL-CIO sponsored advertisement in the summer of 1996. That advertisement ended with the announcer proclaiming: "They're after Medicare again" (Toner 1996).[14]

Embarking on a reform program that made Medicare a partisan issue was always likely to constitute a grave political risk for Republicans. Gingrich admitted that he went against the advice of senior Republican figures in pursuing Medicare reductions. Haley Barbour, then chair of the Republican National Committee, warned that Medicare was too popular with older voters. Gingrich reflected: "Medicare was the only thing we touched this year that could kill us" (DeParle 1996). But if the Republicans had been successful, they would have undermined one of the bulwark pillars of the federal welfare state. The GOP's leadership was primarily motivated by its ideological conviction even when this clashed with majority public preferences (Jacobs and Shapiro 2002, 67).

Medicare and the Budget Wars, Round 2: Incrementally Advancing Conservative Ideas

The Balanced Budget Act of 1997 (BBA) was not a defining conservative moment regarding Medicare, but it is possible to identify aspects of policy layering that were applied to the program. This did not bring dramatic early changes to the way that Medicare worked, but the creation of the Medicare+Choice (M+C) did pave the way for further, distinctively conservative reform as part of the 2003 MMA.

More generally, the BBA saw the protagonists from 1995–96 come to the budget table again. The 1996 election results had left the political and institutional balance of power unchanged, but budget negotiations were significantly helped by the improved fiscal conditions. The White House and congressional leaders finally agreed on a plan to balance the budget by 2002 that included cutting projected Medicare spending by $115 billion (Palazzolo 1999, 128). One aspect of the agreement was to reduce the rate of growth in payments to health maintenance organizations (HMOs) operating in Medicare (ibid., 128); the BBA also anticipated increasing the number of managed care plans in Medicare. To this end the BBA established Medicare Part C.

The new Part C was the M+C program that more formally integrated private managed care plans into Medicare. Managed care plans had been available as an option to Medicare beneficiaries who wanted an alternative to the traditional fee-for-service (FFS) program since the early 1980s. In 1985 nearly half a million beneficiaries were enrolled in managed care plans. By 1998 that number had grown to just over 6 million (Century Foundation 2001). To encourage the growth of managed care within Medicare, Part C relaxed existing restrictions on which managed care plans were allowed to compete for Medicare business.

Under M+C, an insurer would receive a set sum per enrollee per month to cover all services offered by traditional Medicare. The insurer would then bear the risk as to whether the enrollee's costs exceeded that sum. This contrasted with FFS, where Medicare paid health care providers for services rendered. Advocates expected that fostering greater competition among managed care plans would work to drive down costs. Against this, some liberal critics worried that any increase in the participation of managed care plans at the expense of FFS Medicare represented a shift toward marketization that would fragment the provision of health care to seniors (Marmor 2000, 143). This was because the managed care plans that were already operating within Medicare had proved to be more popular among program beneficiaries who were healthier than the norm and who were looking to reduce their out-of-pocket expenses. This feature also meant that the available evidence cast doubt on the assumption that M+C would reduce costs because Medicare beneficiaries who were more likely to need medical care stayed with FFS Medicare. That is, FFS Medicare continued to pay the medical costs of "expensive" Medicare beneficiaries while Medicare paid capitation payments to managed care plans when many of the enrollees in those plans did not incur significant expenses (Century

Foundation 2001, 33). In fact, by 1997 it was already evident that, even though the government paid HMOs only 95 percent of what it cost to insure the average beneficiary in FFS Medicare, the prevailing payment arrangements cost government money as HMOs were being overpaid. Because 5 percent of beneficiaries account for almost half of Medicare spending (Berenson 2007, 14), private insurers targeted healthier beneficiaries who were less likely to require expensive treatments to enroll with them (DeParle 2002, 500).

In 1997 the debate about M+C focused on payment issues rather than the broader ideological implications. So while some liberals did worry that M+C was a foot in the door toward the privatization of Medicare, it was also the case that Part C remained a defined-benefit program rather than marking a shift toward the conservative preference for a defined-contribution program. Hence, as the then-director of the HCFA noted, "The program was heralded by the Clinton administration and Republicans and Democrats in Congress alike as the kind of Medicare reform that they could all embrace" (DeParle 2002, 495).

Ironically, the initial impact of the BBA was to reduce the number of managed care plans competing for business within Medicare. The BBA adjusted the manner in which capitation payments to managed care plans were decided in order to reduce geographical disparities that had emerged with the managed care plans that operated within Medicare concentrated in New York, California, Florida, and Arizona (Century Foundation 2001, 34). Despite considerable efforts to ensure the efficacy of this new formula, however, in practice the resultant payments "seemed inadequate, almost confiscatory" (Smith 2002, 290). This meant that managed care plans were less able to offer attractive add-ons to traditional Medicare, such as prescription drug coverage or sight and hearing tests (Gold 2001). Consequently, the number of managed care plans engaged with Medicare dropped by almost 50 percent between 1998 and 2001 (Brown and Sparer 2003). The drop in the number of enrollees, though less precipitous, was also significant, from a peak of 6.4 million, representing 17 percent of Medicare beneficiaries, in 1999 to 4.6 million, representing 12 percent of beneficiaries, in 2003 (Moon 2006, 187). Therefore, the creation of M+C was at first a largely ineffectual piece of policy layering, but private insurers lobbied intensively to reverse what they saw as effectively being a defunding of their efforts to win customers within Medicare. The 1999 Balanced Budget Refinement Act and the 2000 Benefits Improvement and Protection Act addressed some of the industry's grievances, and the 2003 MMA made extensive and controversial changes that saw the number of private plans and enrollees expand significantly. The increasingly contentious nature of the plans operating under Part C was again illustrated in 2010 when the health care reform included cuts in payments to private providers in Part C.

The BBA also established the National Bipartisan Commission on the Future of Medicare. Cochaired by Democratic senator John Breaux of Louisiana and Republican representative Bill Thomas of California, the commission's mandate was to examine how to fund Medicare's long-term liabilities. As it was, and reflecting how conservative ideas had permeated into the wider debate, the commission predominantly focused on whether to introduce a premium support mechanism. One commission member, the strongly conservative senator Phil Gramm of Texas, emphasized his ideological advocacy of premium support as he declared, "It's going to save money, but I'm for it [even] if it doesn't save a dime" (quoted in Goldstein 1999). Reflecting support for the concept of premium support beyond conservative Republicans, commission members and Democratic senators Breaux and Bob Kerrey of Nebraska also backed a shift to a defined-contribution funding formula.[15] In the end, the commission did not reach a consensus. There was a ten-to-seven majority in favor of premium support, but the rules governing the commission's operation required a supermajority of eleven before a formal report could be issued. Nevertheless, the commission's deliberations illustrated how conservative ideas about reforming the structures of Medicare were gaining elite if not popular credibility.

For all this incremental advance of conservative ideas, the BBA also created the State Children's Health Insurance Program (SCHIP). This program distributed $24 billion over five years in block grants to states so that they could provide insurance coverage to children in households not eligible for Medicaid but without employer-provided insurance and with incomes insufficient to buy private insurance. As with Medicaid, states were to share the costs of SCHIP with the federal government, but in order to encourage participation, the funding formula was more generous to the states than was the funding for Medicaid (Rosenbaum et al. 1998). When enacted, SCHIP was the biggest new government-funded health care program since Medicare and Medicaid were established.

In trying to sum up health care politics and policy throughout the 1990s, it is tempting to conclude that the outcome was an ideological stalemate. But this is too simple, as both liberals and conservatives made advances and suffered retreats. Most obviously, the liberal vision of some sort of national health insurance system was decisively defeated. There was also no sign of a conservative mandate to reduce the scope of existing public programs. Conservatives, nevertheless, had some room for quiet satisfaction at the end of the 1990s, inasmuch as conservative ideas about future Medicare reform had gained elite credibility. While efforts to further marketize Medicare provision, particularly through a premium support system, had not been realized, these ideas had become part of the mainstream policy debate about the program's future.

Overall, the shifting and contradictory politics of Medicare were exemplified by the highly significant legislation enacted in President George W. Bush's first term in office. The 2003 MMA, despite circumventing many institutional obstacles to health care reform, was a curiously unloved law. To many conservatives, it was the fiscally reckless creation of a new government entitlement; yet to many liberals, it embedded conservative principles in Medicare and the wider health insurance market.

The Medicare Prescription Drug, Improvement, and Modernization Act, 2003

As a popular social insurance program, Medicare would seem naturally to be an issue "owned" by the Democrats, and that expectation has clearly played out in the political arena at times, as witnessed throughout the budget battle of 1995. Yet Medicare's politics have been less straightforward at other times. The MCCA affair saw assorted Democratic efforts at credit claiming for enacting the legislation, followed by multiple efforts at blame avoidance as the law was disavowed and then repealed. The MMA of 2003 provides another illustration of the political and ideological confusion that can be thrown up by health care policy. Unlike the MCCA, the MMA produced sharp partisan division, with President George W. Bush and congressional Republicans lining up against Democratic opposition. The case is ideologically disorientating because the division, at least on the surface, saw conservative Republicans voting in favor of an expensive addition to the federal welfare state and liberal Democrats voting against providing a new benefit to the country's seniors. Moreover, when signing the legislation, President Bush celebrated passage of a bill that was considerably more expansive than the one he had originally proposed. In contrast, Democrats opposed to the measure argued that the new benefit was inadequate and that aspects of the legislation were in effect subsidized benefits to the pharmaceutical and insurance industries.

An examination of the enactment of the MMA shows that the key political players acted out of a combination of motives as partisan expediency mixed with ideological principle to produce legislation that created an expensive new entitlement for seniors yet also embedded conservative ideas into both Medicare and the wider health insurance market. When the bill was enacted, the estimated ten-year cost of the new prescription drug benefit was $410 billion. So what happened that a unified Republican federal government produced this apparently most unconservative policy result?

Prescription Drugs for the Elderly: The Battle for Issue Ownership

It had in fact been President Clinton, a Democrat, who had put the idea of adding a prescription drug benefit to Medicare squarely on to the legislative agenda. In his 1999 State of the Union address, Clinton referred to "the greatest growing need of seniors—affordable prescription drugs" and proposed using the then-projected long-term budget surpluses to fund an expansion of Medicare to provide a prescription drug benefit (Clinton 1999). At that point, President Clinton's political capacity was limited by the ongoing Lewinsky scandal, and there was little serious legislative momentum on the issue during the remainder of his term in office, but Vice President Al Gore continued to promote the idea of a prescription drug benefit for seniors through his presidential campaign, and he attacked his Republican opponent, Gov. George W. Bush, for lacking a clear plan to introduce such a benefit. As the campaign progressed and as the idea of adding a prescription drug benefit to Medicare "emerged as a first-order issue" (Oberlander 2003, 189), candidate Bush promised that he too would introduce a drug benefit if elected to the White House and even added that this would be a "priority" for his administration (Carey 2000, 2084). The two candidates then proceeded to trade negative campaign ads attacking each other's prescription drug plans (Toner 2000). As it was, a CNN International exit poll found that Gore still comfortably beat Bush by a margin of 60 percent to 38 percent among the 7 percent of voters who named Medicare and a prescription drug benefit as the most important issue of the election. Yet Bush had made a commitment that would not go away after he moved to the White House. In fact, critically, it was a commitment that did not vanish even as the propitious fiscal circumstances of projected budget surpluses gave way, once again, to budget deficits and a climate of fiscal austerity.

The pressure to add a prescription drug benefit to Medicare reflected the rising costs that some seniors had encountered. In 2003 Medicare beneficiaries spent "an average of $2,322 per year on prescription drugs" (Oliver, Lee, and Lipton 2004, 284). This figure disguised significant variation from individual to individual based on their medical needs and according to the extent of their existing coverage. For example, some seniors had prescription drug coverage provided through a former employer's continuing health insurance coverage while other low-income seniors had their prescription drug bills paid by Medicaid. But significant numbers found their drug costs to be a major out-of-pocket expense. By the early 1990s, partly because of the cost of prescription drugs, seniors' out-of-pocket costs for medical care were as high as a percentage of their income as they had been before Medicare was established (Hacker 2004, 253). Furthermore, one unintended effect of the rules introduced by the 1997 BBA governing the M+C program was to reduce the number of managed care plans in Medicare. These plans had often offered prescription drug coverage as an enticement to attract seniors out of traditional Medicare. Hence, as the number of plans dropped, many former enrollees in these plans found that their drug coverage had disappeared. Even those plans that remained cut back on the drug packages that they offered. In 1999 84 percent of enrollees in managed care plans had basic drug coverage, but that figure had declined to 69 percent by 2003 (Achman and Gold 2003, 6).

Moreover, the proposal to cover prescription drugs was not new. The short-lived MCCA had provided subsidies to seniors to pay their drug costs. Clinton's Health Security Act also included a plan to add a drug benefit to Medicare Part B. In the late 1990s, the National Bipartisan Commission on the Future of Medicare also outlined a drug benefit plan, although this included significant copayments and deductibles for beneficiaries (Smith 2002, 352). In all these cases, however, the prescription drug benefit had been a secondary aspect of a wide-ranging reform proposal. In contrast, the MMA placed the drug benefit at the center of the legislative effort, even though there were other significant aspects to the law.

Despite President Bush's commitment to act, the first two years of his administration saw continued partisan bickering over the shape of a new prescription
drug benefit for seniors, marked by divided government after Republican senator
Jim Jeffords defected in May 2001. Congressional Democrats consistently offered
up the more generous benefit packages, but both congressional Republicans and
the Bush White House shifted from their original positions to put forward more
expansive—and expensive—plans. For example, in 1999 congressional Republicans
advocated spending $61 billion over ten years on an income-tested benefit for low-
income seniors, but by 2002 House Republicans were willing to spend $310–20
billion over ten years to subsidize a benefit for all seniors. In addition, the Bush
White House also initially favored an income-tested plan called Helping Hand,
which would have distributed $48 billion in block grants to the states over four
years. Simultaneously, the Democrats consistently emphasized their credentials
as the party that was committed to expanding access to health care. The public's
receptiveness to this message was confirmed by polls reinforcing the view that the
public trusted the Democrats over their opponents on the prescription drugs issue
(Serafini 2002). As far as issue ownership was concerned, Democrats had a clear,
perceived advantage.

Yet the political dynamics shifted again as the midterm elections of 2002 put
in place a unified Republican government. Republicans could no longer blame
obstruction on the Democrats for continued legislative inaction on the drugs benefit. The chair of the Senate Republican Conference, Rick Santorum of Pennsylvania, acknowledged in the summer of 2003, "If we can't pass it, that is a big problem
for us. . . . There's no question the responsibility falls on a Republican president
and Senate and House Republicans" (Dewar 2003). The administration worked
with Republican leaders in Congress through 2003 to get a bill enacted. This sometimes meant calming the fears of fiscal conservatives concerned about the cost of
the developing legislation. For example, in June and July of 2003, the president
and House Speaker Dennis Hastert met with delegations of Republican members
of Congress to persuade them to stick with the party's leadership and to emphasize that there would be conservative elements to the legislation to compensate for
the expense (Adams with Carey 2003; Nather and Adams 2003). But conservative
unease with the Republican plans cannot be discerned through an examination of
votes in Congress. In both chambers, but especially the House, votes on alternative plans and amendments produced highly partisan roll call divisions (Jaenicke
and Waddan 2006a, 231–38). The final Senate version of the bill did in fact receive
bipartisan support, but that proved to be of little consequence as the Conference
Committee to reconcile the House and Senate versions effectively excluded all
Democrats except two conservative-leaning moderate Democratic senators, Max
Baucus from Montana and John Breaux of Louisiana.

The headline aspect of the bill that emerged from Conference Committee was
the creation of a new prescription drug benefit entitlement, which would be Part
D of Medicare, with projected ten-year costs of $410 billion over ten years. Despite

the price tag, it was still anticipated that when the bill was enacted beneficiaries would pay a $35 monthly premium along with a $250 annual deductible and a 25 percent copayment. In addition, the benefit had a so-called "donut hole" whereby beneficiaries would still bear the full burden of prescription drugs costing between $2,250 and $5,100 annually. Among other things, Democrats complained that the bill forfeited government's capacity to get better value for money by prohibiting government from using its economic muscle to negotiate for cheaper drug prices with the pharmaceutical companies.

The final stages of the bill's legislative progress saw extraordinary scenes on the floor of the House as the effort to push the MMA through that chamber reached its climax. In the end, 89 percent of Republican House members voted for the MMA and 92 percent of Democrats against. In Senate, the numbers were 82 percent and 76 percent, respectively (Jaenicke and Waddan 2006a, 235–36). But these figures do not capture the full story. In an unprecedented fashion, the House Republican leadership kept the final vote open for three hours in order to turn an initial vote of 219 to 215 to defeat the proposal into a 220 to 215 victory margin. It required Speaker Hastert and Health and Human Services Secretary Tommy Thompson to make the rounds throughout the night to "persuade" reluctant House Republicans (Pear and Toner 2003). Meanwhile, President Bush's Legislative Affairs director, David Hobbs, awakened a jet-lagged president at 4 a.m. so he could speak to wavering members and apply some further presidential pressure (Draper 2007, 280). In the Senate there was a final attempted filibuster led by the doyen of Senate liberals, Edward Kennedy from Massachusetts. When the filibuster was broken, Republican Senate majority leader Bill Frist from Tennessee declared: "Today is a historic day and a momentous day. Seniors have waited 38 years for this prescription drug benefit to be added to the Medicare program. Today they are just moments away from the drug coverage they desperately need and deserve" (Pear and Hulse 2003).

When signing the bill, President Bush echoed Frist's sentiments as he declared, "You are here to witness the greatest advance in health coverage for America's seniors since the founding of Medicare" (Bush 2003).[16] Many conservatives, however, did not celebrate, and the reason for their displeasure was straightforward enough. The sheer scale of the MMA drew the wrath of conservative groups and think tanks normally loyal to the Republican cause.[17] Furthermore, in addition to the cost of the drug benefit, there had been a significant ideational change from the White House's Helping Hand proposals advanced in January 2001 through to the bill the president signed in late 2003. In January 2001 the Bush White House had proposed a limited benefit available through the application of a means test, but the MMA made the new prescription drug benefit available to all Medicare beneficiaries. This meant that the new drug benefit was, like the wider Medicare system, a social insurance entitlement rather than a residual safety-net benefit.

Moreover, only two months after the bill was signed, the projected cost had risen to $534 billion over ten years. Remarkably, it also emerged that the administration had been aware of this higher estimate but had kept quiet in order not to further alienate fiscally conservative Republican members of Congress (Aberbach 2005, 141). Just one year later the ten-year cost of the bill was estimated at $724 billion. Nevertheless, President Bush made it clear that he would veto any attempt to scale back the benefit that he continued to hail as a "landmark achievement" (Pear 2005). Nevertheless, some Republicans expressed their regrets. Sen. Trent Lott, for one, lamented, "I think I made a big mistake. . . . That's one of the worst votes I've cast in my 32 years in Congress" (quoted in Carey 2005, 726). In September 2005 Sen. John McCain called for the law to be reversed: "I'm saying cancel it. It was a bad idea to start with" (quoted in Bartlett 2006, 80). Some prominent conservative commentators and pundits also expressed their anger in the most explicit language. Bruce Bartlett, who had worked in the Reagan White House and then in the Treasury under President George H. W. Bush, charged that "the Medicare drug bill may well be the worst piece of legislation ever enacted" because it "will cost vast sums the nation cannot afford," inevitably leading to "higher taxes" (Bartlett 2006, 80).

On the basis of the evidence presented here, it would be easy to conclude that the Bush administration, guided only by political expediency, abandoned conservative ideas and principles in order to defuse a potential Democratic issue. Bruce Reed, a senior domestic policy advisor to President Clinton, saw the effort in these terms when writing at the start of 2004: "As we begin an election year, the paint-by-numbers politics of this White House is wearing thin. The administration threw over conservatives last fall to get a prescription drug bill because elderly voters are crucial in Florida" (Reed 2004). It was certainly the case that there was growing unease within the administration as the original aim of attaching significant reform to a modest benefit saw the ambition of reform scaled down as the size of the benefit increased.[18] But to end the story with this analysis would be to ignore significant aspects of the MMA that had a distinctly conservative twist. Perhaps most obviously, a Democratic alternative would have been unlikely to have contained such a big "donut hole" in the actual benefit, but there were other critical elements to the bill that were an anathema to many liberals.[19]

One indication of the counterintuitive politics involved in the legislation of the drug benefit and of how normal coalitional alignments were disrupted came when the AARP announced its support for the bill. AARP chief executive William Novelli told the New York Times, "This is not a perfect bill, but America cannot wait for perfect." For Novelli, the most important factor was that "two-thirds of Medicare beneficiaries will be better off with regard to drug coverage" (quoted in Pear and Toner 2003). Democratic leaders reacted furiously to the AARP's stance. For example, Nancy Pelosi, Democratic leader in the House, reflected that she was "deeply disappointed that AARP's national leadership has been co-opted by Republicans" (ibid.). Certainly, the MMA did expand the Medicare program while simultaneously advancing long-standing conservative ideas about how to restructure Medicare to make it more market oriented and reliant on private health plans (Hacker and Pierson 2005b, 85–86).

Conservative Policy Ideas and Layering in the MMA

One of the key themes of this book is to emphasize the importance of ideas in explaining incremental change rather than referring only to ideational processes when analyzing "paradigm shifts" and sharp—as opposed to incremental—policy change. One means of advancing an ideological agenda, which is frequently incremental, is through the process of policy layering, whereby the original policy framework is apparently left intact—hence diminishing potential opposition—but new elements are added to that existing policy that potentially undermine the principles of the traditional arrangements (Hacker 2004; Thelen 2004). This type of reform strategy helps bypass the institutional obstacles to reform outlined by Paul Pierson (1994, 2001), which are especially strong in the fragmented institutional context of the American polity (Steinmo and Watts 1995).

With regard to Medicare, while conservatives were thwarted when attempting directly to challenge existing social policy structures in the mid-1990s, they were more successful in advancing their agenda in 2003 even if much of what was done went under the public radar and was overshadowed by the creation of a new prescription drug benefit. The MMA was undoubtedly an expansion of the federal government's role because it established an expensive new benefit entitlement, but, through extensive policy layering, it also legislated a series of favored conservative ideas that had potentially significant long-term implications for health care provision in the United States.

First, regarding the provision of prescription drugs themselves, the MMA prohibited Medicare from directly providing the benefit to Medicare enrollees. Instead private insurers were to offer benefit plans. Plans could be either stand-alone drug benefit plans or part of a Medicare Part C package (M+C was renamed Medicare Advantage as part of the MMA). The MMA even stipulated that, in regions where no private insurer offered a drug benefit plan, a private insurer would nevertheless need to administer the plan, with Medicare paying the costs. According to key players within the administration, this structuring of the benefit to encourage competition between private plans was central to promoting market-based ideas within Medicare.[20] For the first time, a Medicare benefit was to be delivered entirely via private plans without an FFS traditional Medicare option available. If successful in terms of benefit provision and cost control, this reliance on the private sector would potentially provide a model for future program reform.[21] And the organization of the new Part D benefit was critical to those conservatives in the administration who were unhappy with the initial expense involved in paying for the benefit.[22] That is, while the cost to government was high, the delivery of the prescription drug benefit "provide[d] a testing ground for . . . [conservatives] belief that competition, consumer choice, and market forces can govern Medicare much better than the federal government can" (Oberlander 2007, 202). This fit with a conservative view that had emerged in the 1980s. According to this view, contracting out publicly funded social programming functions was a means of introducing market principles into the welfare state (Campbell and Morgan 2011).

Second, even though the administration had to back away from its original proposal that the new drug benefit should be provided on an income-tested basis, the MMA nevertheless introduced an element of income-testing into Part B of Medicare. Prior to the enactment of the MMA, all beneficiaries paid the same premium for Part B coverage. From 2007 onward, however, the MMA determined that higher-income beneficiaries would pay higher premiums.[23] Advocates of introducing income-related premiums portrayed this as a fairer system because it would simply mean that higher-income beneficiaries would contribute more to Medicare's financing than lower-income beneficiaries. Republican representative Nancy Johnson from Connecticut, who was chair of the House Ways and Means Committee's Subcommittee on Health explained: "I do not believe that someone with a $200,000 income living in a gated community should have exactly the same subsidy as someone struggling along on $25,000 or $30,000 of income" (quoted in Pear 2003a). Democrats were divided about the introduction of differential premiums. California senator Dianne Feinstein agreed that "high-income beneficiaries can afford to pay a larger share of Medicare's costs" but Sen. Edward Kennedy expressed his worry that charging higher-income beneficiaries more might erode their support for the overall program (ibid.). The CBO's initial estimate was that about 3 percent of beneficiaries would pay a higher premium in 2007, rising to 6 percent by 2013 (CBO 2005b). While these are relatively small numbers, "this provision could become an entering wedge for greater means testing within Medicare that would undermine the social insurance that has characterized Medicare since its inception" (Jaenicke and Waddan 2006a, 230; Marmor and Hacker 2005).

Third, the MMA further encouraged managed care plans to operate in Medicare when changing the M+C program into Medicare Advantage (MA). In hindsight, conservatives complained that M+C had not been a fair test of the capacity of private plans to compete with traditional FFS Medicare. For example, according to Robert Moffit of the Heritage Foundation, M+C "was compromised from the start. Governed by a new and very different form of financing that capped Medicare payments to health care plans, the program was also burdened with a 900-page regulatory regime that stifled both innovation and plan flexibility" (Moffit 2008, 2N). Revealingly, in contrast to the negotiations about M+C in 1997, the shift to MA released partisan hostilities (Pear 2003b).

In a May 2002 speech to a group called the Coalition for Medicare Choices, President Bush reflected that private plans offered benefits not available through traditional FFS Medicare. He added, "The defined benefit plan in Medicare limits the capacity of seniors to meet their needs. And that doesn't seem right to me" (quoted in Lambrew and Davenport 2006, 2). The creation of the MA program did not herald a switch to a defined-contribution approach, but it did offer private plans the chance to compete with traditional Medicare on terms much more favorable to private plans than had been the case under M+C. Primarily, the MMA abandoned the payment mechanisms to private plans devised in 1997 that had so inhibited their development within Medicare.

Thus, while the original rationale for introducing private insurance into Medicare was that competition among private insurers would control costs, that objective played little part in the discussions about the creation of the MA program in 2003. The new provisions included "a series of financial subsidies and rate increases designed to attract private insurers to the Medicare market" (Oberlander 2007, 204). Accordingly, critics of MA's design concluded, "The ideological goal of privatizing more of Medicare trumped the stated goal of using 'competition' to restrain the rate of growth in Medicare costs" (Park, Greenstein, and Kogan 2004, 4). By 2009 it was evident that MA plans were significantly more expensive than FFS Medicare: "Although private insurers were brought into Medicare to reduce costs, Medicare pays them an average of $1,000 more per beneficiary per year than it costs to treat the same beneficiaries through traditional Medicare. These overpayments threaten Medicare's finances and increase the premiums paid by participants in traditional Medicare" (Angeles and Park 2009, 1).

In this context, liberal analysts worried that the aim was to "make the private health insurance alternatives to Medicare so enticing that beneficiaries voluntarily desert the traditional program, and it perishes from neglect" (Berenson 2007, 13). Conservative analysts were happy to echo that sentiment. Joseph Antos, of the American Enterprise Institute, noted, "The MMA has created an unprecedented opportunity for the growth of private plans in Medicare" (Antos 2006, 9). He added that while the long-term success of MA was far from certain, "the strategy of the MMA is to make MA plans so attractive that most beneficiaries will voluntarily switch out of traditional Medicare" (ibid., 10).

Fourth, and going beyond Medicare to extend a fiercely held but equally fiercely disputed conservative idea about the way to reform the wider health care system, the MMA universalized the availability of health savings accounts (HSAs). HSAs, savings accounts that can be used to pay for out-of-pocket health care expenses, had only been accessible to limited numbers of Americans and, prior to 2003, had already proved to be particularly controversial as legislative attempts to expand their availability produced sharp partisan rancor and ideological cleavage. The controversy surrounding HSAs is tied to their tax-privileged status that allows holders of such accounts to benefit by making tax-deductible contributions to their HSA and by receiving tax-exempt interest on the money in the account.[24] Advocates of HSAs argue that the accounts provide individuals the opportunity to determine their own health care needs, both in the short and long term. Further, by emphasizing the cost of what might be termed regular health care needs (as distinct from catastrophic needs) at the point of use, HSAs are meant to encourage individuals to be more careful consumers of health care. In turn, advocates claim, this individualized incentive structure will contain costs better than either employer- or government-provided insurance packages. Consequently, according to conservative analysts, "HSA-style plans, by design, create incentives for better utilization of services and encourage price and quality comparisons" (D'Angelo and Moffit 2006, 2). The underlying principle was expressed by President Bush in a radio address when he argued that the problem of widespread uninsurance was best remedied by changing incentives and encouraging people to "treat health insurance more like home ownership" (Bush 2007). In this sense, HSAs corresponded with Bush's notion of the "ownership society," which would soon become central to the debate on Social Security privatization (see chapter 3). Celebrating the expanded access to HSAs, conservative commentator Fred Barnes castigated those conservatives who disparaged the overall MMA. Barnes insisted: "Bush and his aides have embraced an insight lost on some other conservatives: what matters is not how big government is, but what it does. . . . Bush realized that a conservative president can use government policies to expand personal freedom . . . and health savings accounts in Medicare aim to do that" (Barnes 2006, 176).

Critics of HSAs argue that this type of savings account will be most appealing to the healthy and wealthy, who are happy to combine an HSA with a high-deductible insurance plan. In turn, this would segment the overall insurance market and encourage a process of adverse selection in both private and public insurance. That is, while it might make sense for a healthy and wealthy individual to take out a high-deductible insurance package to cover catastrophic health costs and to invest in an HSA to cover other expenses, this would mean that that person would opt out of the existing insurance market. If significant numbers of the healthy and wealthy behaved in this fashion, then the redistribution inherent in the big, traditional insurance pools would be lost because those pools would be left with poorer and unhealthier insurees (Cohn 2005). The very different perspectives about HSAs were well captured in the two following—and contrasting—statements from two members of the House in the aftermath of the final House on the MMA. On one hand, according to Wisconsin Republican Paul Ryan, "It will get people shopping with their own dollars for health care." On the other hand, Californian Democrat Pete Stark ridiculed this idea: "Health care is not like other goods. . . . You're not a consumer. How can you shop when you're scared and in pain" (quoted in Rosenbaum 2003a). These two quotes vividly illustrate the contrast between individualistic, pro-market conservative ideas and the liberal belief in social insurance and government-granted economic protection and social solidarity.

Of the various parts of the MMA that were not directly connected to the provision of the prescription drug benefit for seniors, the loosening of the regulations governing the availability of HSAs did the most to affect congressional voting. Prior to the MMA, Republicans had led efforts to push the use of HSAs. The passage of the 1996 Health Insurance and Portability Accountability Act (HIPAA) was nearly derailed by arguments over HSAs (then known as medical savings accounts). In the end, HIPAA passed with a small number of MSAs authorized for individuals and small businesses. Similarly, the BBA of 1997 increased availability a little more, but Democrats remained strongly opposed to further expansion of the savings accounts, which made decisive legislative action difficult. So, in 2003 some conservative Republicans, although unhappy with the drug benefit, were persuaded to stick with the Bush administration and vote for the MMA because of the HSA provision (Rosenbaum 2003a).[25] Addressing the House Republican conference, former Speaker Newt Gingrich maintained that expanding popular access to HSAs would be "the single most important change in health care policy in 60 years" and urged support for the MMA on that basis (quoted in Dreyfuss 2004, 26).

While Gingrich's comments seem hyperbolic, especially if the possible impact of HSAs is compared with the actual impact of Medicare and Medicaid established fewer than forty years earlier, the institutionalization of HSAs and the wider push toward individualistic, consumer-driven health care should not be dismissed (Quadagno and McKelvey 2008). In its review of the likely impact of HSAs, the nonprofit research group Employee Benefit Research Institute noted first that, at the time the MMA was adopted, little was really known about how HSAs would interact with the overall health care system, but added that there were potentially significant outcomes that would need monitoring over an extended period.

> The introduction of HSAs has further spurred interest in account-based health plans. There are many theories and positions on the impact that account-based plans will have on the health care system, but real evidence is lacking. . . . The movement toward account-based plans, as part of the evolution of the financing and delivery of health care, not only has implications for the cost of providing health benefits and utilization of health care services, but also for quality of health care, the use of appropriate and inappropriate health care services, the health status of the population, risk selection, and efforts to expand health insurance coverage. (Fronstin 2004, 14)

Finally, the law contained two provisions that offered further potential for future—conservative—Medicare restructuring. It called for a demonstration project to be set up in 2010 that would have experimented with premium support schemes, meaning that Medicare would have been offered to beneficiaries as a defined-contribution rather than as a defined-benefit scheme. Also, the MMA put in place a mechanism that would trigger an overall review of Medicare funding on the basis that a particular funding "crisis" point had been reached. The law stipulated that when two successive Medicare trustees' reports projected that at least 45 percent of the program's costs would be paid out of general revenues, this constituted a "crisis" that demanded congressional review. Some Republicans were unhappy that the language in the trigger was not strong enough because it only called for congressional consideration of Medicare's financing rather than demanding a legislative remedy (Carey 2003). Nevertheless, the trigger embedded the idea that relying on general revenues to pay for Medicare was in itself problematic, which meant that any changes to the program's financial arrangements were likely to be along the lines preferred by conservatives (Park, Greenstein, and Kogan 2004).

When enacted in 2003, these two provisions, the premium support demonstration project and the fiscal trigger, gave conservatives a potential rationale for the future reorganization of Medicare. For example, a Heritage Foundation memo argued that the 2007 Trustees Report, which repeated the previous year's prediction that more than 45 percent of Medicare's funding would come from general revenues in fiscal year 2013, activated the trigger. The authors urged Congress to do more than "simply" readjust "Medicare payment formulas" or impose "research-killing price regulations on prescription drugs." Instead, legislators should "go back to the drawing board" to redesign Medicare's financing structures (Moffit and Fraser 2008). Unlike other features of the 2003 legislation, however, the demonstration projects and the trigger mechanism did not become embedded in Medicare policy. Officials in the administration who worked on the MMA later acknowledged that these two elements, while expressing genuine conservative principles, were not felt to be serious parts of the bill.[26] They were features that were particularly vulnerable to a shift in the partisan control of government, and Democrats found few institutional or popular obstacles to overcome in undoing these provisions. Thus, the Democratic recapture of Congress in 2006 dramatically reduced the likely impact of the two measures.

Nevertheless, the overall MMA was the most significant piece of legislation affecting the structure of Medicare since the program was established in 1965. It created a major new entitlement for seniors and established an environment designed to entice significantly more managed care plans to compete for business with traditional FFS Medicare. In addition, it contained elements that had potentially important implications for the wider provision of health insurance. Ironically, however, both conservative and liberal commentators have tended to focus on the elements of the law they dislike. Thus, while many fiscal conservatives were unhappy with the expensive new drug benefit in the MMA, many liberals were fearful of the long-term implications of other aspects of the legislation.

When signing the MMA, President Bush commented: "Our government is finally bringing prescription drug coverage to the seniors of America" (Bush 2003). But in a book generally favorable to the administration, Stephen Moore, then president of the conservative Club for Growth, called the MMA "the most fiscally reckless bill to pass the US Congress since Lyndon Johnson was in the White House" (Moore 2004, 105). In contrast to President Bush's cheer at the signing ceremony for the MMA, Senator Kennedy that day addressed a crowd of his supporters and, in an exercise in issue-ownership framing, rhetorically demanded to know from them: "Who do you trust? . . . The H.M.O.-coddling, drug-company-loving, Medicare-destroying, Social Security-hating Bush administration? Or do you trust Democrats, who created Medicare and will fight with you to defend it— every day of every week of every year?" (Rosenbaum 2003b).

Medicare Meets the Affordable Care Act: An Incomplete Policy Reversal

During the 2008 campaign for the Democratic Party's presidential nomination, the leading candidates promised to overhaul existing health care arrangements. Appealing to the party's liberal base, the candidates promised to push for universal health insurance coverage. At the same time, they acknowledged the need to "bend the cost curve" that had seen health care expenses place an increasing burden on both American business and government. The latter commitment had the most significant implications for Medicare because any serious attempt to contain the federal government's health care expenditures necessarily meant restraining the future growth of Medicare spending. This was especially so because the program's cost will inevitably rise in the context of population aging (Baker 2010). In fact, the Affordable Care Act (ACA), signed into law by President Obama in March 2010, affected Medicare in a number of ways, but it was the proposals to restrain costs that produced political tumult.

The politics surrounding the passage of the ACA did follow some predictable partisan and ideational patterns. Democrats put together a plan that, through a variety of means, promises to insure an extra 32 million Americans by 2019, primarily through an extension of Medicaid and the establishment of new health insurance exchanges, through which low-income households will be able to get government-subsidized coverage. The bill also mandates that all individuals must get insurance. Democrats themselves were divided over certain issues such as whether to include a "public option" in the new health exchanges, and Republicans were steadfast in their opposition. In terms of getting the legislation passed, the Democratic Party had bigger congressional majorities in 2009–10 than it did sixteen years before, and interest group opposition was more muted than in the 1990s (Hacker 2010). This situation reflects the fact that the White House sought agreements with key interest groups such as the pharmaceutical industry in the early stages of the legislative process (Jacobs and Skocpol 2010).

While the partisan divisions about the overall principle of health care reform were predictable, the place of Medicare in the argument was decidedly counterintuitive as Republicans attacked Democrats for the projected expenditure cuts. The planned savings from 2010 to 2019, through a variety of measures including cuts to providers (but not physicians) and cuts in payments to Medicare Advantage, were estimated at $533 billion. This savings would be offset somewhat by anticipated new spending of $105 billion. Reflecting liberal preferences, extra revenues would be raised through progressive changes to the tax code (Rice 2011), including an estimated $87 billion from an increase in the Medicare payroll tax from 1.45 percent to 2.35 percent for individuals with an annual income over $200,000 and for couples with an annual income over $250,000 (Kaiser Family Foundation 2010).

Some of the measures in the ACA were policy reversals of aspects of the MMA that Democrats had objected to back in 2003. First, reflecting how Democrats had complained that the MMA drug benefit was not sufficiently encompassing, the ACA partially filled in the so-called "donut hole" in the prescription drug benefit. In 2010 the "donut hole" appeared when a person enrolled in Part D of Medicare spent $2,830 on prescription drugs (Staff of the *Washington Post* 2010, 115). The ACA stipulated that seniors who went over this threshold in 2010 were entitled to a $250 rebate. Beginning in 2011, the ACA then required drug manufacturers to discount prices for seniors who fell into the "donut hole". By 2020, through a combination of those discounts and government subsidies, seniors would be paying only 25 percent of the costs in the "donut hole", as compared to 100 percent prior to the ACA. This element of the new law reflected liberal ideas about how government should offer protection to seniors with high health care expenses, but this was more a revision than a repudiation of the MMA.

The second change from the 2003 law was more controversial and ideologically charged because the ACA, by cutting back on payments to private plans operating in the Medicare Advantage program, partially reversed one of the important aspects of conservative policy layering in the MMA. When the Medicare+Choice program was established in 1997, there was relatively little partisan conflict, but when it was renamed as MA and extensively reshaped through the 2003 law, there was much more argument over the merits of the scheme. Conservatives embraced the expanded participation of private plans in Medicare, and by 2010 nearly one-fourth of Medicare beneficiaries were enrolled in a private plan. Critics contended, however, that there was little evidence to support the claim that the MA program would reduce Medicare costs and that it was "unfair to force those enrolled in traditional Medicare" as well as taxpayers to pay for the extra benefits contained in some MA plans.[27] Kenneth Baer of the Office of Management and Budget reflected: "We should not be subsidizing insurance companies to provide Medicare benefits that cost 14% more" (quoted in Parsons and Zajac 2009). Hence, the cuts contained in the ACA were justified on the grounds that Medicare was overpaying the existing MA plans to the tune of "between 9 and 13 percent more per enrollee than it costs to cover the same person under traditional Medicare" (Angeles 2010, 1). This meant that Medicare was paying the private plans an "average" of over "$1,100 for each Medicare Advantage beneficiary" more than it would have cost to cover those people under traditional Medicare amounting to a total of "nearly $44 billion between 2004 and 2009" (Angeles 2010, 1).

As the plan to reduce MA payments came into focus, insurers and conservative analysts protested. In September 2009 the insurance company Humana sent out more than nine hundred thousand letters warning that if MA payments were reduced, "millions of seniors and disabled individuals could lose many of the important benefits and services that make Medicare Advantage health plans so valuable" (quoted in Pear 2009b). The Obama administration responded by saying that the Humana letters were "misleading to beneficiaries" and therefore breached Medicare's rules (Pear 2009a). When addressing Congress in September 2009, President Obama referred to the "unwarranted subsidies in Medicare that go to insurance companies—subsidies that do everything to pad their profits and nothing to improve your care."[28] In short, the administration constructed "the need to reform" (Cox 2001) MA by charging that the program was wasteful and inefficient. Even so, some Democrats, while generally supportive of health care reform, were anxious about the impact that scaling back MA payments would have on seniors. For example, in September 2009, Democratic senator Bill Nelson of Florida promised to protect seniors who received extra benefits from their MA enrolment (Pear 2009b).

Conservatives protested that the reduction in payments to MA plans was justified by a flawed fiscal logic and would be harmful to seniors because it would cause many plans that offered benefits beyond those contained in traditional Medicare to withdraw from the MA market (Book and Capretta 2010). From this perspective, even the 2003 legislation had not allowed private plans to compete properly in the Medicare market. This is true because the method of assessing MA costs by comparing them with standard Medicare FFS costs in each county was an imperfect means of calculating MA's effectiveness. For instance, it did not take into account cases where county FFS costs were reduced because they followed the practices of a successful local MA plan (ibid.). Clearly, much of the discussion surrounding the future of the MA program emphasized fiscal matters, but the ideational implications of rolling back the MA program and reversing the conservative policy layering that had taken place in 2003 were also apparent. For liberals, the attempt to introduce a greater element of private competition into Medicare had primarily resulted in increasing the profits of the insurance companies. As for conservatives, they emphasized that MA plans had brought extra benefits to seniors and had succeeded in controlling costs in some areas. Joseph Antos, a researcher at the conservative American Enterprise Institute, acknowledged that critics of the MA program "point out that MA plans cost about 13 percent more than conventional fee-for-service Medicare." But Antos maintained this was a misleading piece of data: "That extra cash doesn't just go into the pockets of insurers. Seniors get additional benefits, such as dental and vision coverage or lower out-of-pocket costs—often lower than those of traditional Medicare. It's no wonder the program has proved popular. Since 2003, the number of enrollees in Medicare Advantage has nearly doubled. And as of 2008, 10.1 million people—almost a quarter of all Medicare beneficiaries—are opting for Medicare Advantage" (Antos 2009).

Yet the ACA did proceed to reduce funding for MA plans. Payments for 2011 were to be frozen at 2010 levels with cutbacks in payments scheduled to begin in 2012. The formula for calculating the cutback was a complex one, dependent upon FFS Medicare payments that varied on a county-by-county basis.[29] Overall, estimates were that average payments to MA plans would drop by 12 percent, a saving to government of 132 billion dollars over ten years (Staff of the *Washington Post* 2010, 118). For all the arguments over the MA program, the biggest cuts to Medicare spending contained in the ACA were not the explicit reductions to MA plans but cuts in the future growth rate of payments to health care providers.

The administration claimed that these payment reductions were a necessary response to the escalating expense of Medicare. And apparently giving credibility to this claim, the Medicare Trustees report of August 2010 found that the cost-cutting measures in the ACA meant that Medicare's Trust Fund would remain solvent for twelve extra years than had earlier been predicted through to 2029 (Pear and Calmes, 2010).[30] But the measures to control Medicare's costs provoked a furious reaction and a counterintuitive politics of issue ownership as Republicans claimed the mantle of the party determined to protect Medicare against the reckless and ideologically driven Democratic agenda. Republicans accused Democrats of sacrificing the interests of seniors in pursuit of the wider goal of big government intervention in the health care market. The possible traction of this argument was evidenced in the summer of 2009 when references to "death panels" hit the airwaves. This arose when a provision in a version of a House bill referred to funding doctors to advise patients on "end-of-life-services." The "death panel" phrase itself gained prominence after being used by former vice-presidential candidate Sarah Palin. Fox News channel host Glenn Beck mocked the idea of end-of-life counseling: "Sometimes for the common good, you just have to say, 'Hey Grandpa, you've had a good life'" (quoted in Rutenberg and Calmes 2009). The then–House Republican minority leader John Boehner (Ohio) gave such comments credibility when he reflected, "This provision may start us down a treacherous path toward government-encouraged euthanasia" (quoted in Pear and Herszenhorn 2009).

Some Democrats dismissed the Republican attacks as implausible. For instance, Sen. Robert Menendez of New Jersey predicted: "The very people who fought Medicare don't have the credibility to demagogue on this issue" (quoted in Nagourney 2009). In a speech to Congress in September 2009, President Obama derided the Republican jibes and emphasized the Democratic Party's long-standing commitment to traditional Medicare, in contrast to Republican ideas about fundamentally changing Medicare's structure. Explaining that the reductions in spending were targeted at areas of fraud and waste, he declared:

> These steps will ensure that you—America's seniors—get the benefits you've been promised. They will ensure that Medicare is there for future generations. And we can use some of the savings to fill the gap in coverage that forces too many seniors to pay thousands of dollars a year out of their own pocket for prescription drugs. That's what this plan will do for you. So don't pay attention to those scary stories about how your benefits will be cut— especially since some of the same folks who are spreading these tall tales have fought against Medicare in the past, and just this year supported a budget that would have essentially turned Medicare into a privatized voucher program. That will never happen on my watch. I will protect Medicare.[31]

These protestations did not prevent continued Republican attacks. Some conservative commentators lamented the short-termism of Republican tactics. Ross

Douthat, for example, noted that adopting the role of "champions of old-age entitlements" was "a perilous strategy for the right" because it made future conservative proposals for structural Medicare reform more problematic (Douthat 2009). As the 2010 midterm elections approached, these reservations counted for little as Republicans and conservative groups vigorously attacked the ACA for the damage it would allegedly do to seniors. Newt Gingrich and John Goodman (2010), while acknowledging Medicare's "unsustainable course," protested: "The reform bills passed by the House and Senate cut Medicare by approximately $500 billion. This is wrong." This reversal of normal partisan patterns was highlighted during the 2010 midterm campaign when conservative groups and business organizations, including the US Chamber of Commerce, paid for advertisements condemning Democratic legislators who had voted in favor of the ACA for betraying seniors (Steinhauer 2010).

It is difficult to assess clearly the impact of these advertisements in terms of giving the Republicans issue ownership of Medicare in 2010. Older voters strongly supported the Republicans in 2010, but this age cohort had backed John McCain over Obama in 2008, so this was not a decisive new partisan trend. On the other hand, the New York Times did report that "a fifth of those [older] voters rated health care their most important issue, and more than half said that Congress should repeal the whole health care reform law" (New York Times 2010).[32] Hence, even if intellectual elites puzzled over Republicans defending entitlement spending, the attacks on Medicare expenditure reductions were an effective weapon that put anxious Democrats even more on the defensive over the passage of the controversial ACA. Significantly, the AARP did support the overall health reform package, although there were some signs of divisions in the organization's membership between those already covered by Medicare and those aged between fifty and sixty-five who were still anxious about the source of their health insurance (Harris 2009). Just prior to the 2010 elections John Rother of the AARP acknowledged, "Seniors are a tough audience for Democrats" because the ACA had "given Republicans a way to talk about positioning themselves as defenders of Medicare, which is quite unusual" (quoted in Serafini 2010).

A further, if initially less publicized, aspect of the ACA's plans for cost control in Medicare was the creation of the Independent Payment Advisory Board (IPAB). This organization, scheduled to operate from 2015, would have fifteen members appointed by the president to serve six-year terms subject to Senate ratification. The IPAB's existence would become potentially significant if, after 2014, the increase in per capita Medicare spending was above a specified target. In these circumstances, the IPAB's mandate is to recommend spending reductions that will be implemented unless Congress explicitly overrides the board's recommendations and implements spending reductions to the same value. This rather extraordinary power was limited by the stipulation that the IPAB cannot recommend changes that ration care, modify benefits, change eligibility levels or premiums, or reduce payments to certain types of providers. The nature of the IPAB raises the possibility that politicians could allow Medicare reductions to take place while shifting some of the blame onto Medicare experts, but this would require a bipartisan consensus to stop either party from point scoring by opposing any proposed cuts. Potentially IPAB is a significant government tool, having the status to make recommendations about payments to health care providers in an environment less susceptible to interest group lobbying than normal lawmaking channels. In the initial debate about the ACA, the potential powers of IPAB went somewhat under the radar, but by the summer of 2011 a clamor of opposition had emerged from Republicans and interest groups such as PhRMA, the AMA, and an increasing number of congressional Democrats (Aizenman 2011).

One other noteworthy aspect of the ACA was that it expanded on the principle of income-related premiums within Medicare that had been introduced in the MMA. As described earlier, the MMA had brought in differential premiums for Medicare Part B dependent on income. At the time Republicans had welcomed this prospect of income-testing Medicare beneficiaries while Democrats had been divided between those who saw it as a way of raising funds and those who feared it might lead to a breakdown of the social solidarity that had underpinned the program. By 2010 the conservative preference for income testing had gained ground as liberals struggled to find ways of getting around fiscal constraints. Thus, the ACA effectively introduced a policy of inflationary tax-bracket creep by freezing the income threshold at which beneficiaries paid a higher Part B premium through to 2019. In addition, the ACA introduced a new income-related premium for Medicare Part D. This was set at the same threshold as for Part B ($85,000 for a single person and $170,000 for a couple) with that bracket also frozen through 2019.

Overall, the part that Medicare played in the battle over health care reform through 2009–10 was a significant one. It also reflected how difficult it was for the Obama White House and congressional Democrats to design a coherent health reform plan that achieved their objectives of near-universal insurance coverage and cost-cutting without having, from their perspective, negative spillover effects on some aspects of health provision. The pressure to reduce federal spending commitments inevitably meant that Democrats were going to have to call for reductions in projected Medicare growth that would leave them vulnerable to political attack, especially since these reductions were in part a consequence of the need to free up funds to increase spending on the uninsured (Gitterman and Scott 2011, 557). Nevertheless, the ferocity and apparent success of attacks by Republicans and conservative groups on Democrats for "gutting" Medicare was surprising. The ACA did see some liberal ideas prevail in Medicare as the "donut hole" was partially filled and Medicare Advantage scaled back. The latter issue represents a major example of an incremental reform being reversed when there was a shift in the partisan balance of power. This was so even though MA plans had built up a constituency of users in the years leading up to the ACA, which suggests that, over time, political and partisan shifts can lead to the reversal of previously enacted incremental changes. Yet some controversial conservative principles that had been part of the MMA survived as, for example, the basic structure of the delivery system for the prescription drug benefit that relied exclusively on private providers remained (Campbell and Morgan 2011). From this perspective, the ACA did not fully reverse the incremental processes by which conservative ideas about private provisions have become increasingly embedded in the Medicare program.

Furthermore, in the aftermath of the 2010 midterm elections, the Republican congressional leadership returned to the theme of health care reform. The Republican majority in the House of Representatives voted to repeal the ACA. With Senate still in Democratic hands and President Obama still in the White House, this was a symbolic rather than consequential vote, but it signaled that the battle over health policy had not been resolved by the ACA. In fact, the Republican leadership in the House even promoted the idea of radical reform to the Medicare and Medicaid programs. A Republican-sponsored long-term budget plan, put forward in April 2011, proposed that Medicare effectively be changed, beginning in 2022, to a voucher system with beneficiaries being given an amount to spend to buy an insurance plan. Conservative advocates explained that this would allow seniors to cater more carefully for their own needs (Tanner 2011). Liberals worried that it would mean the end of Medicare as we know it, with many seniors left having to make significant out-of-pocket payments (Krugman 2011).

The architect of the Republican budget plan, Paul Ryan from Wisconsin, argued that major changes were required to restore long-term fiscal order. Ryan reflected in a video: "Washington has not been telling you the truth. . . . If we don't reform spending on government health and retirement programs, we have zero hope of getting our spending—and as a result our debt crisis—under control" (quoted in Calmes 2011). When expressing these sentiments, Ryan illustrated one of the central themes of this book: that is, he insisted that there is an objective "need to reform" (Cox 2001) federal social programs. And that reform is best achieved through methods fitting his conservative ideational preferences.

Conclusion

Medicare is a federal program that provides care to the elderly and disabled and that has a popular legitimacy and high levels of public support. But Medicare has developed a complex politics as ideological, institutional, and political processes interact. As Medicare developed into an increasingly partisan political topic, it in turn heralded a significant but mixed reform package in 2003, and then the program became embroiled in the argument over wider health care reform through 2009 and 2010.

For a long time, the program's initial policy legacies prevented explicit political conflict about Medicare. It was as popular as its founders had expected but evidently more expensive than had been anticipated. It was too politically risky to downsize Medicare but also too costly to expand. This meant that for the first three decades of the program's existence there was an apparent consensus in Washington with regard to the program's development (Marmor 2000; Oberlander 2003). Important changes were made to Medicare's mechanisms, but these were done under the cloak of bipartisanship even when the reforms had manifest political implications. Even the enactment and then repeal of the MCCA saw majorities of both congressional parties voting together. In some ways this consensus was an unhappy one. It reflected conservative timidity in that conservatives refrained from attacking a popular big-government program. It also reflected liberal uncertainty about expanding Medicare in the face of the program's escalating costs. From the mid-1990s onward, however, the Medicare consensus broke down and the program became the subject of intense partisan dispute. The dynamics driving the emerging controversies and the manner in which the issues raised have so far been resolved reflect a complex mix of institutional and ideational factors.

First, it became more and more difficult to suppress the problems inherent in the existing Medicare program and its policy legacies. That is, both the cost of the program and the gaps in health care coverage left by it were demanding political attention. In the mid-1990s congressional Republicans aggressively pushed for substantive cuts in Medicare spending. Yet by the end of the decade the most high-profile issue surrounding Medicare was the question of whether to add an outpatient prescription drug benefit to the program to help those seniors who found paying for their medication an increasing financial burden.

Second, as these issues raged there was a break in the ideological cease-fire that had surrounded Medicare following the program's creation in 1965. From the mid-1990s onward, competing ideas about how best to organize the program made Medicare the focus of intense struggle, reflecting a deep ideological cleavage between those wishing to maintain the underlying principles of a social insurance system against those wanting to move toward a more market-oriented policy. This "new politics" of Medicare (Oberlander 2003) was driven primarily by conservative ideas that emphasized the "flaws" in the existing system and insisted that these would best be remedied by treating Medicare enrollees as active consumers rather than passive beneficiaries. Conservatives were successful inasmuch as these ideas became a part of mainstream policy debate. Indeed, some centrists, while not necessarily advocating the rejection of the social insurance model, did agree that the need for cost containment within Medicare required reforms to the program that went beyond simply seeking savings by further squeezing the usual suspects and cutting projected payments to doctors and hospitals (Schlesinger 2002; White 2007b).

Many liberals steadfastly resisted the conservative promotion of premium support and managed care within Medicare, seeing these ideas as a frontal attack on the idea of solidarity that had guided Medicare's initial advocates (Vladeck 2004). In short, the differences in how conservatives and liberals view publicly organized health care are wide, sincere, and likely unbridgeable (White 2007b). In this context, "The balance between the sides will be determined by elections and, to some extent between elections by pitched battles in the public sphere of political debate, in which the two sides contend for support from often inattentive voters" (ibid., 230–31).

This brings us to the third central theme of this book—issue ownership. The overall debate about health care illustrates a very complex politics that suggests Democrats own health care as an issue until they actually develop substantive plans for how to reform the system. As demonstrated by Clinton's failed reform plan and the political catastrophe entailed by that effort, conservatives have launched effective counterassaults when necessary. President Obama's 2009–10 reform effort also generated intense hostility. More specifically, when only Medicare is concerned, issue ownership has also proved convoluted. The MCCA case at the end of the 1980s illustrated that policymakers need to be careful when judging the sentiments of seniors, but the backlash against Republican efforts in the 1990s to cut projected spending showed that protecting existing benefits, as advocated by Democrats, was the priority of the powerful constituency of seniors (Peterson 1998). Furthermore, the addition of a prescription drug benefit to Medicare, which was the headline aspect of the 2003 Medicare reform, represented an attempt by the Bush administration and congressional Republicans to remove a Democratic issue from the political agenda. The prescription drug benefit was not natural ideational and partisan territory for Republicans, so the fact that a unified Republican federal government was pressured into enacting the benefit shows how political expediency can trump ideological preference.

Yet the MMA was categorically not the legislation that Democrats would have written because it featured significant elements of conservative policy layering. Regardless of the generosity of the benefit and the size of the "donut hole", Democrats would surely have allowed traditional Medicare to deliver the drugs benefit rather than leaving that exclusively to private plans. And as conservatives claim that the use of private plans has been fiscally efficient and has made Medicare beneficiaries think more carefully about their prescription drug plans, so the terms on which Part D was created appear as a form of policy layering that potentially has a similar ideational impact as the pre-1996 welfare waivers, which allowed conservatives to stress the alleged "real world" success of their reform ideas. From this perspective, policy layering and the politics of ideas are once again closely related. In the first place, conservative ideas about workfare and private provision have legitimized the addition of new institutional layers to existing welfare and health care policies. Next, in a self-reinforcing manner, these new institutional layers and their discourse about their perceived "success" are used as a rationale to justify the need for further conservative reforms. So conservatives argue that the exclusive use of private providers to supply the actual prescription drug benefit is a success story illustrating the advantages of private sector competition over public sector delivery. In fact, "the response of private insurers to Part D has been overwhelming. The average Medicare beneficiary has more than 50 different Part D plan choices. Thanks to competition, premiums averaged $24 a month in 2006, one-third lower than experts had predicted" (Antos 2007).

Moreover, Democrats would not have given such preferential terms to the MA program, nor would they have expanded access to HSAs in the way that the MMA did. The success of conservative policy layering in the MMA was perhaps best illustrated by the increased number of Medicare beneficiaries enrolled in managed care plans through the MA program. Nevertheless, many liberals remained unpersuaded about this alleged "success," and as the health care debate raged through 2009, MA became a favorite target for some liberals who complained about its costs. With regard to MA, liberals were able to portray their actions as following a fiscal rather than ideological logic, and cuts to the MA program were enacted. But Democratic reform efforts did not extend to undoing the institutional dynamics put in place by the extended use of HSAs as a means of paying for health care. In short, although many Democrats disliked the incentives put in place by HSAs, they did not have the political capacity to reverse the use of HSAs that have developed their own user constituencies and, as a result, some degree of institutional resilience.

Overall, the examination of the 2003 MMA and the provisions of the ACA that affected Medicare reveal a complex interaction between ideas, institutional processes, and issue ownership. Even though the MMA and the ACA represent two examples of policymaking with successful legislative outcomes, both were fiercely contested with alternative ideational frameworks underpinning the policy debate. Yet both cases also illustrated how the politics of issue ownership can lead to partisans taking some counterintuitive policy positions.

Notes

1. Interviews conducted by Alex Waddan with former Bush White House officials, Washington, DC, September 2009.
2. The following paragraphs draw on Béland 2007c.
3. For an alternative economic explanation focusing of the alleged lack of objective need for public insurance during the Progressive Era, see Emery 2010.
4. For a historical and sociological perspective, see Ruggie 1996.
5. Although problematic (Howard 2006), this perception remained strong in more recent decades (e.g., Skocpol 1990).
6. The disabled in fact accounted for 44.7 percent of Medicaid's benefit payments. The CBO counts elderly disabled enrollees in its "disabled" group calculations rather than the "elderly" group. Hence, the percentage of Medicaid spending on the sixty-five and over age group is likely to be considerably higher even than 25 percent (CBO 2005b, 29).
7. On this issue, see Brown and Sparer (2003). In the early 1970s Congress had expanded Medicare to cover beneficiaries of the federal disability insurance program.
8. On this general dichotomy, see Titmuss (1958).

9. In 2004 "nearly $190 billion" was "spent indirectly in the form of federal tax breaks for employer-provided health benefits" (Hacker 2006, 140).

10. "Free" here means free at the point of use.

11. The following data about supplementary coverage comes from testimony given by Glenn M. Hackbarth before the Subcommittee on Health, Committee on Ways and Means, US House of Representatives. Hackbarth was then chair of the Medicare Payments Advisory Commission. His statement, titled "Medicare Cost Sharing and Supplemental Insurance," was given on May 1, 2003.

12. Importantly, this was before the prescription drug benefit provision of the 2003 MMA had been implemented.

13. The prescription drug benefit covered all outpatient prescription drugs as well as insulin, with a deductible scheduled to be $600 in 1991. Beneficiaries also faced coinsurance payments set at 50 percent of "reasonable charges above the deductible in 1991, 40 percent in 1992, and 20 percent in 1993 and subsequent years" (CBO 1988, 5).

14. The fuller quotation was: "we believe it's going to wither on the vine because we think people are voluntarily going to leave it—voluntarily" (Toner 1995). It is difficult to see how Gingrich could have been referring to the HCFA since individuals are not in a position to leave that institution. The HCFA is now the Centers for Medicare and Medicaid Services.

15. Senator Kerrey, however, should not be seen simply as a conservative leaning Democrat in the same way as Breaux. Part of his argument for Medicare reform was that existing entitlement programs narrowed the opportunity for other federal programs. In particular, he thought that excessive Medicare spending inhibited helping the working aged uninsured. (Interview conducted by Alex Waddan with former aide to Senator Kerrey: Washington, DC, September 2009.)

16. The addition of the disabled to Medicare may have been a more significant expansion of Medicare, but that was not aimed specifically at seniors.

17. The Heritage Foundation, for example, regarded the bill as fiscally irresponsible. The continuing opposition of Heritage's health care experts to the benefit was confirmed in an interview conducted by Alex Waddan in September 2009 (Washington, DC).

18. Interview conducted by Alex Waddan with former Bush White House official (Washington, DC, September 2009).

19. Because nearly three-quarters of Democratic senators voted for the Senate version of the bill, which had similar financial costs for seniors, cost sharing and "donut hole" were not the primary reasons for congressional Democratic opposition to the final form of the MMA.

20. Interview conducted by Alex Waddan with former Bush White House official (Washington, DC, September 2009).

21. Interviews conducted by Alex Waddan with former Bush White House officials (Washington, DC, September 2009).

22. Interview conducted by Alex Waddan with former Bush White House official (Washington, DC, September 2009).

23. According to the Department of Health and Human Services, this would mean that "most people will pay the standard monthly Part B premium of $96.40 in 2009." For single seniors with incomes above $85,000 up to $107,000 per annum and couples with incomes of over $170,000 up to $214,000 per annum, the premium would be $134.90 per month. The maximum premium would be for individuals with incomes over $213,000 and couples over $426,000 who would pay a premium of $308.30 per month (US Department of Health and Human Services 2009).

24. In 2008 individuals and their employers were allowed to put up to $2,900 (or $5,800 for families) into HSAs each year. To qualify for the tax privileges, the account had to join with a high-deductible insurance package. In 2008 the deductibles had to be at least $1,100 for an individual and $2,200 for a family (Employee Benefit Research Institute 2008).

25. This point was confirmed in interviews conducted by Alex Waddan both with former Bush administration officials and critics of the overall MMA in leading conservative think tanks (Washington, DC, September 2009).

26. Interviews conducted by Alex Waddan with former Bush White House officials (Washington, DC, September 2009).

27. "Medicare Scare-Mongering." *New York Times*, September 27, 2009.

28. Quoted in "Text of Obama's Health Care Speech to Congress." *New York Times*, September 9, 2009.

29. For full details of the changes to the MA program contained in the ACA, see Kaiser Family Foundation (2010).

30. Some skepticism was expressed about this optimistic scenario. The chief actuary for Medicare and Medicaid services, Richard Foster, publicly questioned the report's efficacy: "The financial projections shown in this report for Medicare do not represent a reasonable expectation for actual program operations in either the short range . . . or the long range" (quoted in Ross and Walker 2010).

31. "Text of Obama's Health Care Speech to Congress." *New York Times*, September 9, 2009.

32. "Medicare and the Republicans." *New York Times*, November 4, 2010.

Chapter Three
The Failed Attempt at Social Security
Privatization, 2005

ocial Security is the largest and one of the most popular social programs in the United States. Expanded during the postwar era, the program faced significant short-term fiscal challenges from the mid-1970s to the enactment of the 1983 amendments to the Social Security Act. Although the 1983 reform helped improve the program's fiscal situation, demographic challenges lie ahead as the baby boomers retire, and confidence in the future of Social Security remains low. For more than three decades beginning in the 1970s a growing number of experts and political actors have advocated significant changes in the way Social Security works. Traditionally labeled Social Security privatization, which reflects conservative ideational preferences, this approach focuses on the development of personal savings accounts "carved out" of the existing federal payroll tax.

This chapter explores the contemporary politics of Social Security from the conservative "Leninist strategy" aimed at weakening support for the program to President George W. Bush's ill-fated push to transform it. After providing historical background about the program's development, the chapter discusses the advent of the politics of austerity in the late 1970s and early 1980s and the related enactment of the 1983 amendments. The chapter explores conservative ideas and strategies leading to the long-term campaign to develop personal savings accounts as part of the Social Security program, and it shows how Social Security reform and personal accounts became major issues during President Bill Clinton's second term and explains why reform did not materialize at the time. The White House seriously considered fundamental reform before backing off amid the Monica Lewinsky affair. Following this discussion, the chapter focuses on the politics of Social Security during the George W. Bush presidency. After an examination of the controversial 2001 President's Commission to Strengthen Social Security, the chapter analyzes the 2005 case during which President Bush aggressively campaigned to convince both the public and Congress to support a reform centered on personal savings accounts. As we demonstrate, this campaign failed due to a number of related institutional and ideational factors. Focusing on the controversial idea of personal accounts, President Bush faced major obstacles, such as the enduring popularity of the program, growing partisanship in Congress, and attacks from Democrats who had long owned Social Security as an issue. Although the president's campaign failed miserably, major changes affecting private benefits have gradually reshaped the American pension system. As we show, the interaction between ideas, institutional legacies, and issue ownership explains the 2005 episode as well as the current trends in both public and private pensions. These latter trends have become an enduring source of policy drift, and they cannot be explained without an understanding of the impact of conservative ideas on the American pension system. The debate on the future of Social Security is far from over because the long-term fiscal balance in the program has yet to be restored.

Social Security Development

The modern American pension system took shape during the 1930s and in the three decades following World War II. The most important program by far is the federal old-age, survivors, and disability insurance (OASDI)—an earnings-related and centralized pension scheme covering the vast majority of the American workforce. The federal Supplemental Security Income (SSI) offers additional federal assistance benefits to blind, disabled, and elderly people with "little or no income."[1] Finally, private pensions and savings schemes play a major role within the American pension system, which should not hide the fact that they only cover some workers (Hacker 2002; Klein 2003; Sass 1997).

Enacted in 1935 as part of the Social Security Act, OASDI, which is widely known as Social Security, is the true foundation of the modern American pension system (apRoberts 2000). By 2005, when President Bush pushed for reform, more than 30 million retired workers received Social Security benefits. Once the disabled and dependents were also factored in, Social Security had about 48 million beneficiaries who received more than $500 billion from the program (DeWitt, Béland, and Berkowitz 2007). For many retirees, particularly those with a low income, Social Security is a major source of economic security: "Recipients in the two lowest income quartiles receive more than 80 percent of their income from Social Security; those in the middle receive more than 60 percent; and even those just below the top receive almost half. Only voters in the highest quartile can retire without caring a great deal about the size of their monthly check" (Galston 2007, 7). The reliance of millions of retirees on Social Security benefits has helped increase the political awareness and participation of seniors, especially those with a low income (Campbell 2003). Furthermore, just as is the case with Medicare, organizations such as the AARP form a well-organized "gray lobby," which has dramatically expanded since the 1960s (Pratt 1993). But the support for Social Security extends far beyond older voters and interest groups. For example, throughout the 1980s and 1990s, more than 90 percent of the general public believed that the program was spending "too little" or "about the right amount." Overall, "an overwhelming majority . . . of the general public supported Social Security." (Cook, Barabas, and Page 2002, 252). The enduring popularity of Social Security makes it risky for politicians to attack the program explicitly. Known as "the third rail of American politics" ("touch it and you die"), Social Security remains one of the most enduring institutional legacies of the New Deal.[2]

In fact, President Franklin Delano Roosevelt played a key role in shaping Social Security (Richards 1994). As Arthur Altmeyer once stated, without the president's push, "we would probably have today a national noncontributory form of social security in the country" (1965, 268). This is true because FDR opposed financing the new program through general revenues and requested that Social Security become a self-supporting program financed through a dedicated payroll tax (Altmeyer 1965; Béland and Hacker 2004; Campbell and Morgan 2005; Leff 1983; Witte 1962). In fact, the president supported the idea of a strict actuarial relationship between Social Security benefits and contributions (i.e., the payroll tax). For him, the contributory method would give "the contributors a legal, moral, and political right to collect their pensions," which would make it hard for future politicians to dismantle the program (Schlesinger 1959, 308–9; Perkins 1946, 281–83). Although major revisions enacted in 1939 considerably weakened the relationship between benefits and contributions (Berkowitz 1983), the discourse about "earned rights" helped federal officials tie Social Security to traditional "American values" such as self-reliance while drawing a clear ideological line of separation between Social Security and social assistance (Cates 1983; Derthick 1979; Fraser and Gordon 1992). Although payroll contributions legitimized the program, this rhetoric obscured how Social Security actually worked (as a somewhat redistributive social insurance scheme), which in turn reinforced public misunderstandings about its effective functioning (Brain 1991).

After facing an uncertain future throughout the 1940s, incremental reforms enacted between 1950 and 1972 transformed Social Security into the largest social program in the United States (Achenbaum 1986; Béland 2007b; Derthick 1979; Jacobs 2009b; Tynes 1996). First, the 1950 amendments substantially increased benefit levels to compensate for the negative effects of inflation that had reduced the real value of Social Security benefits during the 1940s. Again in the 1950s and the first half of the 1960s Congress adopted further modest benefit increases to maintain the real value of benefits amidst inflation. Second, in the 1950s, occupational categories excluded from coverage in 1935, such as domestic and farm workers, were finally allowed to participate in Social Security. Third, in 1956 Congress enacted a disability insurance scheme as part of Social Security. Fourth, in the late 1960s and early 1970s a change in actuarial assumptions as well as intense political competition between the Nixon White House and Democrats in Congress favored the enactment of large benefit hikes that accumulated to significantly boost the real value of Social Security benefits (Derthick 1979; Weaver 1982). Finally, in 1972 the advent of a flawed automatic indexation scheme further boosted the real value of benefits in the era of stagflation that followed the 1973 oil crisis (Béland 2007b; Myles, 1988; Weaver 1988).

In addition to its incremental nature (Derthick 1979; Tynes 1996), the postwar politics of Social Security expansion had a number of characteristics that inform the contemporary debate on the future of Social Security. First, working with bureaucrats such as Arthur Altmeyer and Robert Ball (Berkowitz 1995, 2003),

Democrats such as President Harry Truman and congressional leader Wilbur Mills identified with the program and claimed credit for its expansion (Zelizer 1998). Considering that FDR himself had launched Social Security and that labor unions supported its expansion, Democrats saw Social Security as a key aspect of their "New Deal coalition." As suggested in the following analysis, this historical trend is important to help grasp the politics of issue ownership in the contemporary Social Security debate. Second, because Social Security became an extremely popular program (Brain 1991) and favorable demographics allowed for its expansion without massive tax increases (Schieber and Shoven 1999), Republicans had little choice but to publicly embrace it. Starting with the 1950 amendments, most Republicans in Congress voted for incremental reforms that favored the expansion of Social Security during the postwar era (Ross 2007, 430). In 1953, facing pressures from Democrats, labor officials, and liberal advocates, President Dwight Eisenhower explicitly defended the program's earnings-related structure (Sanders 1973). As for President Nixon, he praised Social Security and called for the advent of an automatic indexation system as a strategy to prevent Democrats in Congress from claiming credit for ad hoc benefit hikes, which had been used since 1950 to offset cost-of-living increases (Weaver 1988). Additionally, Nixon sought to control costs by making it more difficult politically for Democrats to increase benefits above the inflation rate (Derthick 1979; Weaver 1988; Zelizer 1998).[3] Yet both presidents Eisenhower and Nixon failed in their attempts to slow down the program's expansion (Derthick 1979). President Eisenhower could not prevent the enactment of disability insurance, which he had opposed (Berkowitz 1987; Pratico 2001). President Nixon's push for automatic indexation succeeded only after Congress had enacted significant benefit increases (Weaver 1988; Zelizer 1998). Furthermore, by the 1960s, conservatives such as Milton Friedman (1962), who explicitly called for the dismantlement of Social Security in the name of economic freedom and market efficiency, had become politically marginal. The crushing defeat of Republican nominee and Social Security critic Barry Goldwater in the 1964 presidential election reinforced the political strength of the program.[4]

During the 1964 presidential campaign, Democrats attacked Goldwater on Social Security, claiming that he wanted to destroy the popular program (Barnes 1998). Although Goldwater had condemned Social Security (Goldwater 1960) before suggesting it should be made voluntary (Altman 2005, 200), his 1964 campaign brochure "Barry Goldwater Speaks Out for a Stronger America" shows that his team understood the political risks stemming from Social Security. In the brochure, Goldwater argued that his true goal was to make Social Security stronger: "I favor a sound Social Security system and I want to see it strengthened. I want to see every participant receive all the benefits this system provides. And I want to see these benefits paid in dollars with real purchasing power."[5] Since the 1960s other conservative politicians critical of the program's structure—including President George W. Bush—have argued that their only goal was to *strengthen* Social Security (Béland 2007b). This ideological logic stems from the popularity of Social Security, which makes it politically risky to launch direct attacks against the program. The fact that Democrats own Social Security as an issue further reinforces this logic because conservative Republicans must attempt to reduce the level of potential partisan attacks they face when the time comes to support seemingly radical policy alternatives such as privatization.

The Politics of Austerity

In the mid-1970s an economic downturn and the adoption of a flawed indexation system in 1972 worsened Social Security's fiscal situation.[6] These new realities favored a shift from the politics of expansion to the politics of austerity, thereby increasing the political risks politicians faced when they sought to reform Social Security. Instead of claiming credit for more comprehensive benefits as they did in the postwar era, federal politicians attempted to deflect blame stemming from potentially unpopular measures such as benefit cuts and tax hikes (Light 1995; Myles and Pierson 2001; Pierson 1994; Pierson and Weaver 1993; Weaver 1986).[7] The enduring popularity of Social Security exacerbated this new political reality as worried citizens and interest groups pressured elected officials to act in order to restore the fiscal integrity of the program. In 1977, reacting to such pressures, a Democratic Congress enacted legislation aimed at restoring fiscal balance in Social Security.[8] These new amendments to the Social Security Act significantly raised tax rates while revising the indexation system without penalizing current beneficiaries to avoid a political backlash (Califano 1981, 370). Upon signing the legislation, President Carter described tax hikes as "absolutely mandatory" before claiming that the legislation guaranteed "that from 1980 to the year 2030, the social security funds will be sound" (Carter 1978, 837–38).

In retrospect, the actuarial previsions President Carter referred to in his signing remarks proved too optimistic (Béland 2007b). Not long after the adoption of the 1977 amendments it became increasingly clear that new legislation would prove necessary to rescue the program and make sure all beneficiaries received their full Social Security check every month (Light 1995). This time, a newly elected Republican president, Ronald Reagan, had to address the issue. During the 1980 presidential campaign, the former California governor, who had previously criticized Social Security, made sure not to attack the program in public and even stated that he would not cut benefits (Derthick and Teles 2003, 194). Yet, for the Reagan administration, Social Security rapidly became a key source of political anxiety amidst strategic mistakes and Democratic attacks. In the first months of Reagan's administration, a traumatizing political episode reminded the president and his advisors about the political risks stemming from the politics of Social Security in an era of fiscal austerity (ibid., 194–95; see also Stockman 1986). This episode occurred in May 1981, when Secretary of Health and Human Services Richard Schweiker unveiled Social Security proposals that included a direct cut in early retirement benefits. Worst of all, this benefit reduction would become effective as early as January 1982 and would affect Social Security beneficiaries aged sixty-two and older who had opted for early retirement. Because this proposal contradicted Reagan's 1980 campaign promise not to cut Social Security benefits, it represented a true political opportunity for Democrats, such as House Speaker Thomas P. O'Neill, to publicly denounce the administration. Facing relentless attacks from Democrats, the White House rapidly backed off (Derthick and Teles 2003, 195).

A few months later, in the early fall of 1981, President Reagan officially announced the creation of a bipartisan commission aimed at finding a solution to the fiscal crisis Social Security faced. The launching of this commission represented a clear form of blame avoidance for President Reagan, who used it as an institutional shield against Democratic attacks (Pierson and Weaver 1993). This political shield proved especially necessary because Democrats clearly dominated the debate on Social Security, in part because the public trusted them more than they trusted the Republicans to handle this issue properly. For instance, a November 1981 poll showed that far more people believed that Democrats were doing "a better job protecting the Social Security system" than Republicans (Bowman 2005, 35). Even after the commission was established, Rep. Claude Pepper (D-Fla.) "was quite successful" during the 1982 midterm campaign "in pinning on Reagan the entire blame for any uncertainties about Social Security's future. He helped engineer a net gain of 26 Democrats in the House, many of whom were elected largely on the Social Security issue" (Ball 2010, 33). This suggests that, as in the postwar era, Democrats strongly identified with Social Security, and when its future became uncertain, they successfully framed themselves as the best defenders of the program. In other words, as opposed to the situation in welfare and Medicare, Democrats clearly and durably "own" Social Security as an issue (Ross 2007).

Chaired by Alan Greenspan, the National Commission on Social Security Reform was very different from the postwar advisory councils that helped legitimize the expansion of Social Security under the implicit guidance of the Social Security Administration (Béland 2007b; Derthick 1979). Like the advisory council that paved the way for the 1939 amendments to the Social Security Act (Berkowitz 1983), the Greenspan Commission emerged as a bipartisan tool aimed at formulating a detailed legislative compromise acceptable to both Democrats and Republicans (Ball 2010; Light 1995).[9] Because he favored the emergence of a true bipartisan deal acceptable to Congress, the president appointed only five of the commission's fifteen members, leaving the Democratic House Speaker and the Republican Senate Leader with five appointments each. Thus, although Republicans such as Sen. Robert Dole became members of the commission, Democrats and their supporters were also appointed, including former Social Security commissioner Robert Ball, AFL-CIO president Lane Kirkland, and Claude Pepper, who had a reputation as a strong champion of the program's benefit for America's seniors (Ball 2010). To increase the sense of political emergency surrounding the commission, the Old

Age and Survivors Insurance (OASI) trust fund could borrow from the Medicare and the Disability trust funds, but only until the end of 1982. Thus, in order for the OASI trust fund to keep paying all of the promised Social Security benefits, Congress needed to enact legislation to fix the short-term fiscal challenge facing the program before the summer of 1983 (Light 1995, 96).

Despite this additional pressure to rapidly strike a bipartisan deal, intense policy discussions within the commission only began after the 1982 midterm election (Kingson 1984, 145). A central source of disagreement concerned the proper balance between benefit cuts, which Republicans favored, and revenue increases, which Democrats preferred (Light 1995, 96). In the weeks before the commission's extended deadline (January 15), secret meetings took place between White House officials, congressional leaders, and key members of the Greenspan Commission. Former Social Security commissioner Robert Ball played a crucial role during these secret meetings (Berkowitz 2003, 307–16; see also Ball 2010). Finally, a bipartisan deal was struck behind closed doors, and most members of the commission voted in favor of it on January 15 (Ball 2010). The plan became public several days later with the publication of the commission's report. The report rejected highly controversial proposals such as an increase in the retirement age but included the contentious idea to integrate federal civil servants into the Social Security system, which labor unions vehemently opposed (Light 1995, 65). Overall, this report excluded path-departing reform proposals such as the development of personal savings accounts that could have transformed the program's functioning (Greenspan Commission 1983).

With little time to act, congressional leaders responded swiftly to ensure that the bipartisan package embodied in the commission's report would survive the legislative process and become law by the spring. Although the number of amendments debated in the House was limited to three, a controversial increase in retirement age from sixty-five to sixty-seven—set to take place between 2000 and 2027—was passed. Although organizations such as the AARP and the National Federation of Federal Employees actively lobbied against the legislation (Light 1995), Congress rapidly enacted the 1983 amendments to the Social Security Act, which President Reagan signed on April 20 (Béland 2007b; Svahn and Ross 1983). In his remarks upon signing the legislation, President Reagan explicitly alluded to the bipartisan logic that led to the adoption of the 1983 amendments to the Social Security Act:

> Just a few months ago, there was legitimate alarm that Social Security would soon run out of money. On both sides of the political aisle, there were dark suspicions that opponents from the other party were more interested in playing politics than in solving the problem. But in the eleventh hour, a distinguished bipartisan commission appointed by House Speaker O'Neill, by Senate Majority Leader Baker, and by me began to find a solution that could be enacted into law.

Political leaders of both parties set aside their passions and joined in that search. The result of these labors in the Commission and the Congress are now before us, ready to be signed into law, a monument to the spirit of compassion and commitment that unites us as a people. (Reagan 1984, 560)

This illustrates the political success of President Reagan's bipartisan strategy. In a context in which his party fought against the odds due the Democratic ownership of the Social Security issue, Reagan managed to oversee a compromise agreement, even if it was not in line with the conservative agenda.

Interestingly, several people we interviewed for this book project mentioned that the Greenspan Commission and the bipartisan efforts surrounding it represented a great example of successful bipartisan policymaking that could serve as a model for future Social Security reforms.[10] As we will see, however, this is not the road that President George W. Bush took in 2005 when he launched his ill-fated campaign to transform Social Security. Before examining this crucial episode in greater detail, it is necessary to explore the demographic, ideological, institutional, and political factors that paved the ground to President Bush's disastrous campaign.

The Clinton Administration and the Rise of the Privatization Idea

The 1983 amendments helped improve the fiscal situation of Social Security, which has not faced any short-term fiscal crises since their enactment. On the contrary, since then, Social Security has generated major surpluses because the program collects more money every year than it spends on benefits. In 1990, for example, Social Security collected $315 billion in payroll tax revenues but spent $253 billion in benefits. Fifteen years later, in 2005, the program collected $700 billion while allocating $530 billion in benefits (DeWitt, Béland, and Berkowitz 2007, appendix 4). When the Social Security program collects a surplus through the payroll tax, the extra money is loaned to the federal government: "By law, income to the trust funds is invested, on a daily basis, in securities guaranteed as to both principal and interest by the Federal government. All securities held by the trust funds are 'special issues.' Such securities are available only to the trust funds."[11] In the short run, despite the negative impact of the recession that started in 2008–9, the fiscal situation of the trust funds remains sound. In the long run, however, there are significant fiscal challenges ahead. These challenges are related to demographic change and, more specifically, population aging.

Population aging is a global phenomenon with long historical roots (Congressional Budget Office 2005a). As in other advanced industrial societies, powerful demographic factors such as higher life expectancies have gradually increased the percentage of elderly people (sixty-five and older) living in the United States. According to recent estimates, between 2000 and 2050, the percentage of people aged sixty-five and older will grow from 12.3 to 21 percent of the population. Yet, despite the undeniable scope of this gradual population change, the United States is in a rather favorable demographic situation when compared to countries such as Germany, Italy, and Japan (Gavrilov and Heuveline 2003).

This comparatively auspicious demographic reality should not hide the fact that demographic aging will have a negative impact on Social Security financing in the decades to come. According to the 2010 OASDI Trustees Report:

> Under the intermediate assumptions, OASDI cost generally increases more rapidly than tax income through 2035 because the retirement of the baby-boom generation increases the number of beneficiaries much faster than subsequent relatively low-birth-rate generations increase the labor force. From 2035 to 2050, the cost rate declines somewhat due principally to the aging of the already retired baby-boom generation. Thereafter, increases in life expectancy generally cause OASDI cost to again increase relative to tax income, but more slowly than prior to 2035. . . . The dollar level of the Trust Funds is projected to be drawn down beginning in 2025 until assets are exhausted in 2037. (Board of Trustees 2010)

This long-term fiscal and demographic challenge has provoked considerable debate, but little consensus has emerged (Béland 2007b). Supporters of the existing program argue that addressing this challenge only requires a set of moderate adjustments to Social Security's financing and benefit structure. That is, relatively modest rather than path-departing changes are all that are needed to preserve the program's basic structure in the face of current and future demographic and fiscal challenges (e.g., Aaron and Reischauer 1998; Ball and Bethell 1998; Diamond and Orszag 2003; White 2001). In contrast, advocates who promote path-departing reforms tend to depict demographic change as a "time bomb" that will inevitably crush Social Security. Because the program is unsustainable and inherently flawed, they argue, path-departing reform is unavoidable. In other words: without systematic changes that would alter its nature, Social Security is doomed (e.g., Attarian 2004; Robertson 1997; Ferrara and Tanner 1998; Tanner 2004). For those who defend the existing program, this pessimistic discourse about the impact of demographic aging on Social Security is nothing more than a "false alarm" (White 2001) and a "phony crisis" (Baker and Weisbrot 1999; see also Altman 2005; Skidmore 1999). Overall, the debate about demographic aging and the sustainability of Social Security is grounded in a deep ideological opposition between those who believe that the existing program is basically sound and those who think that its inherent logic is flawed. The differences between the two camps reflect not just alternative accounting methods but substantive ideational clashes about the importance of the principle of social solidarity embedded in the existing Social Security system.

Reflecting this ideological division, among the potential alternatives to the current program, the approach known as "Social Security privatization" is the most widely debated (e.g., Altman 2005; Ferrara and Tanner 1998; Svihula and Estes

2008). This controversial term generally refers to the channeling of payroll tax money to personal savings accounts. Most proposals debated in the United States are about "partial privatization" in the sense that they would only redirect a limited portion of the payroll tax to such personal accounts. The idea—advocated as early as the 1960s by Goldwater and Friedman—of transforming Social Security into a voluntary system remains marginal within federal policy circles. In other words, few people "inside the Beltway" advocate the abolition of the payroll tax and a return to "pure and simple" self-reliance and voluntarism. Instead, Social Security privatization is about favoring a partial shift from defined-benefit to defined-contribution pensions that would alter the nature of the program while maintaining—and in some cases increasing—the federal payroll tax (Béland 2007b). However, according to opponents of this approach, even a partial shift from defined-benefit to defined-contribution pensions could seriously undermine the economic security of workers (e.g., Aaron and Reischauer 1998; Altman 2005; Ball and Bethell 1998; Ghilarducci 2008; White 2001). Although supporters of personal accounts generally used the term "privatization" to define their approach, many of them stopped referring to privatization in the early 2000s when a Republican pollster suggested the term was unpopular and should not be used by Republicans (Altman 2005, 266). Again, this illustrates how conservatives, even when promoting profound changes to Social Security, have acknowledged that they need to be careful about how they frame their reform proposals in a context where Democrats durably "own" Social Security as an issue. This reality should not obscure the fact that the ideological logic of Social Security privatization, which is embedded in promarket and individualistic ideas, is at odds with the very nature of this federal program, which is about government-guaranteed economic security associated with the defined-benefit model that has defined the program since its inception in 1935. From this perspective, the push for Social Security privatization is a direct ideological and institutional challenge to the principles and organizational structure of the existing social insurance program.

Partly because it is grounded in individualistic and promarket ideas that challenge the very foundation of the program, Social Security privatization is a controversial policy alternative that seldom made its way to mainstream federal debates until the mid-1990s. For example, although the idea of privatization was in the public domain at the time (Ferrara 1980), the 1983 report of the Greenspan Commission did not even raise it. As mentioned earlier, the commission's mandate was to formulate a bipartisan compromise, which meant excluding consideration of highly contentious proposals such as personal accounts (Light 1995). Conservative supporters of privatization settled on developing a long-term political strategy. A few months after President Reagan signed the 1983 amendments two influential conservative analysts, Stuart Butler and Peter Germanis, sketched a clever ideological and institutional strategy aimed at promoting their policy alternative while weakening support for Social Security.[12] Provocatively titled "Achieving a 'Leninist'

Strategy," this conservative document outlines an incremental approach to facilitate the transformation of Social Security. The two-pronged strategy outlined in the document aimed to alter both the political balance of power surrounding Social Security and to present a viable alternative to the government-run pension arrangements. First they aimed at weakening the "firm coalition behind the present Social Security system" by providing "assurance to those already retired or nearing retirement that their benefits will be paid in full" (Butler and Germanis 1983, 548–49) while simultaneously persuading younger Americans who have little confidence in the future of the program to embrace Social Security privatization (ibid., 549). In addition, the authors argue that those who support privatization should actively promote the expansion of tax-subsidized individual retirement accounts (IRAs), which are depicted as a model for reform. Butler and Germanis stress the need for "a campaign to achieve small legislative changes that embellish the present IRA system, making it in practice a small-scale private Social Security system that can supplement the federal system. As part of this campaign the natural constituency for an enlarged IRA system must be identified and welded into a coalition for political change" (ibid., 551).

As this quote suggests, Butler and Germanis strategically embrace incrementalism as a way to gradually weaken the institutional support for Social Security. From this angle, incrementalism is not only a set of subtle institutional processes but also a strategic idea that can guide actors who seek to bring about concrete policy change in spite of a constraining political environment. For those who seek to reshape Social Security, the gradual development of personal savings accounts is an authentic institutional and ideational model for reform, which makes the proliferation of these accounts a genuine alternative to the existing federal program (Ferrara and Tanner 1998).

It is impossible to understand the debate on the future of Social Security without taking into account the steady development of tax-sponsored savings schemes, such as IRAs and 401(k)s, which represent a major form of layering in the field of old-age security. For Jacob Hacker, "The explosive growth of 401(k) plans and IRAs" during the 1980s and 1990s "represents one of the most important developments in the political history of US pension policy" (2004, 255).[13] Since the enactment of the Employee Retirement Income Security Act in 1974, the federal government has sponsored the development of IRAs. At first only workers without private pension coverage could start an IRA, but the early 1980s witnessed an expansion of IRAs, which became available to all workers for the first time. "In 1997 and 2001, they were liberalized again, permissible uses of the accounts were broadened to include education and housing expenses, and a new plan—called 'Roth IRAs'—was created that would require account holders to pay taxes up front and then avoid all future taxes on their accounts (including estate taxes)" (Hacker 2004, 255). A further defined-contribution retirement savings scheme, the 401(k) plan, is sponsored by employers. The name comes from the fact that these accounts qualify under section 401(k) of the federal tax code. Made possible by a modestly debated change to the tax code enacted in 1978, 401(k) plans have dramatically expanded since the early 1980s, when the Reagan IRS ruled that the 401(k) "provision extended to pensions in which workers put aside their own wages, much as in an IRA" (ibid.). In 2001, with the support of President George W. Bush, Republicans in Congress successfully pushed for a widespread liberalization of both 401(k)s and IRAs. According to recent estimates, "tax expenditures on pensions cost over $100 billion each year in lost revenues" (Howard and Berkowitz 2008, 121). Overall, the massive, tax-subsidized development of these savings schemes mainly benefited the wealthy since the richest quintile of Americans hold about 70 percent of IRAs and defined-contribution pension assets. Meanwhile, about half of the workforce has access to a defined contribution retirement savings plan (Hacker 2006, 122–23).

As suggested earlier, the dramatic expansion of tax-sponsored savings accounts since the late 1970s has become a major aspect of the debate on the future of Social Security. Those who promote the transformation of Social Security into an individualistic system of personal accounts explicitly depict IRAs and 401(k)s as a key source of progress and even a model for reform. The following statement from a Cato Institute policy brief titled *Social Security Privatization: One Proposal* illustrates the close relationship between IRAs and 401(k)s as well as the push for a comprehensive transformation of Social Security: "Workers under age 32 would be allowed to divert up to 46 percent of their payroll taxes to individually owned, privately invested accounts, similar to individual retirement accounts or 401(k) pension plans. The remainder of the payroll tax would be used to continue to provide benefits for the currently retired and those who will retire soon" (Altig and Gokhale 1997). From this perspective, like the welfare waivers of the late 1980s and early 1990s, incremental policy developments—in this case the gradual expansion of IRAs and 401(k)s—help those who support conservative reform to provide the public with a more tangible image of what it might look like. In this specific case, incremental policy developments alongside Social Security are partly meant to make the idea of privatization look increasingly concrete and familiar to the growing number of individuals enrolled in private savings accounts (Teles 1998).

Overall, privatization advocates believe that personal savings and financial investment are more efficient retirement tools than the existing Social Security system, which they sometimes describe as an old-fashioned program imported from Europe during the 1930s (Piñera 1999, 18). This type of argument is meant to frame Social Security as an essentially un-American program that contradicts "American values" such as personal freedom and responsibility. Referring to "home-grown" institutions such as IRAs and 401(k)s as a model for Social Security restructuring complements another conservative strategy, which is somewhat paradoxically to depict reforms enacted in countries such as Britain and Chile as positive examples of what a transformation of the federal program would look like (Béland and Waddan 2000).[14]

The first time the debate on Social Security privatization became a significant federal policy issue was during the second mandate of President Bill Clinton (Altman 2005; Arnold 1998; Cook, Barabas, and Page 2002; Derthick 2001; Quadagno 1999; Schieber and Shoven 1999; Svihula and Estes 2007; Weaver 2005). A series of factors explain this development (Béland 2007b). First, excellent stock market performances in the late 1990s boosted popular expectations about stock market returns. This in turn seemed to increase popular support for personal accounts. This is true because, based on public opinion data, it is clear that "citizens are especially likely to favor Social Security privatization during times of rising stock prices" (Barabas 2006, 59).[15] Such a concrete trend fed the claim that privatization makes people richer by generating much higher average return rates than the present Social Security system (Ferrara and Tanner 1998).[16] Here, conservatives referred to the performance of 401(k)s and IRAs to justify the "need to reform"(Cox 2001) Social Security. As suggested earlier, like welfare waivers, the incremental development of private savings accounts such as 401(k) and IRAs thus represents a form of institutional layering that feeds conservative claims about the empirical validity of their reform ideas (i.e., workfare, in the case of welfare waivers, and personal investment, in the case of private savings accounts). From this perspective, these savings accounts are to Social Security privatization what waivers became in the early 1990s for welfare reform: a form of layering directly related to ideational and framing processes.

Second, in early 1997 the last Social Security Advisory Council published its report. Established in March 1994, this body turned out to be very different from the advisory councils that had taken place every four years since 1965. This is the case because postwar advisory councils legitimized the expansion of Social Security without challenging the program's basic structure (Derthick 1979). One factor that maintained the program's structure was the indirect control the Social Security Administration exerted over these advisory councils. This control seemed to have weakened in 1994 as critics of the existing Social Security system such as Sylvester Schieber and Carolyn Weaver were appointed to serve on the last Advisory Council (Schieber and Shoven 1999). In the end, traditional supporters of the program such as Robert Ball as well as those who pushed for path-departing reform could not agree on unified set of recommendations.[17] As a result, the 1997 report offered three competing sets of recommendations about how to address future demographic and fiscal challenges.[18]

These three sets of recommendations help map the different reform options that have been debated ever since. Supported in part by six members of the council, the first set of recommendations is grounded in the assumption that Social Security as it exists today is a sound model and that only moderate adjustments are necessary to restore its long-term fiscal balance. These adjustments include provisions such as a small tax increase and the extension of the benefit computation period from thirty-five to thirty-eight years phased over a three-year period. Overall, this plan would not alter the nature of benefits or the program's basic structure.

The second set of recommendations, supported by Chair Edward M. Gramlich and only one other member, called for a significant reduction in benefits through measures such as a further increase in retirement age, which would reach age seventy by 2083. To compensate for the anticipated loss in benefits, this second plan advocated the creation of mandatory defined-contribution accounts alongside the traditional social insurance program. Money channeled to these new accounts would not come from the existing payroll tax but from a new 1.6 percent employee contribution. In the contemporary Social Security debate, such accounts are known as "add-ons." Although controversial, add-on accounts are sometimes described as a moderate, centrist alternative to both the status quo and Social Security privatization.[19]

Tied to the idea of Social Security privatization, accounts "carved out" of the current payroll tax are at the center of the third and final set of proposals formulated in the 1997 report. Supported by five members, this plan favored "reforming Social Security to move toward a system of relatively large individual accounts, making a substantial portion of the new system fully funded."[20] Such accounts would exist on top of what would slowly become a modest flat retirement benefit for full-career workers. Workers aged fifty-five and older as well as current retirees would not be affected by any of the proposed changes. This third set of proposals, however, is a more radical approach to reform aimed explicitly at transforming the nature of the federal Social Security system. Hence, the enactment of this type of plan requires path-departing change. Because Social Security remains a popular program and the shift toward full funding involves potentially large benefit cuts and transition costs, privatization is a widespread source of political risk that makes many politicians nervous, for good reason (Arnold 1998; Weaver 2005).

Despite the failure of the Advisory Council to make a clear set of recommendations, a further factor from early 1998 helped push the idea of Social Security reform onto the federal policy agenda: the apparent willingness of President Clinton to deal with the issue. After the failure of the Health Security blueprint and the signing of the distinctly conservative 1996 welfare reform, the Democratic president was looking to build a positive domestic legacy. As the largest federal social program, Social Security was a major issue the president could tackle to frame a lasting domestic legacy. As Republicans remained in control of both chambers of Congress, White House staff began to secretly examine potential reform alternatives likely to receive significant bipartisan support (Blackburn 2004). These reform ideas included different types of savings accounts ranging from "add-ons" to "carve-outs." In total, staff members spent thousands of hours working on potential reform plans. According to a former Republican congressional staffer, during most of his second presidential mandate, President Clinton seemed "open minded" about Social Security reform, including partial privatization.[21] In a 2008 book, historian Steven Gillon (2008) reveals that, during a secret meeting held in October 1997, President Clinton and Republican Speaker Newt Gingrich struck a deal that included the advent of personal savings accounts as part of the Social Security system. However, the beginning of the Lewinsky affair in early 1998 forced the president to move away from this plan and adopt a more cautious approach to Social Security reform because he could not risk losing the support of the Democratic base, which was suspicious of any move toward Social Security reform (ibid.). This points to the role of timing and contingency in policy development (Pierson 2004).

A major aspect of the Social Security debate during the Clinton years concerned the claim that the time had come to "save Social Security." This argument implied that Social Security faced some major future crisis, a claim that a number of observers rejected (Baker and Weisbrot 1999; White 2001). The 1998 State of the Union address provides a key example of the political rhetoric behind "saving" Social Security. In this address, for the first time in his presidency, President Clinton explicitly made Social Security one of his top policy priorities by arguing that future federal surpluses should be used to "Save Social Security." As this excerpt suggests, the presidential rhetoric on Social Security was related to the ongoing debate about the suitability of major, Republican-led tax cuts:

> We must not go back to unwise spending or untargeted tax cuts that risk reopening the deficit. . . . But whether the issue is tax cuts or spending, I ask all of you to meet this test: Approve only those priorities that can actually be accomplished without adding a dime to the deficit. Now, if we balance the budget for next year, it is projected that we'll then have a sizeable surplus in the years that immediately follow. What should we do with this projected surplus? I have a simple four-word answer: Save Social Security first. Thank you. Tonight, I propose that we reserve 100 percent of the surplus—that's every penny of any surplus—until we have taken all the necessary measures to strengthen the Social Security system for the 21st century. Let us say to all Americans watching tonight —whether you're 70 or 50, or whether you just started paying into the system—Social Security will be there when you need it. Let us make this commitment: Social Security first. Let's do that together. (Clinton 1998)

Although it was clear that President Clinton was using Social Security as a shield against massive Republican tax breaks,[22] his State of the Union address featured a call for a national debate about the future of Social Security that clearly extended beyond the issue of tax cuts:

> I also want to say that all the American people who are watching us tonight should be invited to join in this discussion, in facing these issues squarely, and forming a true consensus on how we should proceed. We'll start by conducting nonpartisan forums in every region of the country—and I hope that lawmakers of both parties will participate. We'll hold a White House Conference on Social Security in December. And one year from now I will

convene the leaders of Congress to craft historic, bipartisan legislation to achieve a landmark for our generation—a Social Security system that is strong in the 21st century. Thank you. (Clinton 1998)

After this address it became clear that President Clinton had an increasingly strong interest in Social Security reform.

The president spoke frequently on the issue during 1998 and 1999. In each of these two years, he referred to Social Security in more than 220 speeches. This represented a major increase, as the president had mentioned the issue fewer than 50 times a year in 1995, 1996, and 1997. In 1999 presidential addresses featured more references to Social Security than in any other year during the three preceding decades (Cook, Barabas, and Page 2002, 241). To make the issue even more visible, President Clinton participated in a number of town hall meetings and other public events on Social Security. In December 1998 the president even held a high-profile White House Conference on Social Security, where both supporters and opponents of personal accounts exchanged views on the future of the program. One panel featured Carolyn Weaver (American Enterprise Institute) and José Piñera (Cato Institute), who backed privatization, as well as Henry Aaron (Brookings Institution) and Robert Ball, who made a case for the preservation of the current defined-benefit system.[23]

Think tanks took a prominent role in the debate on Social Security reform throughout the Clinton years and beyond. In the late 1990s, as in the 2000s, these organizations fed the debate on Social Security by publishing numerous studies and policy proposals. For example, conservative think tanks such as the Cato Institute, the Heritage Foundation, and the American Enterprise Institute promoted Social Security privatization while liberal organizations such as the Center on Budget and Policy Priorities and the Center for Economic and Policy Research defended the existing program and downplayed the idea of a looming Social Security crisis. Beyond think tanks, advocacy groups ranging from the Concord Coalition to the AARP and the National Committee to Preserve Social Security and Medicare entered the debate (Altman 2005; Béland 2007b).

In addition to the growing number of presidential addresses and meetings as well as the growing involvement of think tanks and advocacy groups, the multiplication of congressional hearings devoted to the future of Social Security illustrates the development of this issue in the late 1990s. In 1997, following the publication of the Advisory Council report, Congress held ten different hearings exclusively about the future Social Security. In comparison, during the four previous years, Congress held only four hearings specifically on this issue. After a slight decline in 1998 the number of hearings on the future of the federal program reached eighteen in 1999 (Cook, Barabas, and Page 2002, 244). Moreover, some members of Congress such as senators John Breaux (D-La.) and Judd Gregg (R–N.H.) put forward legislative proposals that included personal savings accounts "carved out" of the payroll tax (Derthick 2001, 206). Despite the multiplication of legislative proposals, most members of Congress remained cautious about Social Security reform, which continued to appear as risky business for federal politicians, especially Republicans (Weaver 2005). Because Social Security remained a popular program and the public trusted Democrats on the issue, which reflected how the party truly "owned" the issue (Ross 2007), serious legislative action on Social Security seemed difficult without the support of the Democratic president.

As mentioned earlier, the Clinton administration had secretly explored the reform options available, including personal accounts "carved out" of the payroll tax. In such a context, some in Washington expected that the president would put forward a reform proposal in late 1998 or early 1999 that would include a "carve out" scheme (Blackburn 2004). Yet during the summer of 1998, the Lewinsky affair emerged as a direct threat to President Clinton. Although this scandal had no direct link to Social Security reform, it forced the president to adopt a more traditional Democratic stance on a number of issues, including retirement policy, in order to strengthen his traditional Democratic base and survive the scandal. In fact, it was the Lewinsky affair that forced the White House to ditch potential bipartisan reform proposals featuring personal savings accounts as part of the Social Security framework (Blackburn 2004; Gillon 2008). Consequently, in his 1999 State of the Union address, the president openly rejected "carved out" accounts before formulating a reform plan more in tune with the traditional Democratic stance on Social Security.

> The best way to keep Social Security a rock-solid guarantee is not to make drastic cuts in benefits, not to raise payroll tax rates, not to drain resources from Social Security in the name of saving it. Instead, I propose that we make an historic decision to invest the surplus to save Social Security. . . . Specifically, I propose that we commit 60 percent of the budget surplus for the next 15 years to Social Security, investing a small portion in the private sector, just as any private or state government pension would do. This will earn a higher return and keep Social Security sound for 55 years. But we must aim higher. We should put Social Security on a sound footing for the next 75 years. We should reduce poverty among elderly women, who are nearly twice as likely to be poor as our other seniors. . . . And we should eliminate the limits on what seniors on Social Security can earn. (Clinton 1999)

Although the president rejected personal accounts "carved out" of the existing payroll tax, he did push for the enactment of new savings accounts alongside the existing Social Security system: "I propose that we use a little over 11 percent of the surplus to establish universal savings accounts—USA accounts—to give all Americans the means to save. With these new accounts Americans can invest as they choose and receive funds to match a portion of their savings, with extra help for those least able to save. USA accounts will help all Americans to share in our nation's wealth and to enjoy a more secure retirement" (ibid.).

Thus, in the end, President Clinton explicitly favored add-ons over carve-outs. Combined with partisan struggles over impeachment that poisoned the relationship between the Clinton administration and Republicans in Congress, Clinton's decision to reject carve-outs and instead support the investment of Social Security surpluses in equity seriously weakened the possibility of a bipartisan legislation on Social Security during the remaining two years of his presidency. Supported by liberals such as Robert Ball (Ball and Bethell 1998), the idea that the federal government should directly invest Social Security surpluses in equity did not fly well with Alan Greenspan and many other economists and conservative experts (John 1999) who had opposed the measure even before the president put it forward in his 1999 State of the Union address (Glassman 1998). From a strictly legislative standpoint, President Clinton's Social Security plan went nowhere, and it mainly served a political purpose: reinforcing the president's support among traditional Democrats and placing Republicans on the defensive regarding an issue that his party durably "owned." Although there was still much talk about Social Security reform in Congress, the Lewinsky affair and the 1999 State of the Union address made Social Security reform increasingly unlikely during the last two years of the Clinton presidency (Béland 2007b).

George W. Bush and the Social Security Debate

In the spring of 2000 future Republican presidential candidate George W. Bush explicitly backed Social Security privatization (Derthick 2001, 208). In his speech to the Republican National Convention on August 3 the presidential candidate made it clear that he supported personal savings accounts "carved out" of the existing payroll tax:

> Social Security has been called the third rail of American politics, the one you're not supposed to touch because it might shock you. But if you don't touch it, you cannot fix it. And I intend to fix it. To the seniors in this country, you earned your benefits, you made your plans, and President George W. Bush will keep the promise of Social Security, no changes, no reductions, no way. Our opponents will say otherwise. This is their last parting ploy, and don't believe a word of it. Now is the time—now is the time for Republicans and Democrats to end the politics of fear and save Social Security together. For younger workers, we will give you the option, your choice, to put part of your payroll taxes into sound, responsible investments. This will mean a higher return on your money in over 30 or 40 years, a nest egg to help your retirement or to pass on to your children. When this money is in your name, in your account, it's just not a program, it's your property. Now is the time to give American workers security and independence that no politician can ever take away. (Bush 2000)

Thus, while attempting to allay fears that reform would mean cutting benefits for current beneficiaries, Bush said that he would touch the third rail in order to "fix it," and during the 2000 campaign he listed Social Security as one of his top domestic priorities. In his "Blueprint for the Middle Class" issued in September 2000, for example, Social Security ranked as a prominent domestic issue alongside education, Medicare, and tax cuts (Bruni 2000). However, facing attacks from Democratic presidential candidate Al Gore (Sack 2000), Bush was put on the defensive. During the first televised presidential debate he had to respond to Gore's claim that personal accounts would deplete the Social Security trust fund:

> I thought it was interesting that on the two minutes [Gore] spent about a minute-and-a-half on my plan, which means he doesn't want you to know what he's doing is loading up IOUs for future generations. He puts no real assets into the Social Security system. The revenues exceed the expenses in Social Security until the year 2015 which means all retirees are going to get the promises made. For those of you who he wants to scare into the voting booth to vote for him, hear me loud and clear. A promise made will be a promise kept. You bet we want to allow younger workers to take some of their own money. That's the difference of opinion. The vice president thinks it's the government's money. The payroll taxes are your money. (Commission on Presidential Debates 2000)

Although Social Security never became the central issue of the campaign, Bush kept defending the idea of personal accounts as the best way to reform this federal program.

Once in power, George W. Bush became the first president to explicitly support a major transformation of Social Security (Béland 2007b). But it soon became clear that education and, more importantly, tax cuts trumped Social Security as the most pressing domestic issues for the new Republican administration. Despite this, and in order to display his long-term commitment to Social Security reform and lay the ground for future legislative action, President Bush announced the creation of a new Social Security commission in February 2001:

> Seven years from now, the baby boom generation will begin to claim Social Security benefits. Everyone in this chamber knows that Social Security is not prepared to fully fund their retirement. And we only have a couple of years to get prepared. Without reform, this country will one day awaken to a stark choice: either a drastic rise in payroll taxes or a radical cut in retirement benefits.
>
> There is a better way. This spring I will form a presidential commission to reform Social Security. The commission will make its recommendations by next fall. Reform should be based on these principles: It must preserve the benefits of all current retirees and those nearing retirement. It must return

> Social Security to sound financial footing. And it must offer personal sav-
> ings accounts to younger workers who want them. (Bush 2001a)

As the last sentence made clear, the commission would have to support the creation of personal savings accounts as part of Social Security. Officially established
by an executive order on May 21, 2001, the President's Commission to Strengthen
Social Security was asked to "make recommendations to modernize and restore
fiscal soundness to Social Security."[24] To ensure that the commission's final report
would not contradict the president's basic stance on Social Security reform, its
members had to acknowledge the following six principles:

- Modernization must not change Social Security benefits for retirees or
  near-retirees.
- The entire Social Security surplus must be dedicated to Social Security only.
- Social Security payroll taxes must not be increased.
- Government must not invest Social Security funds in the stock market.
- Modernization must preserve Social Security's disability and survivors
  components.
- Modernization must include individually controlled, voluntary personal
  retirement accounts, which will augment the Social Security safety net.
  (President's Commission to Strengthen Social Security 2001, 13)

Consequently, the Bush administration nominated sixteen people—eight Democrats and eight Republicans—who already agreed with the president on these key
principles, including the need to integrate personal accounts into the Social Security system.

In part for this reason, despite the bipartisan label attached to the commission,
many Democrats in Congress did not see it as a legitimate source of policy advice
but as an ideological tool aimed at promoting the president's agenda.[25] Another
factor that weakened the potential legislative influence of the commission was
the absence of elected officials on it. Instead, the commission only involved several former members of Congress, including Bill Frenzel, Tim Penny, and cochair
Daniel Patrick Moynihan. According to a former White House official, no current
elected officials were appointed to the commission largely because it would have
been harder for the White House to control them and make sure they adhered to
the six basic principles outlined by the president.[26]

The absence of elected members of Congress differentiates the 2001 commission from the Greenspan Commission appointed by President Reagan two decades
earlier. In contrast to the Greenspan Commission, the 2001 commission did not
aim to formulate a genuine bipartisan compromise suitable for rapid legislative
adoption. While the Greenspan Commission operated in a context of short-term
fiscal crisis that pressured both President Reagan and Congress to strike a deal on
Social Security, the timeframe in 2001 was far less constraining. Clearly, there was

no perceived need for immediate action and the administration had other, more pressing priorities in mind, such as tax cuts and Medicare reform.

The commission proposals were made public three months after the terrorist attacks of September 11, 2001, which shifted the federal policy agenda away from long-term domestic issues such as Social Security reform (Béland 2007b). When the final report appeared in December 2001, there was little political opportunity for the Social Security debate to gain voice simply because national security and fighting a new recession had become the main policy priorities. Moreover, because 2002 was a midterm year, Republicans in Congress rejected even the possibility of a legislative debate on Social Security: "they had no intention of taking it up next year, when the midterm Congressional elections will be held, out of concern that Mr. Bush's support for personal accounts would bring intense attacks from Democrats" (Stevenson 2001b). As a result, the role of the commission's final report was simply to lay the ground for future potential reform initiatives. Meanwhile, the major social policy initiative in President Bush's first mandate emerged as the 2003 Medicare legislation described in the previous chapter. Interestingly, that reform, through its expansion of the availability of health savings accounts, illustrated the principle of individualism embedded in Social Security privatization.

Overall, the President's Commission to Strengthen Social Security had little short-term political impact. But because the Bush administration saw its final report as a foundation for future reform, it is important to briefly examine the commission's recommendations, which took the form of three distinct plans. The decision to let its members formulate three plans, rather than a unified reform model, stemmed from the administration's desire to have several options available.[27] This basic strategy was consistent with the will of Republicans in Congress, who did not want to embrace a detailed reform plan before the 2002 midterms (Stevenson 2001a).

Despite the lack of a unified plan, the three sets of recommendations are consistent with the six principles formulated by the White House. Thus, personal savings accounts "carved out" of the existing payroll tax were a key component of the three plans. But in contrast to the first two plans, the third set of recommendations (Model 3) included a 1 percent add-on contribution to finance the voluntary accounts (President's Commission to Strengthen Social Security 2001, 16). At the request of the White House, which wanted one of the reform alternatives to adopt a "pain free" approach, the first plan (Model 1) formulated a personal account option without recommending other changes to Social Security that could help restore the program's long-term fiscal balance (ibid., 14). According to this plan, "Workers can voluntarily invest 2 percent of their taxable wages in a personal account. In exchange, traditional Social Security benefits are offset by the worker's personal account contributions compounded at an interest rate of 3.5 percent above inflation" (ibid., 14). The two other plans would have each restored fiscal balance to Social Security. Using measures such as changes in the indexation system, these adjustments would have resulted in sizable benefit cuts that would have affected a number of people, including those who did choose to start a personal account. Furthermore, to offset the negative impact of personal accounts on the Social Security trust fund, these two plans recommended "the infusion of substantial amounts of revenue into Social Security from the rest of the budget" (Diamond and Orszag 2002, 5). From a political and electoral standpoint and in light of these significant benefit cuts and general revenue financing recommendations, it is easier to understand why the White House insisted on the addition of a pain-free option (Model 1).

As soon as the commission's recommendations became public, organizations defending the current Social Security system loudly denounced them. For instance, in December 2001 AARP's chief executive officer, Bill Novelli, issued a statement that condemned the commission: "The initial premise of the Commission to Strengthen Social Security has led to a missed opportunity and a flawed set of options in its report. For a commission to reach solutions that can be embraced by the public, it takes broad public input, thorough evaluation of all options and most importantly, consensus forged among members who represent diverse points of view—all of which the Commission lacked" (Novelli 2001). In hindsight, the President's Commission to Strengthen Social Security provided an opportunity for those opposing Social Security privatization to organize politically against the Bush administration and get ready for the political battle that would take place several years later.[28]

The "Ownership Society" and the Push to Transform Social Security

In 2003, following the midterms, the federal debate on social policy reform essentially focused on Medicare. Toward the end of the year and throughout 2004, however, President Bush began regularly referring to the "ownership society," a set of policy ideas featuring Social Security privatization that became central to the Bush administration's policy discourse (Kosterlitz 2004, 230; Serafini 2005).[29] As an ideational blueprint, the ownership society featured influential principles rooted in promarket thinking.[30] One assumption at the center of this blueprint is that personal ownership is the best source of economic prosperity and security. Consequently, the ownership society discourse promoted the idea that personal savings accounts are superior to social insurance programs like Social Security. Thus, despite its emphasis on equal opportunity, the ownership society represented an alternative to the social insurance model developed in the United States during the New Deal and the postwar era.[31] Because social insurance programs such as Social Security are historically tied to the Democratic Party, weakening them through the promotion of personal savings and ownership directly served the Republican coalition-building agenda.

Grover Norquist, then president of the conservative group Americans for Tax Reform, vividly illustrated how the ownership society appeared as a Republican coalition-building tool: "You can't have a hate-and-envy class if 80 percent of the public owns stock. That makes it impossible for Democrats to govern. It spells the end of their world" (quoted in Kosterlitz 2004, 231). In this context, the idea of an ownership society formed the centerpiece of a political strategy aimed at justifying the creation of a "capital investment welfare state" that gradually moves away from the social insurance logic (Quadagno 1999). As E. J. Dionne puts it, "The president's 'ownership society' was a political project designed to increase Americans' reliance on private markets for their retirements and, over the longer run, on their own resources for health coverage. The idea was that broadening the 'investor class,' a totemic phrase among tax-cutting conservatives, would change the economic basis of politics—and create more Republicans" (Dionne 2006). Directly associated with the idea of personal ownership, Social Security privatization became the key element of this blueprint rooted in both conservative policy ideas and Republican coalition-building strategies. One confidante of the White House, the conservative journalist Fred Barnes, acknowledged the political risks in pursuing reform of big and popular social programs but maintained that, if successful, Bush could reorder the foundations of American politics and public policy and "the phrase *ownership society* could someday enter the lexicon of presidential trademarks" along with "New Deal" and "Great Society" (Barnes 2006, 126).

The ownership model drew on Margaret Thatcher's idea of "popular capitalism."[32] The president's chief advisor, Karl Rove, even mentioned a book about Thatcherism during private White House discussions about the ownership society (Charter 2005). In the United States, the prevalence of home ownership and financial participation made the idea of an ownership society seem more credible. According to a 2005 survey, "72% [of the respondents] said they own their house and 60% have money invested in the stock market."[33] Moreover, in a 2003 poll, more than 50 percent of Americans said they dreamed of owning a business, while 10 percent already possessed one (Breeden 2003).

As early as May 2001 President Bush stressed the ideological relationship between Social Security privatization and the individualistic and promarket approach he would later call the "ownership society." "Personal savings accounts will transform Social Security from a government IOU into personal property and real assets; property that workers will own in their own names and that they can pass along to their children. Ownership, independence, access to wealth should not be the privilege of a few. They're the hope of every American, and we must make them the foundation of Social Security" (Bush 2001b). Over the years this connection between personal ownership and Social Security reform would remain a major aspect of the president's discourse. For example, President Bush stated in his 2004 State of the Union address: "Younger workers should have the opportunity to build a nest egg by saving part of their Social Security taxes in a personal retirement account. . . . We should make the Social Security system a source of ownership for the American people" (Bush 2004b).[34] Even if that State of the Union address focused mainly on national security issues, the fact that the president mentioned personal accounts showed that Social Security reform remained something his administration planned to tackle during a second term.

Although the issue remained outside the public federal policy agenda, the White House continued to contemplate possible changes to Social Security that aligned with the six principles that guided the 2001 commission. Throughout 2004 a small group of experts working secretly out of the SSA's Office of Policy spent countless hours studying Social Security proposals that the White House forwarded to them on a regular basis. Working with a number of actuaries, these experts ran simulations and provided feedback to the White House on potential reform plans that included personal savings accounts.[35]

Debating Social Security Reform

In spite of the many studies conducted within and outside the White House, Social Security reform seldom became a central issue during the 2004 presidential campaign as national security and the situation in Iraq dominated the debates throughout. Moreover, despite all of the talk disputing the notion that Social Security was an untouchable "third rail," it was clear that Social Security reform remained a risky issue for Republicans for the simple reason that Democrats continued to "own" this issue as they had since the New Deal. Public opinion data tracing back to the early 1980s constantly put Democrats ahead of Republicans in terms of popular trust in dealing with Social Security (Ross 2007). This is perhaps why, considering this Republican disadvantage, President Bush never attempted to make Social Security reform the most prominent issue of his reelection campaign (Altman 2005). Nonetheless, the issue became more visible toward the end of the campaign, especially during the third televised debate between President Bush and Senator John Kerry. During that debate, President Bush stated that he would tackle the issue during his second term:

I believe that younger workers ought to be allowed to take some of their own money and put it in a personal savings account, because I understand that they need to get better rates of return than the rates of return being given in the current Social Security trust. . . . It'll be a vital issue in my second term. It is an issue that I am willing to take on, so I'll bring Republicans and Democrats together. And we're of course going to have to consider the costs. But I want to warn my fellow citizens: The cost of doing nothing, the cost of saying the current system is OK, far exceeds the costs of trying to make sure we save the system for our children. (Commission on Presidential Debates 2004)

In response to President Bush's statement, Senator Kerry stated that this push for personal accounts as part of Social Security was "an invitation to disaster."

> The [Congressional Budget Office] said very clearly that if you were to adopt the president's plan, there would be a $2 trillion hole in Social Security, because today's workers pay in to the system for today's retirees. And the CBO said—that's the Congressional Budget Office; it's bipartisan—they said that there would have to be a cut in benefits of 25 percent to 40 percent. Now, the president has never explained to America, ever, hasn't done it tonight, where does the transitional money, that $2 trillion, come from? (ibid.)

This was not the only time during the campaign that John Kerry questioned the president's stance on Social Security. In mid-October, for example, the Kerry team ran a campaign commercial on Social Security that accused President Bush of seeking to cut benefits. The commercial ended with this question and answer: "The real Bush agenda? Cutting Social Security" (Halbfinger 2004). Interestingly, at the same time that the Kerry team attacked Bush on Social Security, the *New York Times* cited a private speech the president had given to key Republican donors in September 2004. Bush was quoted saying that, immediately after his reelection, he would push for Social Security reform, among other things: "We have to move quickly, because after that I'll be quacking like a duck" (quoted in ibid.). Although the Bush team decided not to make this controversial issue a central aspect of the 2004 presidential campaign, it was clear to that gathering of donors that Social Security reform would become a prominent second-term issue for President Bush.

After his reelection, the president immediately pushed Social Security to the center of his second-term agenda (Weiner 2007). During a press conference that took place only two days after his reelection, President Bush stated that "the President must have the will to take on the issue—not only in the campaign, but now that I'm elected. And this will—reforming Social Security will be a priority of my administration" (Bush 2004a). A genuine "bombshell" (Altman 2005, 273), this announcement surprised even some Republicans in Congress, who did not expect President Bush to tackle the issue so quickly after his reelection.[36] At a meeting with congressional Republicans in January 2005, Bush insisted to a somewhat apprehensive audience that Social Security reform was to be the first major domestic policy goal of the second term on the basis that "I've got political capital, and now I'm going to spend it" (quoted in Draper 2007, 296).

Obstacles to Reform

Although the 2004 elections increased the Republican majorities in both houses of Congress, the situation was not ideal for the president and his allies. The fact that President Bush had not made Social Security a prominent aspect of his reelection campaign weakened the claim that he had received a popular mandate to reform the program (Edwards 2007, 286). As his second term began, the president "enjoyed the lowest approval rating—just 50 percent—of any just-reelected president since modern polling began. That was 9 points lower than Clinton and Nixon, 12 points lower than Reagan, and 21 points lower than Johnson—hardly the foundation for crushing a united opposition" (Galston 2007, 3). After the 2004 election there were fewer conservative and moderate Democrats left in Congress that might potentially have supported the president on Social Security. Ironically, the heightened partisan approach of the Republican leadership in Congress throughout the first half of the 2000s (Hacker and Pierson 2005b) reduced the potential for a bipartisan deal on Social Security. By attacking moderate and conservative Democrats from the South to expand the Republican coalition, Tom DeLay and his White House allies alienated many Democrats in Congress while sending the implicit message that even Democrats who supported the president on issues such as Social Security could become the target of systematic Republican electoral attacks. The Republican drive to defeat Charles Stenholm through redistricting illustrates this political logic (Bickerstaff 2007). Stenholm, a conservative Democrat from Texas, who had been reelected to the House thirteen times since 1979, became a target for DeLay, who used redistricting efforts in his home state to defeat Stenholm despite the fact that he had already worked with Republican representative Jim Kolbe on a Social Security plan that included personal savings accounts (Lemieux 2004). DeLay's efforts were successful, and Stenholm was defeated in November 2004, thus removing a Democrat from Congress who might have cooperated with Republicans on Social Security reform barely two days before President Bush declared that Social Security would become one of the top priorities of his second mandate. Beyond this example, the increased partisanship and ideological polarization witnessed during the first mandate of President Bush represented an obstacle to a bipartisan deal on Social Security during his second term. The reluctance of Democrats to offer political cover for Social Security reform is something that the administration seems to have misjudged. At one point, the moderate Democratic senator Max Baucus of Montana, who had worked across party lines previously, told Karl Rove that no Democrat would accept the idea of carving personal accounts out of the existing Social Security payroll tax. Rove replied: 'You're wrong. There'll be people who have to come on this' (quoted in Draper 2007, 298).

Many of Republicans in Congress failed to show support for the administration on the issue. In late November 2004, for instance, Republican representative Tom Davis of Virginia told the *Wall Street Journal* that "roughly 30 House Republicans, including him, are already inclined to oppose Mr. Bush. That would be little more than 10% of the party's House caucus—but too many defections to allow Mr. Bush to succeed."[37] Reflecting how Democrats "own" Social Security as an issue, many Republicans saw Social Security reform as a huge political risk that could easily turn against them, as had happened to President Reagan at the beginning of his presidency (Ross 2007). In fact, George W. Bush recalls in *Decision Points* that he only received "lukewarm" support from Republican members of Congress when he met with them to discuss Social Security reform in January 2005 (2010, 298). Despite this, the administration seems to have overestimated its capacity to direct members of Congress (Edwards 2007, 264) In fact, drawing on the example of the passage of the Medicare Modernization Act, discussed in chapter 2, key figures in the White House, notably Chief of Staff Andrew Card, thought that the administration could again push controversial social policy reform through Congress (Draper 2007, 294).

A couple of weeks after the reelection of President Bush, the AARP took a strong public stance against the president's plans for Social Security. As the organization's policy director, John C. Rother, put it, "We favor private accounts when they are in addition to Social Security, but not as a substitute" (quoted in Pear 2004). The AARP had angered many Democrats back in 2003 when it collaborated with the Bush administration on Medicare reform, but it soon became clear that this scenario would not be repeated with Social Security. Perhaps in part because many of its own members as well as Democrats in Congress had strongly criticized the organization for endorsing the Medicare Modernization Act in 2003, the AARP made it clear from the start that it would defend the existing Social Security system and, if necessary, campaign against the president over the issue (Pear 2004). The AFL-CIO, the National Organization for Women, and other liberal-leaning organizations soon joined the AARP in opposition to the president's approach to Social Security reform (Cooper and Calmes 2004). For the AFL-CIO, attacking the president's plan on Social Security was crucial because the union movement wanted to help its political allies, the Democrats, while defending the idea of defined-benefit pensions, which it had long supported. AFL-CIO officials also believed that personal savings accounts for Social Security "would flood the markets with money controlled by individuals, not organized labor. That would tend to dilute labor's voting strength on shareholder issues in general" (Birnbaum 2005). This once again stresses the relationship between the politics of Social Security and the development of private benefits and pension funds.

The Battle of Ideas over Social Security

This list of adversaries and potential foes should not hide the fact that many people and organizations supported the president's push for path-departing Social Security reform. First, many Republicans in Congress explicitly backed the president's individualistic approach centered on carved-out personal accounts. As for the Republican congressional leadership, it prepared its troops for the Social Security battle. For instance, in late January 2005 Republican members of Congress received a confidential document titled "Saving Social Security: A Guide to Social Security Reform" (House Republican Conference and Senate Republican Conference 2005). This document explained how Republicans should frame the Social Security debate and legitimize the "need to reform" (Cox 2001) this program. Specifically, Republicans were told not to mention the term "privatization," which conservatives had long used to depict personal savings accounts "carved out" of the payroll tax (Altman 2005, 267).[38] Conservative think tanks such as the Cato Institute and the Heritage Foundation also supported the president's Social Security efforts. This is consistent with the behavior they adopted in the late 1990s, when Social Security restructuring first moved onto the agenda (Béland 2007b). And business coalitions such as the Alliance for Worker Retirement Security and the Coalition to Modernize and Protect America's Social Security received millions of dollars from organizations such as the Business Roundtable and the National Association of Manufacturers to promote the "modernization" of Social Security through the implementation of personal accounts while attacking liberal groups that opposed the president's push to transform the program (Edwards 2007, 264–65; Justice 2005).

Although the president participated in a number of Social Security events in January, his campaign to reform the program only took shape after the State of the Union address. This address is especially interesting because it illustrates the major arguments that the president put forward to convince the population to support his Social Security approach. Calling Social Security "a great moral success of the 20th century," President Bush began his discussion of the program by reassuring older Americans. "I have a message for every American who is 55 or older: Do not let anyone mislead you; for you, the Social Security system will not change in any way" (Bush 2005f). Then, focusing on younger workers and stressing the negative impact of population aging on the program, the president claimed that Social Security faced "serious problems that will grow worse with time" (ibid.). Although the president argued that the time had come to "solve the financial problems of Social Security once and for all," he did not explicitly support any particular way of restoring long-term fiscal balance to the program. Instead he simply referred to a number of policy alternatives associated with centrist Democrats no longer in office: "Former Congressman Tim Penny has raised the possibility of indexing benefits to prices rather than wages. During the 1990s, my predecessor, President Clinton, spoke of increasing the retirement age. Former Senator John Breaux suggested discouraging early collection of Social Security benefits. The late Senator Daniel Patrick Moynihan recommended changing the way benefits are calculated. All these ideas are on the table" (ibid.). After these general remarks, the president focused on the virtues of private savings accounts for younger workers: "Your money will grow, over time, at a greater rate than anything the current system can deliver—and your account will provide money for retirement over and above the check you will receive from Social Security" (ibid.). This quote is a typical example of the individualistic and promarket discourse ever present in the fierce ideological debate over Social Security privatization. Finally, the president stressed that these accounts would offer more—rather than less—retirement security than the existing system.

Overall, the president's discourse about Social Security reform borrowed from two ideological streams that had been central to the conservative discourse on privatization since the 1990s: demographic pessimism (i.e., the idea of an imminent demographic crisis making the program unsustainable in the long run) and financial optimism (i.e., the claim that personal savings account are a much better deal for younger workers than the existing Social Security system).[39] Interestingly, financial optimism extended to minorities as the president and his allies argued that partial privatization would benefit economically disadvantaged groups such as African Americans, who have a shorter average life expectancy than that of whites and, consequently, collect Social Security benefits for a shorter period on average (Edwards 2007, 281). Throughout his 2005 reform campaign, a mix of demographic pessimism and financial optimism remained a key feature of the president's discourse on Social Security reform.

In 2005, like in the late 1990s, supporters of the existing Social Security system put forward two main arguments to oppose the development of personal savings accounts carved out of the payroll tax. First, liberals and organizations such as the AARP downplayed the idea of an imminent crisis in Social Security, arguing that a set of moderate changes would restore long-term balance in the program: "If you had a problem with the kitchen sink, you wouldn't tear down the entire house. So why dismantle Social Security when it can be fixed with just a few moderate changes? Reform is necessary, but diverting money into private accounts is just too drastic, could add up to $2 trillion in more debt and lead to huge benefit cuts."[40] Opponents of the idea of diverting part of the Social Security payroll tax into personal accounts also depicted the Bush administration's assumption about the return rates expected from personal accounts as overly optimistic (Weisman and White 2005). Second, opponents of the president claimed that personal accounts carved out of the payroll tax would weaken the economic security of the elderly, worsen the fiscal situation of the program, and increase federal debt due to the borrowing that would be necessary to set up the personal savings accounts and cover the cost of the transition from the old to the new Social Security system (Varian 2005). According to supporters of the existing program, President Bush and his allies promoted the development of personal accounts as a way to advance the interests of Wall Street brokers and the financial industry at large. The direct ties between members of the White House and organizations promoting the perceived interests of the financial industry made these accusations seem more plausible (Thomas 2004). To reduce support from the financial sector for President Bush's Social Security initiative, labor unions even launched an aggressive campaign against firms affiliated with the Alliance for Worker Retirement Security (Edwards 2007, 272–73).

To reassure the public and promote his vision for Social Security reform, President Bush launched a spectacular public relations effort that led him to travel across the country and attend dozens of "town hall meetings." This effort was "perhaps the most extensive public relations campaign in the history of the presidency on behalf of reforming Social Security" (ibid., 284). The White House campaign culminated in the "60 Stops in 60 Days" tour, which began in early March 2005. During that month alone, members of the administration "participated in 108 events in 32 states, including more than 40 town meetings with senators and representatives. Mr. Bush had 12 Social Security rallies in March, (Rosenbaum 2005a).

A key component of the White House's campaign was the "town hall meeting," a device used throughout the Bush presidency to attract local news coverage while promoting the administration's policies (Altman 2005, 290). Although the term "town hall meeting" evokes the image of lively debates and open participation, the meetings sponsored by the White House were carefully staged events that only simulated grassroots deliberation. In fact, "the audiences at these events have been carefully screened supporters. The meeting organizers deny entry to anyone who seems likely to ask a critical question, so the president always speaks to sympathetic listeners" (Edwards 2007, 39).

Despite these extensive efforts, many things went wrong with the White House's public relations drive, and it became increasingly difficult for the administration to defend its stance on Social Security. For example, because the president refused to unveil a detailed reform plan at the beginning of his Social Security campaign, opponents argued that the administration had "things to hide" regarding potential benefit cuts. The fact that the president decided to focus mainly on the individualistic and promarket virtues of personal accounts rather than addressing potential benefit cuts exacerbated this problem. When President Bush finally unveiled his plan concerning benefit cuts, things went very wrong. This unveiling took place at an April 28 press conference, during which the president endorsed the idea of "progressive indexation" developed by investment executive Robert C. Pozen, a Democrat who had served on the 2001 Social Security commission (Stevenson and Bumiller 2005). As the president put it, "I believe a reform system should protect those who depend on Social Security the most. So I propose a Social Security system in the future where benefits for low-income workers will grow faster than benefits for people who are better off. By providing more generous benefits for low-income retirees, we'll make this commitment: If you work hard and pay into Social Security your entire life, you will not retire into poverty" (Bush 2005c).

Democrats and their liberal allies immediately denounced "progressive indexation" as an attack against the middle class. In a *USA Today* interview published hours before the president's press conference, for example, vocal liberal economist Jason Furman stated: "There's nothing progressive about deep benefits cuts for middle-class families" (quoted in Page and Dorell 2005). Although the administration depicted "progressive indexation" as a social justice device that protected the poor, Democrats and their allies successfully framed this proposal as a way to take money away from the middle class. Less than a week after the April 28 press conference, the administration implicitly backed off, arguing that President Bush would remain open to other ideas about how to restore long-term fiscal balance in Social Security (Edwards 2007, 259). In the end, the White House retreated from the concept of "progressive indexation," having failed to make a convincing case for the necessity to—and the legitimacy of—benefit cuts affecting the middle class.

More generally, according to two former members of the Bush administration, the White House was not well organized to answer questions from journalists and respond to criticisms about the more technical aspects of the Social Security debate.[41] As for the president, he struggled to explain some of the issues at stake, especially when he could not rely on a written script and had to answer direct questions from journalists or members of the public attending his town hall meetings. This difficulty in conveying the issues to the public was illustrated by a Doonesbury cartoon published on April 10, 2005, titled "Confused about the Bush Plan for Social Security?"[42] The cartoon pokes fun at the president by featuring excerpts of an answer he gave to a woman at a White House Social Security public gathering that took place in Tampa on April 2. Asked about how his plan would fix Social Security's problem, the president offered a confused and disjointed reply:

Because the—all which is on the table begins to address the big cost drivers. For example, how benefits are calculate, for example, is on the table; whether or not benefits rise based upon wage increases or price increases. There's a series of parts of the formula that are being considered. And when you couple that, those different cost drivers, affecting those—changing those with personal accounts, the idea is to get what has been promised more likely to be—or closer delivered to what has been promised. Does that make any sense to you? It's kind of muddled. Look, there's a series of things that cause the—like, for example, benefits are calculated based upon the increase of wages, as opposed to the increase of prices. Some have suggested that we calculate—the benefits will rise based upon inflation, as opposed to wage increases. There is a reform that would help solve the red if that were put into effect. In other words, how fast benefits grow, how fast the promised benefits grow, it will help on the red. (Bush 2005b)

Cartoonist Garry Trudeau did not need to add anything to this long quote to make the reader "get the point." Obviously, the president found it hard to spontaneously answer basic questions about Social Security reform, which weakened the effectiveness of the conservative framing campaign in favor of privatization.

Overall, the White House's public relations campaign did not increase popular support for its Social Security initiative. In fact, in contrast to the White House's expectations, support for the president's proposal somewhat declined over the course of the sixty-day tour (Ross 2007, 423). From January to April, in fact, the percentage of Americans who approved of the president's handling of Social Security dropped from 38 percent to 31 percent (Bowman 2005, 37). Because Social Security as an issue is "owned" by Democrats, the White House had to fight an uphill battle to convince the public to support their reform plans (Ross 2007), but in the end the administration failed to alter the long-term partisan dynamics associated with Social Security, leaving the Democrats as the clear winners of the battle of ideas surrounding this program.

"Quacking Like a [Lame] Duck"

This failure to convince most members of the public that reform was necessary clearly did not help the White House to persuade members of Congress to enact a Social Security legislation modeled on the administration's vague proposals. The situation was particularly complicated in the Senate. "Because it would take 60 votes to overcome a Democratic filibuster, no Social Security legislation can clear the Senate without a solid Republican front and some Democratic support" (Rosenbaum 2005b). Unfortunately for the president, efforts to reach that number of potentially favorable votes in the Senate failed, but not without trying. For instance, starting in January 2005 informal staff meetings were held once a week in the Senate in order to tackle Social Security reform. Once a month, members from both parties interested in the president's Social Security proposals also gathered. These talks did not go very far, however, because it seemed impossible to agree on a detailed plan that could have a fair chance at surviving the legislative process. As mentioned earlier, many Democrats in Congress rejected the president's call for reform right from the beginning and united against his Social Security initiative in a context of exacerbated partisanship that Republicans had ironically encouraged earlier in the decade (Hacker and Pierson 2005b).

Meanwhile, Republicans struggled to agree on a detailed legislative plan. Sources of disagreement included the size of the "carve out" and the nature of benefit cuts, which "free-lunch conservatives" opposed (Calmes 2005). Over time, a growing number of Republicans distanced themselves from the president because they found it increasingly difficult to answer the many questions about potential benefit cuts asked by their constituents. For many members of Congress, this difficulty was exacerbated by the relative lack of expert advice available to them. According to a Senate Republican staffer, there are few Social Security experts on congressional staff, which makes it hard for members to get the support they need to answer tough questions from the public. In this context, saying "no" to reform became much easier than defending the president's vague—and potentially painful—proposals. In the end, reform became increasingly elusive in the Senate, especially after the April 28 conference and the president's talk about "progressive indexation," which was poorly received by some influential Republicans in Congress (Altman 2005, 294). By late spring 2005 congressional hearings and "reform talk" could not hide the fact that Social Security legislation inspired by the president's proposals seemed increasingly unlikely. As House Republican E. Clay Shaw Jr. from the Ways and Means Committee put it in late May, "I don't think you could get a third of the Congress to vote for any one plan at this point" (Weisman 2005a).

Considering the united opposition of Democrats and insufficient support for the president's proposals in the Senate, the Republican leadership began considering a potential "exit strategy." In June White House aides debated the possibility of Social Security reform without personal accounts. But Karl Rove and others opposed the idea, arguing that "it would be unwise, both from a political and policy standpoint, to reduce benefits without offering people the potential of bet-ter returns through personal accounts" (Weisman and VandeHei 2005). Instead of taking the controversial idea of personal accounts off the table, President Bush blamed Democrats for the legislative stalemate on Social Security: "On issue after issue, they stand for nothing except obstruction, and this is not leadership. It is the philosophy of the stop sign, the agenda of the roadblock, and our country and our children deserve better. Political parties that choose the path of obstruction will not gain the trust of the American people. If leaders of the other party have inno-vative ideas, let's hear them. But if they have no ideas or policies except obstruc-tion, they should step aside and let others lead" (Bush 2005a). But Democrats did not step aside, and the opposition to his vision for Social Security reform remained strong. By mid-July, the situation in Congress was so dire for supporters of the president's proposals that "the chairmen of the Senate and House committees with jurisdiction over Social Security . . . decided to postpone further consideration of the issue at least until September" (Rosenbaum 2005a). After Hurricane Katrina destroyed large parts of New Orleans in late August, Social Security reform was removed from the federal policy agenda (Weisman 2005b). Facing mounting crit-icisms about the federal response to Katrina and the situation in Iraq, President Bush simply could not revive Social Security as an issue. Without any doubt, the administration had lost the Social Security battle. Ironically, less than a year after declaring that he needed to move quickly on Social Security so that he could accomplish something meaningful before "quacking like a duck," President Bush became an early "lame duck" largely because of his ill-fated Social Security cam-paign. Social Security, the object of his last serious attempt at domestic policy leg-acy building, ended up making him "quack like a duck" much earlier than he had expected. In light of this, it is not surprising that, although he devotes only a few pages to this issue in his 2010 memoir, the former president writes that "the col-lapse of Social Security reform is one of the greatest disappointments of my presi-dency" (Bush 2010, 300).

The Aftermath and the Obama Presidency

The defeat suffered by the White House in its bid to restructure Social Security does not mean that the overall context of the American pension system has remained unchanged.[43] Rather, there have been incremental yet path-departing changes in the government-subsidized private sector. As mentioned in the earlier discussion about layering, the push to privatize Social Security was closely tied to the expan-sion of 401(k)s and other tax-sponsored savings schemes (Hacker 2004; Teles 1998). Along the same lines, traditional defined-benefit private pensions have declined in recent decades.[44] Such decline potentially weakens the economic security of future retirees because the multiplication of defined-contribution plans means that employers shift financial risks onto workers (Hacker 2004; Klein 2003). In the long run, the movement away from defined-benefit plans and the expansion of additional layers of government-subsidized savings schemes in the private sector could further diffuse "popular finance" among the middle class (Teles 1998). Because these tax-subsidized provisions operate according to a different institutional logic than Social Security's defined-benefit approach, this raises the possibility of wealthier Americans embracing private retirement accounts at the expense of supporting the social insurance model inherent in Social Security. Hence, the ownership logic promoted by conservative supporters of change could gain further ground in the future, making existing Social Security arrangements more vulnerable to future conservative reform efforts.

This discussion points to the existence of massive policy drift in the American pension system (Hacker 2004). This policy drift stems not only from changing social and economic trends but from the ideational shift in the way employers perceive the labor contract between them and their workers as well as the relative domination of the conservative belief in the virtues of personal, individualized savings tied to the individualistic, promarket ideas of self-reliance and "popular finance" (Teles 1998), which both remain influential despite the 2008 financial crisis and its negative impact on 401(k)s and other savings vehicles.

With the relative absence of reforms aimed at countering policy drift associated with the reduction in the traditional employer-granted social benefits, future retirees are likely to have significantly less economic security than current retirees enjoy.[45] Thus, by forcing liberals to adopt a defensive stance on Social Security, the ongoing conservative "Leninist strategy" and the more recent White House campaign to transform Social Security succeeded in marginalizing proposals that could have improved the protection granted by Social Security and by the lesser-known but important Supplemental Security Income (SSI) program. Ironically, the decline of private defined-benefit pensions means that the federal government is more crucial than ever as a source of economic security for seniors, especially low-income ones (Béland 2007b). Considering that old-age poverty is already higher in the United States than in many other advanced industrial countries (Wiseman and Yčas 2008), the fact that so few federal politicians push for an *expansion* of the federal public pension system is a little-acknowledged source of concern as far as the future of old-age security in the United States is concerned. This reflects the ideological ascendancy of the austerity discourse that has dominated the Social Security debate since the mid-late 1970s. Finally, the 2005 push for personal accounts carved out of the payroll tax intensified ideological and partisan polarization over Social Security, a situation hardly conducive to the type of bipartisan, 1983-style legislation that could improve the long-term fiscal situation of the program.

During the 2008 presidential campaign, Social Security seldom became a high-profile issue (Espo 2008; Sherman 2008). Furthermore, health care and, during the last stretch of the campaign, the international fiscal crisis truly dominated domestic policy debates. Throughout the Democratic campaign, Barack Obama made it clear that he opposed Social Security privatization and any further increase in retirement age.[46] To address the long-term imbalance in Social Security financing, Obama advocated an increase of the earnings cap for the Social Security payroll tax. Unsurprisingly, Republicans attacked this proposal as a genuine tax hike (McGurn 2008).

As for John McCain, after the failure of President Bush's 2005 campaign, he and his Republican colleagues adopted a cautious approach to Social Security reform.[47] His official website did not even list "Social Security" among the fifteen most prominent issues of his campaign. Instead, under the umbrella concept of "economic policy," his website only devoted a single paragraph to Social Security. This paragraph claimed that Senator McCain simply backed the implementation of new savings accounts alongside the current Social Security system. As suggested earlier, such an add-on model is different from Social Security privatization and, interestingly, closer to the proposal President Clinton had put forward in his 1999 State of the Union address. Further, although his campaign website featured a vague statement about possible benefit cuts, it did not refer to concrete, unpopular measures such as a new increase in the Social Security retirement age (McCain website 2008).[48] Overall, in the mirror of President Bush's humiliating 2005 Social Security defeat, McCain's careful approach during the 2008 campaign is understandable.

During the first two years of the Obama presidency, issues such as health care reform and the "Great Recession" largely kept Social Security outside the federal policy agenda. The only exception concerned the absence of costs-of-living benefit increases in 2009 due to low inflation figures, an issue President Obama raised to justify the special, one-time $250 payment to seniors that became part of federal efforts to stimulate the economy (Obama 2009). Nevertheless, the growing size of the federal deficit as well as the deterioration of the program's actuarial situation caused by the recession that started in 2008 exacerbated the perceived anxiety over the program's future. More important, the creation of the bipartisan National Commission on Fiscal Responsibility and Reform in February 2010 rapidly became a source of concern among citizens, experts, and interests groups who opposed future cuts in Social Security benefits. This is true partly because of the presence of many conservative lawmakers on the commission, with its mission to identify "policies to improve the fiscal situation in the medium term and to achieve fiscal sustainability over the long run" as well as the formulation of "recommendations that meaningfully improve the long-run fiscal outlook, including changes to address the growth of entitlement spending and the gap between the projected revenues and expenditures of the Federal Government" (Obama 2010). For instance, liberal experts Nancy Altman and Eric Kingson (2010) claimed that the commission could become a Social Security "death panel" aimed at promoting major benefit cuts. Throughout the 2010 midterm campaign, Democrats used Social Security as an issue to attack Republican candidates who had expressed support for privatization at one point or another. For example, Nevada senator and majority leader Harry Reid ran ads attacking his Republican opponent and Tea

Party supporter Sharron Angle (Espo 2010), who had talked of the "need to phase Medicare and Social Security out in favor of something privatized" (quoted in Schwartz 2010). Reid's attack ads served to remind the public that Social Security remains an issue largely "owned" by Democrats, who are committed to protect the program against conservative attacks. Yet following the Republican gains at the 2010 midterm election (e.g., their control of the House and significantly larger representation in the Senate) and considering the ideological rise of fiscal austerity, pressures to reform Social Security and possibly reduce benefits further increases, which put President Obama in a delicate political situation in 2011 as he attempted simultaneously to appear serious about so-called "entitlement reform" while also adopting the traditional Democratic stance as the ultimate defender of Social Security.

As the 2010 midterm campaign advertisements suggest, although the idea of Social Security privatization has not made a true political comeback yet, discussions about how to improve the long-term fiscal stability of the program remain as passionate and polarized as ever. As in the past, this debate concerns the proper balance between tax increases and benefit cuts, including indirect ones such as a new increase in Social Security's retirement age. This last option is advocated in the report of the National Commission on Fiscal Responsibility and Reform, which appeared in December 2010. "After the Normal Retirement Age (NRA) reaches 67 in 2027 under current law," the commission proposed to "index both the NRA and Early Eligibility Age (EEA) to increases in life expectancy, effectively increasing the NRA to 68 by about 2050 and 69 by about 2075, and the EEA to 63 and 64 in lock step." Other measures proposed by the commission regarding Social Security include making the benefit structure more progressive and gradually increasing "the taxable maximum so that it covers 90 percent of wages by 2050," compared to only 86 percent in 2009 (National Commission on Fiscal Responsibility and Reform 2010, 51). Predictably, the commission's ideas, which feature many unpopular proposals while attempting to "spread the pain," generated much criticism from both the left and the right, even before the report appeared: "The liberal and conservative media universally panned the proposal as too regressive and too progressive; destroying Social Security but also turning it into a welfare program; raising taxes too little and raising them over their historical average" (Thomson 2010). It remains to be seen whether the controversial work of the National Commission on Fiscal Responsibility and Reform will help pave the ground for a major Social Security reform, which would be the first since 1983.

Conclusion

President Bush's push to reform Social Security was the culmination of a conservative campaign to redirect Social Security toward financial investment and personal ownership. With Social Security's reputation as the "third rail of American politics," conservatives have developed a long-term strategy to weaken support for the program by promoting the expansion of savings schemes layered alongside the federal program. As evidenced in this chapter, President Bush's attempt to crown this strategy with legislative action on Social Security failed. A mix of institutional, ideological, and partisan factors explains this outcome.

First, Social Security remains a most popular program that has created a large army of politically active beneficiaries over time (Campbell 2003; Pierson 1994). Although the overall confidence of the public in the long-term sustainability of the program has declined since the mid-1970s, few politicians in Washington dare take a stance against the program, and even people who want to transform Social Security claim that their goal is to "save" or "strengthen" it (Béland 2007b). Considering the growing electoral and political clout of the elderly and increasing support for Social Security generally, reforming this program has remained a risky business for politicians since the shift from expansion to austerity and retrenchment that took place in the late 1970s and early 1980s (Light 1995; Pierson 1994). In short, and in contrast to welfare policy, the policy feedback generated by the development of the Social Security system has been highly self-reinforcing. This remark illustrates the powerful institutional logics that help shape the contemporary politics of Social Security.

Second, because the public trust Democrats more than Republicans on Social Security, the political risks that Republicans face when trying to make reforms are much greater on average (Ross 2007). To reduce these risks, Republicans have a strong incentive to reach out to Democrats to forge bipartisan coalitions that protect them against popular discontent. This is exactly what President Reagan accomplished in the early 1980s when he put together the Greenspan Commission and forced Democrats and Republicans in Congress to work with the White House to achieve a compromise on the issue. Because most Democrats saw President Bush's 2001 Social Security commission as a staged attempt to legitimize his push for personal accounts, its report did not favor genuine bipartisan coalition-building.

Third, back in 2005 growing partisanship stemming from the electoral strategy of the Republican leadership in Congress made a genuine bipartisan deal on Social Security unlikely. After what happened to people such as Charles Stenholm, who was prepared to work across the partisan aisle, few Democrats in Congress seemed interested in bargaining with Republicans on Social Security. The partisan polarization created by the Iraq War and the 2004 presidential campaign added to the mix to create a poisonous political climate hardly suitable for bipartisan efforts.

Finally, regarding the role of ideas, the Bush administration's unilateral push for personal accounts made a compromise with Democrats on Social Security even more difficult. The president and his conservative allies truly believed in the virtues of ownership and personal accounts for both ideological and strategic reasons. On one hand, the ownership society formed a coherent promarket set of ideas that articulated an economic and social vision whereby personal accounts represented a better model than the current Social Security system.

This conservative belief in both the moral and economic superiority of personal accounts became part of the conservative and Republican creed. During one of our interviews, a former member of the Bush administration clearly articulated this identification between conservatism and personal accounts: "I'm a conservative, I'm a Republican and [therefore] I support personal accounts."[49] Believing in the irresistible popularity of personal accounts, members of the White House clearly thought that the administration should sell this idea to the public despite the political risks involved. Moreover, many conservatives thought the implementation of the ownership society blueprint through Social Security privatization would help create a new generation of citizen-investors who would be more likely to support Republicans than Democrats on key economic and political issues. This strategic belief is crucial to understanding why conservatives put Social Security reform on the top of their policy agenda. But conservatives underestimated the popularity of the existing program and the capacity of Democrats to effectively turn the public against the need for conservative Social Security restructuring, particularly in the absence of short-term fiscal crisis. Public opinion data suggest that, although many citizens are sympathetic to the idea of personal accounts in general, support for it declines dramatically when they are told about the potential financial risks associated with such accounts (Cook, Barabas, and Page 2002, 254–55).

What Democrats and their allies did in 2005 was simply to remind the public about these potential risks, which helped reduced support for the president's proposals and reflected how Democrats have maintained clear "ownership" of Social Security as a political question (Ross 2007). Beyond issue ownership, something about the nature of the idea of personal accounts makes that idea especially vulnerable to political attacks. In addition to the issue of financial risks typically associated with privatization, the promarket and individualistic discourse on personal accounts was inherently flawed because conservatives attempted to sell the accounts to the public as a way to "save Social Security" even as it became increasingly clear that—far from helping to restore the program's fiscal balance—these accounts would increase costs and, thus, would generate new fiscal problems that would require large borrowings or benefit cuts.

By pushing aggressively for one of the most controversial policy alternatives available, President Bush made it more difficult to establish a bipartisan agreement on Social Security while helping his opponents depict him as an enemy of the enduringly popular program he claimed to support. Instead of working with Democrats to help solve the long-term financing challenges facing the program, the White House referred to such challenges to justify the enactment of controversial personal accounts that Democrats could portray as a threat to both the economic security of retirees and the long-term survival of the program.

Overall, a combination of institutional, ideological, and partisan factors led to the crushing defeat of President Bush's 2005 Social Security campaign. This defeat, however, should not hide the fact that the focus on personal accounts helped prevent the enactment of more moderate measures that could have restored long-term fiscal balance to the program while tackling other issues such as gender equality, the decline of employment-based economic security, and the enduring reality of old-age poverty.[50] In other words, in a changing economic and social context, the domination of conservative ideas has contributed to massive policy drift stemming from legislative inaction and the related failure to offset the gradual decline in employer-provided retirement security.

From a political standpoint, President Bush's failed attempt to reshape Social Security may have killed short-term prospects for the implementation of personal accounts carved out of the payroll tax. Many of the people we interviewed back in 2008, including conservatives, stated that privatization was politically dead in the short run because few politicians were then willing to spend their political capital advocating such a controversial proposal. But the ideological push for such accounts continues as a number of conservative politicians and organizations such as the Cato Institute are willing to keep the privatization flame alive. While the push for privatization is a long-term game, especially if the Democrats remain in an institutional position to block unwanted reform efforts, it is likely that Social Security reform will return to the center of the federal agenda sooner rather than later. As indicated by the report of the 2010 National Commission on Fiscal Responsibility and Reform, there is ongoing concern about the fiscal sustainability of the program, especially given the significant demographic and fiscal challenges facing it. This raises the possibility that advocates of change will again attempt to frame the debate around the "need to reform" (Cox 2001) the existing system in a manner that reduces or even discards its inherent social solidarity.

Notes

1. "Supplemental Security Income." *Social Security Online*, www.ssa.gov/ssi/.
2. For a more systematic analysis of the history of Social Security, see Achenbaum 1986; Altman 2005; Béland 2007b; Berkowitz 1995, 2003; Cates 1983; Derthick 1979; DeWitt, Béland, and Berkowitz 2007; Quadagno 1988; Schieber and Shoven 1999; Tynes 1996; Weaver 1982. For a comparative perspective focusing on long-term governance, see Jacobs 2011. The following discussion draws on Béland 2007b.
3. On credit claiming, see Mayhew 1974.
4. For a detailed historical analysis of conservative attitudes toward Social Security, see chapters 2, 5, and 8 in Glenn and Teles 2009.
5. Interestingly, in the same campaign brochure, Goldwater lashes out at the "welfare state": "We, the people, can change all of this. We can unite. We can reject appeasement. We can deny self-indulgence. We can restrain our pressure groups from seeking special privilege favors at the expense of the general public taxpayer."
6. The main issue with the 1972 indexation system was that the benefit formula's percentages that set benefit levels for future Social Security recipients also changed to reflect consumer prices. In periods of high inflation such as during the mid-1970s,

both the consumer price index and the wage rates would increase, "with the result of producing larger than anticipated initial benefit levels for future beneficiaries" (Berkowitz 2003, 238–39).

7. On blame avoidance in general, see Weaver (1986).

8. There were 61 Democrats and 39 Republicans in the Senate, and 292 Democrats and 143 Republicans in the House.

9. For an insider's view, see Ball (2010).

10. For example, this view was expressed by a White House official in an interview conducted by Daniel Béland (Washington DC, February 2008). For a cautionary tale about the idea of a "new" Greenspan Commission, see Ball (2010).

11. "Frequently Asked Questions about the Social Security Trust Funds," *Social Security Administration*, www.ssa.gov/OACT/ProgData/fundFAQ.html. In 1990 Sen. Daniel Patrick Moynihan of New York, who was a strong supporter of Social Security, introduced a proposal in Senate to reduce the Social Security payroll tax. He did this to highlight his argument that funds in the Social Security trust fund should only be used for Social Security rather than transferred to finance overall government debt. This plan provoked a divided response but was defeated in the Senate and did not come to a vote in the House (Patashnik 2000, 88–89).

12. On this strategy, see also Teles (1998).

13. This paragraph draws extensively on Hacker (2004).

14. Since the 1960s, however, "foreign models" have played a lesser role in American social policy debates than during the Progressive Era, the New Deal, and the 1940s, for example (Berkowitz 1996). On the global campaign in favor of pension privatization, see Blackburn (2002) and Orenstein (2008).

15. For a critical and comparative perspective on the relationship between Social Security and the stock markets, see Munnell and Sass (2006).

16. Because Social Security is a defined-benefit system, actuaries and other social insurance experts generally use the term "replacement rate" (the proportion of the average salary being replaced) rather than "return rate" (proportion of returns on an investment) when they describe how the program works (e.g., Myers 1993).

17. For a personal recollection of the 1994–96 Advisory Council from one of its members, see Schieber and Shoven (1999). A detailed analysis of the 1994–96 Advisory Council is found in Gibson (2007). On the role of recent pension commissions in other countries, see Marier (2009).

18. "Report of the 1994–1996 Advisory Council on Social Security," January 1997. Available at *Social Security Online*, www.ssa.gov/history/reports/adcouncil/report/toc.htm. For an analysis of the political implications of each set of proposals, see Arnold (1998).

19. "Add-On Accounts Add no Value," *New York Times*, March 26, 2005, Editorial, A12; John 2005; and "Social Security 'Add-On' Accounts with Benefit Offset." Available at *Centrist.org*.

20. "Report of the 1994–1996 Advisory Council on Social Security," January 1997. Available at *Social Security Online*, www.ssa.gov/history/reports/adcouncil/report/toc.htm.

21. Interview with a former Republican staffer now working for a conservative think tank conducted by Daniel Béland (Washington, DC, March 2008).

22. Interview with a former Democratic Senate staffer conducted by Daniel Béland (Washington, DC, March 2008).

23. "White House Conference on Social Security," *C-Span*, Live televised event, December 8, 1998.

24. Website of the President's Commission to Strengthen Social Security, http://gov-info.library.unt.edu/csss/index.htm.

25. Interview with a Republican congressional staffer conducted by Daniel Béland (Washington, DC, March 2008).

26. Interview with a former member of the Bush administration conducted by Daniel Béland (Washington, DC, March 2008).

27. Interview with a former member of the Bush administration conducted by Daniel Béland (Washington, DC, March 2008).

28. Interview with a Democratic House staffer conducted by Daniel Béland (Washington, DC, March 2008).

29. The following paragraphs on the "ownership society" draw extensively on Béland and Waddan (2007).

30. For an ideational take on the concept of blueprint, see Blyth (2002).

31. On the social insurance model, see Marmor and Mashaw (2006).

32. For a comparative discussion of the pension reform debate in Britain and in the United States that stresses the role of "popular capitalism," see Teles (1998).

33. "Some Decisions Easier to 'Own,' New Poll Finds." *USA Today*, March 22, 2005.

34. For additional examples, see Bush (2005d, 2005e).

35. Interview with a former member of the Bush administration conducted by Daniel Béland (Washington, DC, March 2008).

36. A Republican congressional staffer told us that she almost "fell off her chair" when she heard the president's November 4 press conference; interview with a Republican congressional staffer conducted by Daniel Béland (Washington, DC, March 2008). Another Republican staffer found the timing of the announcement "surprising"; interview with a Republican congressional staffer conducted by Daniel Béland (Washington DC, February 2008).

37. "Bush Faces Obstacle From Republicans On Social Security," *Wall Street Journal*, December 1, 2004.

38. For a different and highly detailed analysis of the framing processes surrounding the Social Security privatization debate see Asen (2009). On the ideological polarization of the Social Security debate analyzed through a study of congressional hearings, see Svihula and Estes (2007).

39. On these two issues, see Béland (2007b).

40. AARP ad quoted in "AARP's Double Game," *Wall Street Journal*, April 18, A18.

41. Interviews with two former members of the Bush administration conducted by Daniel Béland (Washington, DC, February 2008).

42. We would like to thank one of our interviewees for telling us about this most vivid cartoon.

43. The two following paragraphs draw on Béland and Waddan (2007).
44. In 2003 the Pension Benefit Guaranty Corporation (PBGC) "insured about 29,500 single-employer defined benefit plans, down from an all-time high of 112,000 plans in 1985. This decline primarily reflects a large number of terminations among small plans" (PBGC 2003, 11).
45. This paragraph partly draws on Béland (2007b).
46. "Learn Where Barack Stands on Issues Important to Seniors." Barack Obama campaign website, http://ia.barackobama.com/page/s/IAseniors.
47. The following discussion draws extensively on Béland (2009).
48. "The Issues." John McCain official campaign website. www.johnmccain.com/Informing/Issues/ (website has since been taken down).
49. Interview with a former White House staff conducted by Daniel Béland (Washington, DC, March 2008).
50. On this issue, see Béland (2007b).

Conclusion

This book has explored the politics of policy change in the federal welfare state through the analysis of three major policy episodes and, where relevant, subsequent developments: the 1996 welfare reform, the 2003 Medicare reform, and the 2005 push for Social Security privatization. The analysis presented of these three cases illustrates the main argument of this book, which is that paying systematic attention to ideas is necessary to explain both sharp and incremental policy change. Beyond the claim that "ideas matter," this book has formulated and applied an integrated framework that explains both how and why ideas matter in policy change as well as how ideas can interact with other causal factors, namely institutions and issue ownership, to produce specific types of policy change over time. The analysis of three distinct policy areas and episodes demonstrates the added value of the integrated framework outlined in the introduction while explaining the contrasting ways in which specific social programs located within the same national welfare state can evolve over time.

Assessing Policy Change

In the introduction, we observed that scholars need to define policy change before trying to explain it. For us, policy change is primarily about the consequential alteration of institutional rules and norms, which does not exclude the role of perceptions in change processes. One of the things that make our three cases particularly interesting is that each one illustrates a specific pattern of policy change, a situation that reinforces the worth of our integrated framework as it helps explain why there are different types of policy change.

The 1996 welfare reform is a clear example of sharp and comprehensive path-departing change taking place through legislative revision. Although, like in most cases of policy change, there is some continuity with the past (e.g., the persistence of the "deserving"/"undeserving" poor categories), the introduction of time limits and the decisions to distribute federal monies through block grants profoundly altered the institutional "rules of the game" in the field of social assistance for both beneficiaries and state governments. The 1996 welfare reform effectively ended a major entitlement and replaced it with a program that only offers conditional and limited support to eligible citizens. Even if the 1996 reform was not a complete departure from the past, the actors involved in the reform process clearly judged that something important had happened, and that "welfare as they knew it" had been replaced by a different type of program altogether. The 2005 reauthorization of the TANF program reinforced the logic of the 1996 reform and, by changing the basis on which states count the composition of their welfare population, put increased pressure on the states to move people off TANF regardless of whether those people had the capacity to provide for themselves and their children. Ironically, conservatives who denounced federal "big government" ended up using it to impose their economic and moral ideas upon welfare recipients across the country.[1] Furthermore, despite some extra resources being granted to states as part of ARRA to fund emergency TANF payments in response to the economic downturn from 2008 (Pavetti 2009), there is no evidence of any significant political or ideational challenge to the welfare policy settlement that was reached in 1996.

If it is possible to depict the 1996 welfare reform as a sharp, path-departing reform that reflected an explicit triumph of conservative ideas, the 2003 Medicare reform is an ideologically ambiguous piece of legislation that expanded a popular program while promoting policy mechanisms such as health savings accounts that are consistent with a conservative, promarket, individualistic agenda. Written with the perceived interests of the pharmaceutical industry and private insurance companies in mind, this legislation also created Medicare Part D as an apparent benefit to seniors explicitly supported by the powerful AARP. This points to the complexity of both Medicare as a program and the health care field in general. Considering this, it is possible to describe the 2003 reform as both an expansion of government entitlements and a subtle push to move Medicare further in the direction of a promarket logic. Yet, since some of the Medicare provisions introduced as part of the 2010 health insurance reform reverse a number of changes introduced in 2003, we must always keep in mind that incremental changes can be at least partially reversed over time, especially under new ideological and partisan circumstances. The potentially unstable nature of Medicare policy that resulted from a change in the partisan balance of power was illustrated again in early 2011 when the new Republican majority in the House of Representatives laid out its budget proposals that promoted conservative ideas about health policy reform, including turning Medicaid into a block grant program and changing the Medicare system so that the government would pay money toward a premium for private health coverage rather than reimburse health care providers directly (Pear 2011a). The possible reversal of incremental changes suggests that we cannot assume that specific forms of layering, conversion and policy drift will necessarily keep accumulating over time until they inevitably produce major institutional transformations. A long-term approach to policy change and caution about the alleged cumulative effects of recent incremental changes over time are needed.[2]

At first sight, compared to the legislatively successful 2003 Medicare reform, the case of the 2005 Social Security campaign is completely different because it led to a humiliating defeat for President Bush and his allies. Clearly, as far as public social policy is concerned, little has changed in the institutional rules of Social Security since Ronald Reagan signed the 1983 amendments to the Social Security

Act. Yet it is important to understand Social Security in the context of the rapidly changing field of private pensions, in which incremental yet path-departing change has been taking place since the 1980s (Hacker 2004). With the shift from defined-benefit to defined-contribution plans facilitated in part by federal legislation that has expanded private savings accounts, the world of private pensions and retirement savings is increasingly at odds with the institutional logic of Social Security, a social insurance program that remains grounded in the defined-benefit logic established during the New Deal (Béland 2007b). Thus far, however, in opposition to the expectations of some scholars (e.g., Teles 1998), this shift in the field of occupational pensions and private savings has not tipped the ideological and political balance in favor of privatization advocates. It is not clear that these advocates have a real chance to convince the public and most policymakers to follow their advice in a world where different institutional logics (i.e., defined-benefit and defined-contribution models) can coexist for long periods. For the time being, the failure of the 2005 Bush initiative, combined with rapid changes in private benefits, have exacerbated institutional dualism within the American pension system because the contrast between the defined-benefit federal social insurance program (Social Security) and the defined-contribution model now prevalent in private benefits remains stronger than ever, which suggests that highly different policy instruments can cohabitate within the same institutional environment and, in the case of retirement benefits, the same policy area.

Institutions

Consistent with a key insight from historical institutionalism at the center of our integrated framework, our three case studies confirm the enduring weight of institutional factors in federal politics. First, power fragmentation and the lack of formal party discipline often become direct obstacles to comprehensive reform because they force party leaders to forge loose legislative coalitions that are typically hard to sustain over time. Even when a party controls both Congress and the White House, as the Republicans did during part of the George W. Bush presidency, the lack of formal party discipline in Congress means that party leaders have to struggle to get votes from their own colleagues, which can seriously complicate their reform efforts. This is particularly true in the Senate, where members are elected for six years and often have a political base of their own, beyond their party's. In addition, the use of the filibuster in the Senate has increasingly meant that in some policy areas a de facto majority of sixty votes is required (Wawro and Schickler 2006). Although such institutional features can become opportunities to build bipartisan coalitions that help elected officials share the blame for unpopular measures such as benefit cuts (Pierson and Weaver 1993), when ideological and partisan conflict became widespread as it did during much of the Bill Clinton and George W. Bush presidencies, these opportunities become rare. In its examination of the 1996 welfare reform and the 2003 Medicare reform, this book has investigated two episodes where important policy change was enacted, but in both cases the legislative process was long and complex. The difficulty in enacting legislation, even in a period of unified government, was seen again as the Obama administration struggled to win support for the Affordable Care Act (Béland and Waddan, in press). These institutional obstacles to reform have exacerbated policy drift by making it even harder to enact comprehensive reforms aimed at adapting the federal welfare state to changing social and economic circumstances (Hacker and Pierson, 2010).

Formal political institutions, which are not purely static, as the example of the increasing use of the filibuster shows, form the inescapable background of the three policy cases studied in this book. Even if these institutions typically help explain outcomes, when we consider how they interact with other potential causal factors such as ideas, there is strong evidence that the institutional features of the federal government (in this case the division of power between Congress and the presidency) considerably delayed the enactment of comprehensive welfare reform, even after the "need to reform" (Cox 2001) had been clearly established. In the case of Medicare reform, the White House had to work hard to convince some congressional Republicans to support the legislation in 2003. As far as political institutions are concerned, however, the 2005 attempt to privatize Social Security showed once more that presidents are severely constrained even when their party controls both chambers of Congress. When public opinion and key constituencies turned against President Bush, a number of Republican senators decided not to support his efforts, which killed any chance of legislative success for the White House. This does not mean that political institutions alone explain Bush's humiliating defeat in 2005, or that Social Security reform is more or less impossible because of the separation of powers. Instead, our analysis simply suggests that considering institutions alongside—and in relationship to—other factors such as ideas and issue ownership is often necessary to explain policy outcomes.

Second, like political institutions, existing policy legacies can both constrain and empower actors who seek to alter them. Here it is useful to compare these legacies across policy areas (Pierson 1994). For example, it is clear that the expansion of Social Security during the postwar era created a bolder "army of beneficiaries" with loyalty to the program than was ever the case with AFDC. The latter program disproportionately supported minority women and increasingly from the 1960s onwards faced much gendered and racial stigma. Furthermore, elderly voters have a higher level of political participation than the average population and, according to Andrea Louise Campbell (2003), this situation is related to the very existence of programs such as Medicare and Social Security, which give a good reason for seniors to vote and organize politically. As a feedback effect, greater electoral participation among seniors as well as the role of organizations such as the AARP does send a strong message to conservative politicians who dare attack programs like Medicare and Social Security in a frontal way. Although our analysis suggests that subtle forms of change like the ones adopted as part of the 2003 Medicare reform can help officials alter large social programs without getting punished for it by the electorate, the example of Social Security is a powerful reminder that constituencies shaped at least in part by existing policy legacies play a direct role in the federal politics of welfare state change in the United States.

Mechanisms of Policy Change

Following insight from our integrated framework, the empirical and comparative analysis also suggests that subtle mechanisms of policy change, such as layering, conversion, and policy drift (Hacker 2004; Thelen 2004), are influential in all the three policy areas at stake. Although these mechanisms do not explain policy outcomes on their own, they help describe various patterns of change with greater accuracy while pointing to the incremental strategies actors use to bring about change when they face apparently formidable obstacles such as large constituencies likely to oppose their reform ideas. Our three policy areas illustrate the role of incremental yet potentially transformative forms of change in policy development.

First, in the field of welfare reform, while the 1996 reform represented comprehensive change through sharp legislative revision, it was preceded by the adoption of federal waivers that allowed states to experiment in a way generally consistent with the workfare logic. These waivers represented an implicit form of layering, according to which new policy elements developed alongside the existing AFDC model serving as a Trojan horse for conservative policy change at the federal level. Because of these waivers, conservatives could depict workfare programs enacted in the states as successful models for reform. There is evidence that the policy layering associated with the welfare waivers directly impacted policy outcomes by paving the ideological and institutional road to the 1996 reform (Rogers-Dillon 2004).

Second, in the field of health care the 2003 reform features examples of conversion and layering evidenced by the conservative priorities that made their way into a bill where the headline feature was a major expansion of Medicare, not the promotion of individualistic and promarket forms of health coverage. Clearly, although they were explicitly expanding Medicare, conservatives found low-profile ways to promote market principles and delivery while layering health savings accounts alongside existing public health care programs. Although conservatives did not privatize Medicare in the strict sense of the term, they extended the role of market-friendly mechanisms in the context of a highly complex policy area where distinct and even competing institutional logics have long coexisted (Campbell and Morgan 2011). The complexity of health care as a field where public and private schemes interact in intricate ways, even within the realms of Medicare, clearly leaves much room for policy layering and other forms of incremental, but over time potentially transformative, forms of policy change.

Finally, in the field of Social Security, the attempt to introduce private savings accounts as part of the Social Security program failed. The high level of political visibility of this not-so-subtle form of layering explains why liberals successfully undercut the bold reform efforts of the Bush White House. Nevertheless, in the case of Social Security, the expansion of defined-contribution schemes and the over- all decline of traditional occupational pension plans have exacerbated policy drift (Hacker 2004).

Ideas

Our book shows that, in the challenging institutional context of the American polity, political actors are willing to pursue incremental strategies that, in the long run, can have a strong and even transformative impact on the welfare state. Yet this book also demonstrates that to explain policy change, including incremental change, scholars must pay close attention to the policy ideas of policymakers and the ideological frames they articulate. This claim is a direct challenge to the work of authors such as Kathleen Thelen (2004; Mahoney and Thelen 2009), who tend to neglect ideational processes, which prevents them from truly explaining why policy actors pursue certain strategies and promote particular types of change at specific moments in time. Our three case studies clearly show that turning to ideas helps explain the direction of policy change and the strategies and goals of actors, including when path-departing processes are identified. As suggested, ideas help actors define the problems of the day (Kingdon 1995; Mehta 2011; Stone 1997), articulate the policy alternatives available to address them (Blyth 2002; Hall 1993), and provide the apparent "need to reform" (Cox 2001) existing policy legacies. This is how ideas matter in policy change and why they are an essential compo- nent of social policy reform that can interact with other potential causal factors to explain both patterns and episodes of policy change (Campbell 2004; Padamsee 2009; Parsons 2007). Although ideas may simply legitimize the status quo, they can also help actors imagine alternatives to existing policies they see as ineffec- tive, inappropriate, or inconsistent with their perceived interests (Blyth 2002). Our three cases provide much evidence that turning to ideas helps explain both sharp and incremental policy change. From this perspective, the role of ideas in policy change is not only about sudden paradigm shifts but also about gradual processes that slowly alter both the ideological and the institutional landscapes to produce path-departing change over time.

As far as subtle mechanisms of change are concerned, exploring the ideas of prominent policy actors helps explain why conversion, layering, and policy drift can take a specific, dominant institutional and political direction. For instance, it is impossible to account for the politics of welfare waivers or the layering of per- sonal savings accounts as part of the 2003 Medicare reform without at least refer- ring to the conservative ideas that informed these processes of change. In health care, as in Social Security, private savings accounts are part of a broad conserva-tive ideology that promotes risk taking and personal responsibility at the expense of economic solidarity and social insurance (defined-benefit) security. To help explain why layering takes place, for example, we must systematically trace the ideas that orient and give meaning to such a policy process and strategy. Without doing this, it is much harder to explain why actors want to bring about change in the first place. Although institutional legacies may convince actors to pursue a spe-cific policy change strategy to reach some of their goals, the decision to actually embrace this particular strategy largely stems from ideational processes that help actors make sense of their preferences and their position within their institutional and political environment.

Concerning legislative revision, ideas are crucial because they help make a strong case for the need to explicitly bring about sharp, comprehensive change, notably by denigrating existing policy legacies (Berman 2011) and by proposing a credible policy alternative susceptible to act as a political coalition magnet. Doing this does not mean that reform efforts will succeed, but the creation of policy alter-natives and blueprints is a necessary condition for comprehensive reform (Blyth 2002). In the case of the 1996 welfare reform, conservatives won the political bat-tle at least in part because they successfully pushed Bill Clinton, other Democrats, and large segments of the public to embrace their definition of the problem (wel-fare as *the* problem) and to see workfare as the only possible solution to this prob-lem. In the case of Social Security, massive ideological efforts on the part of the Bush White House and conservative think tanks helped transform privatization into a prominent policy alternative on the federal agenda, but these actors failed to make a winning case for conservative reform largely because the public trusted their Democratic opponents better on this issue, thus demonstrating the relation-ship between the politics of ideas and issue ownership.

Issue Ownership

As our three case studies show, understanding the role of issue ownership (Damore 2004; Petrocik 1996; Ross 2007) sheds light on the role of ideas in policy change because the public discourse of politicians is assessed by the public and specific constituencies in the mirror of their party's track record regarding the specific pro-gram they attempt to transform, abolish, or preserve. But, as argued, for the con-cept of issue ownership to adequately inform the political analysis of policy change, we must adopt a subtle—and largely qualitative—view about how issue owner-ship works. Where American welfare state politics is concerned, issue ownership is a rather complex reality because it is not always obvious who "owns" a specific issue. On one hand, in the case of Social Security, it is clear that people generally trust Democrats more than they trust Republicans to preserve this popular pro-gram, which means that the impact of issue ownership on Social Security reform is relatively straightforward. Republicans are at a clear disadvantage when the time comes to deal with Social Security as an issue (Ross 2007). On the other hand, turning to health care and welfare reform demonstrates that issue ownership is potentially complex and unstable; over time, actors who are most trusted in a specific policy area can lose the advantage in public support they hold. For instance, beyond Medicare, health insurance reform is risky for politicians in general, including Democrats, who must deal with the anxieties of people who already have coverage and are afraid that measures aimed at covering other people could lead to a decline in the care they can currently access. The highly contentious debate over health insurance reform in 2009–10 provides more ground to this claim with some analysts suggesting that the passage of "Obamacare," as opponents derided the ACA, was a significant factor in explaining why Democrats did so badly in the 2010 midterms (Saldin 2010). In the field of welfare reform, the enduring conservative ideological campaign against welfare weakened the Democratic position and image within this policy area by depicting them as permissive liberals who failed to enforce "hard work" and "family values" in American society. Even if welfare reform remained a source of political risks for Republicans, they forced "Third Way" Democrats such as Clinton to recognize explicitly the value of key conservative ideas about work and time limits, which increasingly appeared as "mainstream" ideas by the mid-1990s.

In general, issue ownership is a dynamic process that is largely shaped by the agency and strategies of political actors. But issue ownership is also related to existing institutions and policy legacies; voters can positively associate a party with a concrete policy issue because the party in question is deemed responsible for the existence of a popular program. In the case of Social Security, FDR is widely known as the founder of this popular program. In recent decades Democrats have successfully depicted themselves as the legitimate protectors of Social Security, which their political ancestors initiated during the New Deal. In the case of welfare, being seen as the main force behind the development of the increasingly controversial AFDC program did not necessarily help traditional Democrats retain associated ownership of this policy area. In fact, being tied to a contentious policy legacy made it more difficult for them to sell their welfare reform ideas to the public and other political actors. In 1992 candidate Clinton attempted to offset the increasing electoral disadvantage of his party over welfare as a political issue by very publicly challenging public perception of where his own party stood on the issue and by adopting key conservative ideas. This helped him establish his "New Democrat" identity, but conservatives were unwilling to relinquish this policy domain, particularly after the Republicans captured Congress in the 1994 midterm elections. In the end, President Clinton signed a welfare reform that was considerably more conservative than his initial proposals.

The Integrated Framework and the Role of Ideas

Just as with ideas and institutions, issue ownership on its own does not explain the developments in the three policy areas under consideration in this book. Instead this book shows that several distinct types of factors interacted to produce or prevent policy change—namely, ideational and institutional factors and issue ownership. By drawing analytical lines between these distinct types of causal factors (Parsons 2007), we have shown how they interact over time. For instance, the fact that conservatives successfully redefined welfare as *the* problem (ideational factor), the reality that AFDC had created much weaker constituencies than Medicare and Social Security (institutional factor), and the related decline in the public trust in traditional Democrats who had long been associated with the program (issue ownership) reinforced one another to facilitate the enactment of the 1996 reform. We have explored the interaction of issue ownership, the ideas of actors, and the institutional environment they operate in, which create both obstacles and opportunities for reform. Additionally, we have shown how, taking these factors into account, we can explain the basic direction of policy change mechanisms and strategies such as layering and legislative revision, which actors pursue to promote their ideas in a competitive partisan environment and a fragmented polity where social policy reform is a potentially difficult and risky business for federal politicians of both parties.

Clearly, without paying close attention to ideas, it is impossible to explain the direction of policy change or even the will of concrete actors to introduce or oppose change in the first place. Thus, our integrated framework starts and ends with the role of ideas, which does not prevent us from recognizing that ideas interact with institutions and partisan effects such as issue ownership. It is only by focusing on the ideas and motivations of actors that we can explain why those actors pursue specific types of policy change, including incremental yet potentially transforming strategies. This broad claim contrasts with the lack of ideational focus of the most recent and prominent institutionalist approach to incremental change (Thelen 2004; Mahoney and Thelen 2009). Recognizing that ideas and incremental strategies are closely related not only helps explain the direction and nature of change but also contributes to a perspective on ideational processes that moves us beyond an exclusive focus on "crises" and "paradigm shifts," which is legitimate but too narrow to account for the full range of ideational processes that can impact political behaviors and policy outcomes (Carstensen 2011). Overall, our integrated framework formulates a more subtle and systematic model to explain policy change from both an ideational and an institutionalist perspective.

Because this book has emphasized the importance of ideas in the process of policy change, it is fitting to finish with some brief comments about the overall state of play in the battle of ideas between liberals and conservatives in the United States with regard to social policy. As our three case studies illustrate, there has not been a single, consistent direction of ideational influence, but conservative views promoting individualism and market-oriented reform since the 1980s have been more boldly advanced, even if some of these advances have been rebuffed. Without doubt, conservative ideas triumphed with regard to welfare reform. President Clinton was keen to share credit with Republicans in 1996 when he signed PRWORA, but even moderate liberals who had joined his administration to reform what they perceived to be the flawed AFDC program protested that he had conceded too much ground to conservative advocates (Ellwood 1996).[3] However, conservatives were defeated when they attempted to reorient Social Security, which is a hugely more costly component of the American welfare state than AFDC ever had been. Certainly, if President Bush had succeeded in his effort at Social Security reform in 2005, then his administration would have significantly shifted social policy to the right. The defeat of that reform effort illustrates the institutional resilience of the Social Security program, but in the world of employer-based pensions, policy drift has led to the decline of defined-benefit pensions with new arrangements shifting the risk (i.e., the value of the pension) from employer to employee (Hacker 2004). Furthermore, while the 2005 episode reinforced the image of Social Security as a political "third rail," the program is still subject to debates about the reform that is likely necessary due to long-term fiscal projections that suggest the program's trust fund will eventually be unable to fully meet its obligations. Even though privatization is off the political agenda for the foreseeable future, other types of program retrenchment such as raising the retirement age are on the table.

Fiscal constraints illustrate an important backdrop to debates about social policy development since the 1980s. The era of "permanent austerity" (Pierson 2001) makes it hard for liberals to pursue expansionary social policy initiatives. Interestingly, the costliest expansion of a social policy program in the Clinton and Bush era came during the latter's presidency and at a time when Republicans controlled Congress. Nevertheless, while the 2003 Medicare reform did create a new prescription drug benefit, it also expanded the role of private health insurance in Medicare and promoted the use of more individualized risk in the wider private insurance market through the use of HSAs (Quadagno and McKelvey 2008). And while the federal deficit grew during the Bush presidency, conservatives and Republican members of Congress quickly rediscovered their fiscal probity once Barack Obama entered the White House. The pressure to restrict federal spending in light of the budget deficit is honored more in the breach than in reality, but fiscal constraints are a powerful weapon that conservatives use when constructing the "need to reform" (Cox 2001) social policy programs such as Medicare and Medicaid in line with their ideational preferences.

A major problem for liberals who wish to respond boldly to this conservative critique and revitalize their social policy agenda is that Democrats have become increasingly nervous about funding programs through tax increases, or even opposing tax cuts that significantly reduce government revenues. The major tax cuts enacted in 2001 were a "once-in-a-decade event, a chance to shape the fundamental priorities of government" (Hacker and Pierson 2010, 245). The impact of these tax cuts is illustrated by the fact the projected loss of revenue from these cuts is greater than the projected long-term deficit in the Social Security trust fund (Hacker and Pierson 2005b, 33). Rather than letting these cuts, including the ones benefiting the very wealthiest Americans, expire as scheduled at the end of 2010, the Obama administration agreed to extend them in a deal with congressional Republicans in the lame duck session of Congress following the 2010 midterm elections (Herszenhorn and Stolberg 2010). In exchange, Republicans conceded an extension of the payment of unemployment benefits to the long-term unemployed and a temporary cut in the payroll tax. These were important parts of the administration's economic stimulus agenda, but the overall effect was to leave relatively unchallenged the continuing growth of income inequality in the United States (Bartels 2008).

The most significant counterexample to this narrative of relative conservative triumph was the passage of the Affordable Care Act (ACA) in 2010. In aggregate, this was the most redistributive legislative measure enacted in a generation (Leonhardt 2010), and, if fully implemented, it will bring greater health and economic security to millions of Americans (Jacobs 2011). But even this liberal success, at a time of unified Democratic government in Washington, involved compromise with powerful health care interests that restricted the scope of the reform. Furthermore, the administration's room for maneuver was consistently undercut by the need to demonstrate that the overall reform would save the federal government money. Conservatives have questioned the efficacy of the numbers used by the Democrats (Nix 2010), but even so the need to satisfy the Congressional Budget Office that the ACA would at least nominally reduce the deficit created political difficulties. In particular, it was necessary to propose reductions in the rate of growth of Medicare spending that opponents used to attack the plan. And, importantly, conservatives did not accept the passage of the ACA as a final settlement because Republicans made their rejection of ACA a centerpiece of their campaign for the 2010 elections (Saldin 2010). Then, shortly after assuming their majority in the House of Representatives in January 2011, Republicans in that chamber voted to repeal the ACA. There was not a repeat of this vote in Senate, and President Obama will surely veto any repeal of the measure as long as he remains in office. Nevertheless, this ongoing battle over the ACA illustrates how unstable this liberal reform was even after passage. Overall, the enactment of ACA has not reversed the relative domination of conservative ideas in contemporary federal social policy. In September 2011 the Census Bureau released data on the rise of poverty in the United States since the start of the recession in 2008. In 2010 poverty rate of Americans was 15.1 percent, which was the highest since 1993 (US Census Bureau 2011b, 14). Yet, reflecting how political discussion was framed by the discourse about austerity, debate in Washington, DC, focused on the perceived necessity to reform existing welfare state programs in order to reduce overall government spending (Pear 2011b).

In future research on policy change in the federal welfare state and well beyond, scholars should keep in mind that turning to ideational processes is the best way to explain the direction of policy change and the strategies actors develop in specific institutional and partisan contexts. While doing this, scholars should reject the assumption that paradigm shifts are the only source of ideational change that matters in the policymaking process. Finally, only the careful analysis of the interaction between the ideas of actors, institutional legacies, and partisan effects such as issue ownership can lead to a comprehensive analysis of policy change, which needs to be defined in a systematic manner, something that too many students of public policy fail to do (Capano and Howlett 2009). We hope that our integrated framework will help students of policy develop more insightful empirical analyses in the field of welfare state research and far beyond.

Notes

1. On this issue, see also Béland and Vergniolle de Chantal (2004).
2. On the importance of the analytical time frame in the analysis of institutional and policy change, see Campbell (2004).
3. Two other former advisors on welfare policy to the Clinton administration confirmed in interviews their frustration at Clinton's decision to sign PRWORA (interviews conducted by Alex Waddan, Washington, DC, March 1999 and Boston, April 1999).

References

Aaron, Henry J., and Robert D. Reischauer. 1998. *Countdown to Reform: The Great Social Security Debate.* New York: Century Foundation Press.

Aberbach, Joel. 2005. "The Political Significance of the George W. Bush Administration." *Social Policy and Administration* 39, no. 2: 130–49.

Achenbaum, W. Andrew. 1986. *Social Security: Visions and Revisions.* New York: Cambridge University Press.

Achman, Lori, and Marsha Gold. 2003. "Trends in Medicare+Choice Benefits and Premiums, 1999–2003," *Mathematica Policy Research*, December 19. www .mathematica-mpr.com/publications/PDFs/trends99t003.pdf.

Adams, Rebecca, with Mary Agnes Carey. 2003. "Compromise Will Come Hard." *Congressional Weekly Quarterly*, June 28, p. 1611.

Administration for Children and Families. 2000. "Changes in TANF Caseloads since the Enactment of New Welfare Law." Washington, DC: US Department of Health and Human Services.

Aizenman, Nurith C. 2011. "Republicans, Health Industry Lobbyists Target Medicare Cost-Cutting Board." *Washington Post*, August 12.

Albrekt Larsen, Christian, and Jørgen Goul Andersen. 2009. "How New Economic Ideas Changed the Danish Welfare State: The Case of Neoliberal Ideas and Highly Organized Social Democratic Interests." *Governance* 22, no. 2: 239–61.

Aldrich, J. H., and D. W. Rohde. 1997–98. "The Transition to Republican Rule in the House." *Political Science Quarterly* 112, no. 4: 541–67.

———. 2001. "The Logic of Conditional Party Government: Revisiting the Electoral Connection." In *Congress Reconsidered*, 7th ed., edited by L. C. Dodd and B. L. Oppenheimer, 269–92. Washington, DC: CQ Press.

Altig, David, and Jagadeesh Gokhale. 1997. "Social Security Privatization: One Proposal." *The Cato Project on Social Security Privatization*, no. 9 (May 29). www.cato.org/pubs/ssps/ssp9.html.

Altman, Nancy. 2005. *The Battle for Social Security: From FDR's Vision to Bush's Gamble.* Hoboken, NJ: Wiley.

Altman, Nancy, and Eric Kingson. 2010. "Has Obama Created a Social Security 'Death Panel'?" *Nieman Watchdog*, May 21. www.niemanwatchdog.org/index .cfm?fuseaction=ask_this.view&askthisid=456.

Altmeyer, Arthur J. 1965. *The Formative Years of Social Security.* Madison: Wisconsin University Press.

Amenta, Edwin. 1998. *Bold Relief: Institutional Politics and the Origins of Modern Social Policy.* Princeton, NJ: Princeton University Press.

————. 2006. *When Movements Matter: The Townsend Plan and the Rise of Social Security*. Princeton, NJ: Princeton University Press.

Anderson, Martin. 1978. *Revolution*. New York: Harcourt Press.

Angeles, January. 2010. "Health Reform Changes to Medicare Advantage Strengthen Medicare and Protect Beneficiaries," July 27. *Center on Budget and Policy Priorities*, www.cbpp.org/cms/index.cfm?fa=view&id=3243.

Angeles, January, and Edwin Park. 2009. "Curbing Medicare Advantage Overpayments Could Benefit Millions of Low-Income and Minority Americans," February 19. *Center for Budget and Policy Priorities*, www.cbpp.org/files/2-19-09health.pdf.

Antos, Joseph. 2006. "Will Competition Return to Medicare?" Working Paper Number 125. *American Enterprise Institute*, www.aei.org/docLib/20060207_AEIWP125Antos .pdf.

————. 2007. "Everything You Wanted to Know about Medicare But Were Afraid to Ask." *The American: The Journal of the American Enterprise Institute*, March/April.

————. 2009. "Spending Our Way to Health Care Reform." *San Diego Tribune*, May 5.

apRoberts, Lucy. 2000. *Les retraites aux États-Unis: sécurité sociale et fonds de pension*. Paris: La Dispute.

Arnold, Douglas R. 1998. "The Politics of Reforming Social Security." *Political Science Quarterly* 113, no. 2: 213–40.

Asen, Robert. 2009. *Invoking the Invisible Hand: Social Security and the Privatization Debates*. East Lansing: Michigan State University Press.

Atkinson, Michael M. 2011. "Lindblom's Lament: Incrementalism and the Persistent Pull of the Status Quo." *Policy and Society* 30, no. 1: 9–18.

Attarian, John. 2004. *Social Security: False Consciousness and Crisis*. New Brunswick, NJ: Transaction Publishers.

Baer, Kenneth S. 2000. *Reinventing Democrats: The Politics of Liberalism from Reagan to Clinton*. Lawrence: University of Kansas Press.

Baker, Dean. 2010. "The Bipartisan Attack on Medicare." *American Prospect*, October 11. www.prospect.org/cs/articles?article=the_bipartisan_attack_on_medicare.

Baker, Dean, and Mark Weisbrot. 1999. *Social Security: The Phony Crisis*. Chicago: University of Chicago Press.

Ball, Robert M. 2010. *The Greenspan Commission: What Really Happened*. New York: Century Foundation Press.

Ball, Robert M., and Thomas N. Bethell. 1998. *Straight Talk about Social Security: An Analysis of the Issues in the Current Debate*. New York: Century Foundation/ Twentieth Century Fund.

Bane, Mary Jo. 1992. "Welfare Policy after Welfare Reform." In *Fulfilling America's Promise: Social Policies for the 1990s*, edited by Joseph A. Pechman and M. S. McPherson, 109–28. Ithaca, NY: Cornell University Press.

Bane, Mary Jo, and David Ellwood. 1983. "Slipping Into and Out of Poverty: The Dynamics of Spells." *Journal of Human Resources* 21:1–23.

————. 1994. *Welfare Realities: From Rhetoric to Reform*. Cambridge, MA: Harvard University Press.

Banfield, Edward. 1968. *The Unheavenly City: The Nature and Future of Our Urban Crisis*. Boston: Little, Brown.

Barabas, Jason. 2006. "Rational Exuberance: The Stock Market and Public Support for Social Security Privatization." *Journal of Politics* 68, no. 1: 50–61.

Barnes, Bart. 1998. "Barry Goldwater, GOP Hero, Dies." *Washington Post*, May 30, A1.

Barnes, Fred. 2006. *Rebel-in-Chief: Inside the Bold and Controversial Presidency of George W. Bush*. New York: Crown Forum Barnes.

Barr, Nicholas. 1993. *The Economics of the Welfare State*. Stanford, CA: Stanford University Press.

Bartels, Larry. 2008. *Unequal Democracy: The Political Economy of the New Gilded Age*. Princeton, NJ: Princeton University Press.

Bartlett, Bruce. 2006. *Impostor: How George W. Bush Bankrupted America and Betrayed the Reagan Legacy*. New York: Doubleday.

Baumgartner, Frank R., and Bryan D. Jones. 1993. *Agendas and Instability in American Politics*. Chicago: University of Chicago Press.

Beer, Samuel. 1999. "Welfare Reform: Revolution or Retrenchement." In *Welfare Reform: A Race to the Bottom?*, edited by Sanford Schram and Samuel Beer, 13—19, Washington DC: Woodrow Wilson Center Press.

Béland, Daniel. 2005. Ideas and Social Policy: An Institutionalist Perspective." *Social Policy & Administration* 39, no. 1: 1–18.

———. 2007a. "Ideas and Institutional Change in Social Security." *Social Science Quarterly* 88, no. 1: 20–38.

———. 2007b. *Social Security: History and Politics from the New Deal to the Privatization Debate*, rev. ed. Lawrence: University Press of Kansas.

———. 2007c. *States of Global Insecurity*. New York: Worth Publishers.

———. 2009. "The Great Social Security Debate." *International Journal* 64, no. 1: 115–23.

———. 2010a. "Policy Change and Health Care Research." *Journal of Health Politics, Policy and Law* 35, no. 4: 615–41.

———. 2010b. *What Is Social Policy? Understanding the Welfare State*. Cambridge: Polity Press.

Béland, Daniel, and Robert Henry Cox, eds. 2011. *Ideas and Politics in Social Science Research*. New York: Oxford University Press.

Béland, Daniel, and Brian Gran, eds. 2008. *Public and Private Social Policy: Health and Pensions in a New Era*. Basingstoke, UK: Palgrave Macmillan.

Béland, Daniel, and Jacob S. Hacker. 2004. "Ideas, Private Institutions, and American Welfare State 'Exceptionalism': The Case of Health and Old-Age Insurance in the United States, 1915–1965." *International Journal of Social Welfare* 13, no. 1: 42–54.

Béland, Daniel, and Patrik Marier. 2006. "The Politics of Protest Avoidance: Labor Mobilization and Social Policy Reform in France." *Mobilization* 11, no. 3: 297–311.

Béland, Daniel, and François Vergniolle de Chantal. 2004. "Fighting 'Big Government': Frames, Federalism, and Social Policy Reform in the United States." *Canadian Journal of Sociology* 29, no. 2: 241–64.

Béland, Daniel, Francois Vergniolle de Chantal, and Alex Waddan. 2002. "Third Way Social Policy: Clinton's Legacy?" *Policy and Politics* 30, no. 1: 19–30.

Béland, Daniel, and Alex Waddan. 2000. "From Thatcher (and Pinochet) to Clinton? Conservative Think Tanks, Foreign Models and US pensions reform." *Political Quarterly* 71, no. 1: 202–10.

———. 2006. "The Social Policies Presidents Make: Pre-emptive Leadership under Nixon and Clinton." *Political Studies* 54, no. 1: 65–83.

———. 2007. "Conservative Ideas and Social Policy in the United States." *Social Policy & Administration* 41, no. 7: 768–86.

———. 2010. "The Politics of Social Policy Change: Lessons of the Clinton and Bush Presidencies." *Policy & Politics* 38, no. 2: 217–33.

———. In press. "The Obama Presidency and Health Insurance Reform: Assessing Continuity and Change." *Social Policy and Society.*

Bélanger, Éric. 2003. "Issue Ownership by Canadian Political Parties 1953–2001." *Canadian Journal of Political Science* 36, no. 3: 539–58.

Berenson, Robert. 2007. "Doctoring Health Care, II." *The American Prospect*, January/February, 13–14.

Berkowitz, Edward D. 1983. "The First Social Security Crisis." *Prologue* 15, no. 3: 133–49.

———. 1987. *Disabled Policy: America's Programs for the Handicapped.* New York: Cambridge University Press.

———. 1991. *America's Welfare State: From Roosevelt to Reagan.* Baltimore: John Hopkins University Press.

———. 1995. *Mr. Social Security: The Life of Wilbur J. Cohen.* Lawrence: University of Kansas Press.

———. 1996. "Current Developments in the Welfare State: An International and Historical Perspective." In *Social and Secure? Politics and Culture of the Welfare State: A Comparative Inquiry*, edited by Hans Bak, Frits Van Holthoon, and Hans Krabbendam. 160–72. Amsterdam: VU University Press.

———. 2000. "History and Social Security Reform." In *Social Security and Medicare: Individual vs. Collective Risk and Responsibility*, edited by Eric Kingdon, Sheila Burke, and Uwe Reinhardt, 31–55. Washington, DC: Brookings Institution Press.

———. 2003. *Robert Ball and the Politics of Social Security.* Madison: University of Wisconsin Press.

Berkowitz, Edward D., and Kim McQuaid. 1980. *Creating the Welfare State: The Political Economy of Twentieth-Century Reform.* Westport, CT: Praeger.

Berman, Sheri. 2006. *The Primacy of Politics: Social Democracy and the Ideological Dynamics of the Twentieth Century.* New York: Cambridge University Press.

———. 2011. "Ideational Theorizing in Political Science: The Evolution of the Field since Peter Hall's 'Policy Paradigms, Social Learning and the State.'" Paper presented at the Symposium on Policy Paradigms and Social Learning, February 11. Boston: Suffolk University Law School.

Bernstein, Blanche, Douglas J. Besharov, Barbara Blum, Allan Carlson, John Cogan, Leslie Lenkowsky, Lawrence Mead, et al. 1987. *A Community of Self-Reliance:*

The New Consensus on Family and Welfare. Washington, DC: American Enterprise Institute for Public Policy Research.

Bhatia, Vandna. 2010. "Social Rights, Civil Rights, and Health Reform in Canada." *Governance* 23, no. 1: 37–58.

Bhatia, Vandna, and William D. Coleman. 2003. "Ideas and Discourse: Reform and Resistance in the Canadian and German Health Systems." *Canadian Journal of Political Science* 36, no. 4: 715–39.

Bickerstaff, Steve. 2007. *Lines in the Sand: Congressional Redistricting in Texas and the Downfall of Tom DeLay.* Austin: University of Texas Press.

Binder, Sarah. 1999. "The Dynamics of Legislative Gridlock." *American Political Science Review* 93:519–34.

Birnbaum, Jeffrey H. 2005. "For Labor Unions, Social Security Is a Matter of Clout." *Washington Post*, May 16, E1.

Blackburn, Robin. 2002. *Banking on Death: Or Investing in Life: The History and Future of Pensions.* London: Verso.

———. 2004. "How Monica Lewinsky Saved Social Security." In *Dime's Worth of Difference*, edited by Alexander Cockburn and Jeffrey St. Clair, 31–60. Oakland: AK Press.

Blank, Rebecca M. 2002. *Evaluating Welfare Reform in the United States*, National Bureau of Economic Research Working Paper 8983. Cambridge, MA: National Bureau of Economic Research.

Bleich, Erik. 2002. "Integrating Ideas into Policy-Making Analysis: Frames and Race Policies in Britain and France." *Comparative Political Studies* 35, no. 9: 1054–76.

Blyth, Mark. 2002. *Great Transformations: Economic Ideas and Institutional Change in the Twentieth Century.* Cambridge: Cambridge University Press.

Board of Trustees. 2010. *The 2010 Annual Report of the Board of Trustees of the Federal Old-Age and Survivors Insurance and Federal Disability Insurance Trust Funds.* Washington, DC: US Government Printing Office.

Bonoli, Giuliano. 2000. *The Politics of Pension Reform: Institutions and Policy Change in Western Europe.* Cambridge: Cambridge University Press.

Book, Robert, and James Capretta. 2010. "Reductions in Medicare Advantage Payments: The Impact on Seniors by Region," Backgrounder No. 2464, September 14, *The Heritage Foundation*, www.heritage.org/research/reports/2010/09/reductions-in-medicare-advantage-payments-the-impact-on-seniors-by-region.

Bowler, M. K. 1974. *The Nixon Guaranteed Income Proposal: Substance and Process in Policy Change.* Cambridge, MA: Ballinger.

Bowman, Karlyn H. 2005. "Attitudes about Social Security Reform," *AEI Studies in Public Opinion* (American Enterprise Institute), August 2, www.aei.org/paper/14884.

Boychuk, Gerard. 2008. *National Health Insurance in the United States and Canada Race, Territory, and the Roots of Difference.* Washington, DC: Georgetown University Press.

Bradley, Katherine, and Robert Rector. 2010. "How President Obama's Budget Will Demolish Welfare Reform." *Heritage Foundation*, WebMemo No. 2819, February 25, http://thf_media.s3.amazonaws.com/2010/pdf/wm2819.pdf.

Brain, Charles M. 1991. *Social Security at the Crossroads: Public Opinion and Public Policy*. New York: Garland Publishing.

Breeden, Richard. 2003. "Ownership Values." *Wall Street Journal*, November 18, B4.

Brooks, Clem, and Jeff Manza. 2007. *Why Welfare States Persist: The Importance of Public Opinion in Democracies*. Chicago: University of Chicago Press.

Brown, Lawrence D. 2005. "Incrementalism Adds Up?" In *Healthy Wealthy and Fair: Health Care and the Good Society*, edited by James Morone and Lawrence Jacobs, 315–36. New York: Oxford University Press.

———. 2010. "Pedestrian Paths: Why Path-Dependence Theory Leaves Health Policy Analysis Lost in Space." *Journal of Health Politics, Policy and Law* 35, no. 4: 643–61.

Brown, Lawrence D., and Michael S. Sparer. 2003. "Poor Program's Progress: The Unanticipated Politics of Medicaid Policy." *Health Affairs* 22, no. 1: 31–44.

Brown, Lawrence D., Michael S. Sparer, Lorraine Frisina, and Mirella Cacace, eds. 2010. "Beyond Path Dependency: Explaining Health Care System Change." Special Issue of the *Journal of Health Politics, Policy, and Law* 35(4): 449–688.

Bruni, Frank. 2000. "Bush Campaign Turns Attention to Middle Class." *New York Times*, September 18.

———. 2001. "Bush Pushes Role of Private Sector in Aiding the Poor." *New York Times*, May 21.

Bumiller, Elizabeth. 2002. "Bush Promotes Changes in Welfare Rules and a Senator's Re-election Bid in Arkansas." *New York Times*, June 4.

Burke, Vincent J., and Vee Burke. 1974. *Nixon's Good Deed: Welfare Reform*. New York: Columbia University Press.

Bush, George H. W. 1989. Inaugural Address, January 20. Nationalcenter.org. www .nationalcenter.org/BushInaugural.html.

Bush, George W. 2000. "Governor Bush Delivers Remarks at the Republican National Convention." *Enter Stage Right*, www.enterstageright.com/archive /articles/0800bushaccept.htm.

———. 2001a. "Address of the President to the Joint Session of Congress." Washington, DC: The White House (Office of the Press Secretary), February 27.

———. 2001b. "Remarks by the President in Social Security Announcement," Washington, DC: The White House (Office of the Press Secretary), May 2.

———. 2003. "Remarks by the President at Signing of the Medicare Prescription Drug Improvement and Modernization Act of 2003." Washington, DC: The White House (Office of the Press Secretary), December 8.

———. 2004a. "President Holds a Press Conference." Washington, DC: The White House (Office of the Press Secretary), November 4.

———. 2004b. "State of the Union Address." Washington, DC: The White House (Office of the Press Secretary), January 20.

———. 2005a. "President Attends 2005 President's Dinner." Washington, DC: The White House (Office of the Press Secretary), June 14.

———. 2005b. "President Discusses Strengthening Social Security in Florida." Washington, DC: The White House (Office of the Press Secretary), February 4.

——. 2005c. "Press Conference of the President." Washington, DC: The White House (Office of the Press Secretary), April 28.

——. 2005d. "Speech to Social Security Conversation in New York," (Greece, NY). Washington, DC: The White House (Office of the Press Secretary), May 24.

——. 2005e. "Speech on Strengthening Social Security for Younger Workers," (Milwaukee). Washington, DC: The White House (Office of the Press Secretary), May 19.

——. 2005f. "State of the Union Address." Washington, DC: The White House (Office of the Press Secretary), February 2.

——. 2007. "President's Radio Address," January 20. Available at http://georgewbush-whitehouse.archives.gov/rss/radioaddress.xml.

——. 2010. *Decision Points*. New York: Crown Publishers.

Butler, Stuart, and Peter Germanis. 1983. "Achieving a 'Leninist' Strategy." *Cato Journal* 3, no. 2: 547–61.

Califano, Joseph A., Jr. 1981. *Governing America: An Insider's Report from the White House and Cabinet*. New York: Simon and Schuster.

Calmes, Jackie. 2005. "'Free Lunchers' Take on the 'Pain Caucus.'" *The Wall Street Journal*, May 31.

——. 2011. "A Conservative Vision, with Bipartisan Risks." *New York Times*, April 5.

Campbell, Andrea Louise. 2003. *How Policies Make Citizens: Senior Political Activism and the American Welfare State*. Princeton, NJ: Princeton University Press.

Campbell, Andrea Louise, and Kimberly J. Morgan. 2005. "Financing the Welfare State: Elite Politics and the Decline of the Social Insurance Model in America." *Studies in American Political Development* 19 (Fall): 173–95.

——. 2011. *The Delegated Welfare State: Medicare, Markets and the Governance of Social Policy*. New York: Oxford University Press.

Campbell, John L. 1998. "Institutional Analysis and the Role of Ideas in Political Economy." *Theory and Society* 27:377–409.

——. 2004. *Institutional Change and Globalization*. Princeton, NJ: Princeton University Press.

Cannon, Michael, and Michael Tanner. 2007. *Healthy Competition: What's Holding Back Health Care and How to Free It*. Washington, DC: Cato Institute.

Capano, Giliberto. 2009. "Understanding Policy Change as an Epistemological and Theoretical Problem." *Journal of Comparative Policy Analysis* 11, no. 1: 7–31.

Capano, Giliberto, and Michael Howlett. 2009. "Introduction: The Determinants of Policy Change: Advancing the Debate." *Journal of Comparative Policy Analysis* 11, no. 1: 1–5.

Carey, Mary Agnes. 2000. "Bush's Medicare Drug Plan." *Congressional Quarterly Weekly*, September 9, p. 2084.

——. 2003. "GOP Wins Battle, Not War." *Congressional Quarterly Weekly*, November 29, p. 2956.

——. 2005. "Lott Laments His Medicare Vote." *Congressional Quarterly Weekly*, March 27, p. 726.

Carstensen, Martin B. 2011. "Paradigm Man vs. the Bricoleur: Bricolage as an Alternative Vision of Agency in Ideational Change." *European Political Science Review* 3, no. 1: 147–67.

Carter, Jimmy. 1978. "Social Security Amendments of 1977 (December 20, 1977)." In *Public Papers of the Presidents of the United States: Jimmy Carter*, vol. 1. Washington, DC: United States Government Printing Office.

Cates, Jerry R. 1983. *Insuring Inequality: Administrative Leadership in Social Security, 1935–1954.* Ann Arbor: University of Michigan Press.

Century Foundation. 2001. *Medicare Reform: A Century Foundation Guide to the Issues.* New York: Century Foundation Press.

Charter, David. 2005. "Which Tory Mother Has the White House in Her Grip?" *London Times*, February 17.

Clasen, Jochen, and Nico A. Siegel. 2007. "Comparative Welfare State Analysis and the 'Dependent Variable Problem.'" In *Investigating Welfare State Change: The 'Dependent Variable Problem' in Comparative Analysis*, edited Jochen Clasen and Nico A. Siegel, 3–12. Cheltenham, UK: Edward Elgar.

Clemens, Elisabeth S., and James M. Cook. 1999. "Politics and Institutionalism: Explaining Durability and Change." *Annual Review of Sociology* 25:441–66.

Clinton, William J. 1998. "State of the Union Address." Washington, DC: The White House (Office of the Press Secretary), January 27.

———. 1999. "State of the Union Address." Washington, DC: The White House (Office of the Press Secretary), January 19. Available at www.cnn.com/ALLPOLITICS /stories/1999/01/19/sotu.transcript/.

———. 2004. *My Life.* London: Hutchinson.

———. 2006. "How We Ended Welfare, Together." *New York Times*, August 22.

Clinton, Hillary. 2002. "Senator Clinton on Welfare Reform." *New York Times*, May 16, letter to the editor.

———. 2003. *Living History*, updated ed. London: Headline Publishing.

Clinton, Hillary, and Joe Lieberman. 2002. "Welfare Backsliding." *Washington Post*, May 3

Clinton, William J., and Al Gore. 1992. *Putting People First: A Strategy for Change.* New York: Times Books..

Clymer, Adam. 1996. "Politics: The Message: Clinton Will Limit Those on Welfare to 2 Years of Aid." *New York Times*, July 17.

———. 2000. "Two Democrats Fire Broadsides in Testy Debate." *New York Times*, January 27.

Cohn, Jonathon. 2005. "Crash Course: The Danger of Consumer Driven Health Care." *New Republic Online*, November 7, www.tnr.com/article/politics /crash-course.

Commission on Presidential Debates. 2000. "The First Gore-Bush Presidential Debate: Unofficial Debate Transcript," October 3. *Debates.org*, www.debates.org /index.php?page=october-3-2000-transcript.

———. 2004. "The Third Bush-Kerry Presidential Debate: Debate Transcript," October 13. *Debates.org*, www.debates.org/index.php?page=october-13-2004-debate-transcript.

Congressional Budget Office (CBO). 1988. "The Medicare Catastrophic Coverage Act of 1988," Staff Working Paper, October. Washington, DC: Congressional Budget Office.

———. 2005a. "Global Population Aging in the 21st Century and Its Economic Implications." Washington, DC: Congressional Budget Office. www.cbo.gov /ftpdocs/69xx/doc6952/12-12-Global.pdf.

———. 2005b. "Long Term Budget Outlook." Washington, DC: Congressional Budget Office. www.cbo.gov/ftpdocs/69xx/doc6982/12-15-LongTermOutlook.pdf.

Congressional Quarterly Weekly Report. 1972a. Democratic Party Platform, 1972, *Congressional Quarterly Weekly Report*, July 15, p. 1727.

———. 1972b. Republican Party Platform, 1972, *Congressional Quarterly Weekly Report*, August 26, p. 2160–61.

Cook, Fay Lomax, Jason Barabas, and Benjamin I. Page. 2002. "Invoking Public Opinion: Policy Elites and Social Security." *Public Opinion Quarterly* 66, no. 2: 235–64.

Cook, Fay Lomax, and Edith J. Barrett. 1992. *Support for the American Welfare State*. New York: Columbia University Press.

Cook, R. 1992. "Arkansan Travels Well Nationally as Campaign Heads for Test." *Congressional Quarterly Weekly Report*, December 10, p. 3516.

Cooper, Christopher, and Jackie Calmes. 2004. "Bush Seeks Bipartisan Backing For His Social Security Plan; Democrats, Interest Groups Mobilize against the Cost of Transition, New Accounts." *Wall Street Journal*, December 17, A2.

Cox, Robert Henry. 2001. "The Social Construction of an Imperative: Why Welfare Reform Happened in Denmark and the Netherlands but Not in Germany." *World Politics* 53:463–98.

D'Angelo, Greg, and Robert Moffit. 2006. "Building on the Success of Health Savings Accounts," *The Heritage Foundation*, WebMemo No. 1239, October 20, www.heritage.org/research/reports/2006/10/building-on-the-successes-of-health-savings-accounts.

Daguerre, Anne. 2008. "The Second Phase of US Welfare Reform, 2000–2006: Blaming the Poor Again?" *Social Policy and Administration* 42, no. 4: 362–78.

Damore, David F. 2004. "The Dynamics of Issue Ownership in Presidential Campaigns." *Political Research Quarterly* 57, no. 3: 391–97.

Danziger, Sheldon, and Peter Gottschalk. 1985. *America Unequal*. New York: Russell Sage Foundation.

Davies, Gareth. 1996. *From Opportunity to Entitlement: The Transformation and Decline of Great Society Liberalism*. Lawrence: University of Kansas Press.

———. 2003. "The Welfare State." In *The Reagan Presidency: Pragmatic Conservatism and Its Legacies*, edited by W. Elliot Brownlee and Hugh Davis Graham, 209–32. Lawrence: University of Kansas Press.

DeParle, Jason. 1996. "Rant, Listen, Exploit, Learn, Scare, Help, Manipulate, Lead." *New York Times Sunday Magazine*, January 28.

———. 2004. *American Dream: Three Women, Ten Kids and a Nation's Drive to End Welfare*. New York: Penguin Books.

DeParle, Nancy-Anne. 2002. "As Good as It Gets? The Future of Medicare+Choice." *Journal of Health Politics, Policy and Law* 27, no. 3: 495–512.

Derthick, Martha. 1979. *Policymaking for Social Security*. Washington, DC: Brookings Institution.

———. 2001. "The Evolving Old Politics of Social Security." In *Seeking the Center: Politics and Policymaking at the New Century*, edited by Martin A. Levin, Marc K. Landy, and Martin Shapiro, 193–214. Washington, DC: Georgetown University Press.

Derthick, Martha, and Steven Teles. 2003. "Riding the Third Rail: Social Security Reform." In *The Reagan Presidency: Pragmatic Conservatism and Its Legacies*, edited by W. Elliot Brownlee and Hugh Davis Graham, 182–232. Lawrence: University Press of Kansas.

Dewar, Helen 2003. "Both Parties Face Huge Risks in Prescription Drug Bill Fight." *Washington Post*, June 11, A6.

DeWitt, Larry, Daniel Béland, and Edward D. Berkowitz. 2007. *Social Security: A Documentary History*. Washington, DC: Congressional Quarterly Press.

Diamond, Peter A., and Peter R. Orszag. 2002. "Reducing Benefits and Subsidizing Individual Accounts: An Analysis of the Plans Proposed by the President's Commission to Strengthen Social Security," July. *Center on Budget and Policy Priorities and the Century Foundation*, http://tcf.org/publications/pdfs/pb409/Diamond_Orszag.pdf.

———. 2003. *Saving Social Security: A Balanced Approach*. Washington, DC: Brookings Institution Press.

Dionne, E. J. 2006. "Rove's New Mission: Survival." *Washington Post*, April 21, A23.

Dobbin, Frank. 1994. *Forging Industrial Policy: The United States, Britain, and France in the Railway Age*. Cambridge: Cambridge University Press.

Douthat, Ross. 2009. "Telling Grandma 'No.'" *New York Times*, August 17.

Draper, R. 2007. *Dead Certain: The Presidency of George W. Bush*. New York: Free Press.

Drew, Elizabeth. 1997. *Showdown: The Struggle between the Gingrich Congress and the Clinton White House*. New York: Simon and Schuster.

Dreyfuss, Barbara T. 2004. "Cheap Trick." *American Prospect*, September 26, http://prospect.org/cs/articles?articleId=8345.

Edelman, Peter. 1997. "The Worst Thing Bill Clinton Has Done." *Atlantic Monthly*, March, 43–58.

Edin, Kathryn, and Laura Lein. 1997. *Making Ends Meet: How Single Mothers Survive Welfare and Low Wage Work*. New York: Russell Sage Foundation.

Edwards, George C., III. 2007. *Governing by Campaigning: The Politics of the Bush Presidency*. New York: Pearson Longman.

Egan, Patrick. 2006. "Issue Ownership and Representation." Working paper. Berkeley, CA: Institute of Governmental Studies, UC Berkeley.

Ellwood, David. 1988. *Poor Support: Poverty in the American Family*. New York: Basic Books.

———. 1996. "Welfare Reform as I Knew It." *American Prospect* 26:22–29.

Emery, J. C. Herbert. 2010. "'Un-American' or Unnecessary? America's Rejection of Compulsory Government Health Insurance in the Progressive Era." *Explorations in Economic History* 47, no. 1: 68–81.

Employee Benefit Research Institute. 2008. "HSAs Play Minor Part in Saving for Retiree Medical Expenses." *EBRI News*, August 7, www.ebri.org/pdf/PR_810_07Aug08.pdf.

Erskine, H. 1975. "The Polls: Government Role in Welfare." *Public Opinion Quarterly* 39, no. 2: 257–74.

Espo, David. 2008. "Candidates' Social Security Plans Lack Details." *USA Today*, October 18, www.usatoday.com/news/topstories/2008-10-18-269568608_x.htm.

———. 2010. "Reid Struggles against Bad Economy, GOP Rival." *Washington Post*, October 19.

Feldman, Stanley, and J. Zaller. 1992. "The Political Culture of Ambivalence: Ideological Responses to the Welfare State." *American Journal of Political Science* 36 (February): 268–307.

Ferrara, Peter J. 1980. *Social Security: The Inherent Contradiction*. San Francisco: Cato Institute.

Ferrara, Peter J., and Michael D. Tanner. 1998. *Common Cents, Common Dreams: A Layman's Guide to Social Security Privatization*. Washington, DC: Cato Institute.

Field, M. 1978. "Sending a Message: Californians Strike Back." *Public Opinion* 1, no. 3: 3–8.

Fischer, Frank. 2003. *Reframing Public Policy: Discursive Politics and Deliberative Practices*. Oxford: Oxford University Press.

Fleisher, R., and J. R. Bond. 2004. "The Shrinking Middle in the US Congress." *British Journal of Political Science* 34, no. 3: 429–51.

Fox, S. 1969. "Rockefeller Calls Nixon's Proposal Unfair to State." *New York Times*, August 11, 1.

Fraser, Nancy, and Linda Gordon. 1992. "Contract versus Charity: Why Is There No Social Citizenship in the United States?" *Socialist Review* 22 (July): 45–68.

———. 1994. "'Dependency' Demystified: Inscriptions of Power in a Keyword of the Welfare State." *Social Politics* 1, no. 1: 4–31.

Freeden, Michael. 2003. *Ideology: A Very Short Introduction*. Oxford: Oxford University Press.

Friedman, Milton. 1962. *Capitalism and Freedom*. Chicago: University of Chicago Press.

Fronstin, Paul. 2004. "Health Savings Accounts and Other Account Based Health Plans." *EBRI Issue Brief*, No. 273 (September). Employee Benefit Research Institute, www.ebri.org/publications/ib/index.cfm?fa=ibDisp&content_id=3504.

Galbraith, John K. 1958. *The Affluent Society*. Boston: Houghton Mifflin.

Galston, William A. 2007. "Why President Bush's 2005 Social Security Initiative Failed, and What It Means for the Future of the Program," Research Brief No 1. New York: John Brademas Center for the Study of Congress, New York University.

Garfinkel, Irvin, and Sarah S. McLanahan. 1986. *Single Mothers and Their Children: A New American Dilemma*. Washington, DC: Urban Institute Press.

Gavrilov, Leonid A., and Patrick Heuveline. 2003. "Aging of Population." In *The Encyclopedia of Population*, edited by Paul Demeny and Geoffrey McNicoll, 32–37. New York: Macmillan Reference.

Genieys, William, and Mark Smyrl, eds. 2008. *Elites, Ideas, and the Evolution of Public Policy*. Basingstoke, UK: Palgrave.

Ghilarducci, Teresa. 2008. *When I'm Sixty-Four: The Plot against Pensions and the Plan to Save Them*. Princeton, NJ: Princeton University Press.

Gibson, James Edward III. 2007. "The Last Council: Social Security Policymaking as Coalitional Consensus and the 1994–1996 Advisory Council as Institutional Turning Point." PhD diss., Virginia Tech.

Gilbert, Neil. 2002. *Transformation of the Welfare State: The Silent Surrender of Public Responsibility*. New York: Oxford University Press.

———. 2009. "US Welfare Reform: Rewriting the Social Contract." *Journal of Social Policy* 38, no. 3: 383–99.

Gilbert, Neil, and Barbara Gilbert. 1989. *The Enabling State: Modem Welfare Capitalism in America*. New York: Oxford University Press.

Gilder, George. 1981. *Wealth and Poverty*. New York: Basic Books.

Gilens, Martin. 1996. "Race Coding and White Opposition to Welfare." *American Political Science Review* 90, no. 3: 593–604.

———. 1999. *Why Americans Hate Welfare: Race, Media and the Politics of Antipoverty Policy*. Chicago: University of Chicago Press.

Gillon, Steven M. 2008. *The Pact: Bill Clinton, Newt Gingrich, and the Rivalry that Defined a Generation*. New York: Oxford University Press.

Gingrich, Newt, and John Goodman. 2010. "Ten GOP Health Ideas for Obama." *Wall Street Journal*, February 10.

Ginsburg, N. 1989. *Race and the Media: The Enduring Life of the Moynihan Report*. New York: Institute for Media Analysis.

Gitterman, Daniel, and John Scott. 2011. "'Obama Lies, Grandma Dies': The Uncertain Politics of Medicare and the Patient Protection and Affordable Care Act." *Journal of Health Policy, Politics and Law* 36, no. 3: 555–63.

Glassman, James K. 1998. "Uncle Sam on Wall Street? No." *Washington Post*, December 8, A21.

Glenn, Brian J., and Steven M. Teles, eds. 2009. *Conservatism and American Political Development*. New York: Oxford University Press.

Gofas, Andreas, and Colin Hay, eds. 2010. *The Role of Ideas in Political Analysis: A Portrait of Contemporary Debates*. London: Routledge.

Gold, Marsha. 2001. "Medicare+Choice: An Interim Report Card." *Health Affairs* 20, no. 4: 120–38.

Goldstein, Amy. 1999. "Impasse Over Medicare Reform Looks Likely." *Washington Post*, February 25, A12.

Goldstein, Judith, and Robert O. Keohane, eds. 1993. "Ideas and Foreign Policy: An Analytical Framework." In *Ideas and Foreign Policy: Beliefs, Institutions, and Political Change*, 3–30. Ithaca, NY: Cornell University Press.

Goldwater, Barry. 1960. *The Conscience of a Conservative*. Shepherdsville, KY: Victor Publishing.

Goodman, Peter. 2008. "From Welfare Shift in '96: A Reminder for Clinton." *New York Times*, April 11.

———. 2010. "Cuts to Child Care Subsidy Thwart More Job Seekers." *New York Times*, May 23.

Gordon, Colin. 1997. "Why No Health Insurance in the US? The Limits of Social Provision in War and Peace, 1941–1948." *Journal of Policy History* 9, no. 3: 277–310.

Gordon, Linda. 1994. *Pitied but Not Entitled: Single Mothers and the History of Welfare*. New York: Free Press.

Gottschalk, Marie. 2000. *The Shadow Welfare State: Labor, Business, and the Politics of Health Care in the United States*. Ithaca, NY: Cornell University Press.

Greenberg, Stanley. 1995. *Middle Class Dreams: The Politics and Power of the New American Majority*. New Haven, CT: Yale University Press.

Greenspan Commission. 1983. "Report of the National Commission on Social Security Reform." *SocialSecurity.gov*, www.ssa.gov/history/reports/gspan.html.

Grogan, Colleen, and Eric Patashnik. 2005. "Medicaid at the Crossroads." In *Healthy Wealthy and Fair: Health Care and the Good Society*, edited by James Morone and Lawrence Jacobs, 267–96. New York: Oxford University Press.

Gueron, Judith M. 1996. "A Research Context for Welfare Reform." *Journal of Policy Analysis and Management* 15, no. 4: 547–61.

Hacker, Jacob S. 1996. "National Health Care Reform: An Idea Whose Time Came and Went." *Journal of Health Policy, Politics and Law* 21:647–96.

———. 1997. *The Road to Nowhere: The Genesis of President Clinton's Plan for Health Security*. Princeton, NJ: Princeton University Press.

———. 1998. "The Historical Logic of National Health Insurance: Structure and Sequence in the Development of British, Canadian, and US Medical Policy." *Studies in American Political Development* 12:57–130.

———. 2002. *The Divided Welfare State: The Battle over Public and Private Social Benefits in the United States*. New York: Cambridge University Press.

———. 2004. "Privatizing Risk without Privatizing the Welfare State: The Hidden Politics of Welfare State Retrenchment in the United States." *American Political Science Review* 98:243–60.

———. 2006. *The Great Risk Shift; The Assault on American Jobs, Families, Health Care, and Retirement and How You Can Fight Back*. New York: Oxford University Press.

———. 2010. "The Road to Somewhere: Why Health Reform Happened, or Why Political Scientists Who Write about Public Policy Shouldn't Assume They Know How to Shape It." *Perspectives on Politics* 8, no. 3: 861–76.

Hacker, Jacob S., and Paul Pierson. 2002. "Business Power and Social Policy: Employers and the Formation of the American Welfare State." *Politics and Society* 30, no. 2: 277–325.

———. 2005a. "Abandoning the Middle: The Bush Tax Cuts and the Limits of Democratic Control." *Perspectives on Politics* 3, no. 1: 33–54.

———. 2005b. *Off Center: The Republican Revolution and the Erosion of American Democracy*. New Haven, CT: Yale University Press.

———. 2010. *Winner-Take-All Politics. How Washington Made the Rich Richer—And Turned Its Back on the Middle Class*. New York: Simon & Schuster.

Hager, G. 1995. "Harsh Rhetoric on Budget Spells a Dismal Outlook." *Congressional Quarterly Weekly Report*, December 9, pp. 3721–25.

Halbfinger, David M. 2004. "Campaigning Furiously, with Social Security in Tow." *New York Times*, October 18.

Hale, Jon. 1995. "The Making of the New Democrats." *Political Science Quarterly* 110, no. 2: 207–32.

Hall, Peter A. 1993. "Policy Paradigms, Social Learning and the State: The Case of Economic Policymaking in Britain." *Comparative Politics* 25, no. 3: 275–96.

Hall, Peter A., and Rosemary C. R. Taylor. 1996. "Political Science and the Three Institutionalisms." *Political Studies* 44, no. 5: 936–57.

Handler, Joel F., and Yeheskel Hasenfeld. 1997. *We the Poor People: Work, Poverty and Welfare*. New Haven, CT: Yale University Press.

———. 2007. *Blame Welfare: Ignore Poverty and Inequality*. New York: Cambridge University Press.

Hansen, Randall, and Desmond King. 2001. "Eugenic Ideas, Political Interests, and Policy Variance: Immigration and Sterilization Policy in Britain and the US." *World Politics* 53, no. 2: 237–63.

Harrington, Michael. 1962. *The Other America: Poverty in the United States*. New York: MacMillan.

Harris, Gardner. 2009. "A Heated Debate Is Dividing Generations in AARP." *New York Times*, October 4.

Haskins, Ron. 1991. "Congress Writes a Law: Research and Welfare Reform." *Journal of Policy Analysis and Management* 10, no. 4: 616–32.

———. 2006. *Work over Welfare: The Inside Story of the 196 Welfare Reform Law*. Washington, DC: Brookings Institution Press.

Haskins, Ron, and Isabel Sawhill. 2009. *Creating an Opportunity Society*. Washington, DC: Brookings Institution Press.

Haskins, Ron, Isabel Sawhill, and Kent Weaver. 2001. *Welfare Reform: An Overview of Effects to Date*. Washington, DC: Brookings Institution Press.

Hattam, Victoria C. 1993. *Labor Visions and State Power: The Origins of Business Unionism in the United States*. Princeton, NJ: Princeton University Press.

Hay, Colin. 2011. "Ideas and the Construction of Interests." In *Ideas and Politics in Social Science Research*, edited by Daniel Béland and Robert Henry Cox, 65–82. New York: Oxford University Press.

Hay, Colin, and Daniel Wincott. 1998. "Structure, Agency and Historical Institutionalism." *Political Studies* 46, no. 5: 951–57.

Hayes, M. T. 2001. *The Limits of Policy Change: Incrementalism, World View and the Rule of Law.* Washington, DC: Georgetown University Press.

Heclo, Hugh. 1974. *Modern Social Politics in Britain and Sweden: From Relief to Income Maintenance.* New Haven, CT: Yale University Press.

———. 2001. "The Politics of Welfare Reform." In *The New World of Welfare*, edited by Rebecca Blank and Ron Haskins, 169–200. Washington, DC: Brookings Institution Press.

Hernandez, Raymond. 2002. "With a Step Right, Senator Clinton Agitates the Left." *New York Times*, May 22.

Herszenhorn, David, and Sheryl Stolberg. 2010. "Obama Defends Tax Deal, but His Party Stays Hostile." *New York Times*, December 7.

Himelfarb, Richard. 1995. *Catastrophic Politics: The Rise and Fall of the Medicare Catastrophic Coverage Act of 1988.* University Park: Pennsylvania State University Press.

Himmelfarb, Gertrude. 1984. *The Idea of Poverty: England in the Early Industrial Ages.* New York: Knopf.

Hinrichs, Karl, and Olli Kangas. 2003. "When Is a Change Big Enough to Be a System Shift? Small System-shifting Changes in German and Finnish Pension Policies." *Social Policy & Administration* 37, no. 6: 573–91.

House Republican Conference and Senate Republican Conference. 2005. "Saving Social Security: A Guide to Social Security Reform." Washington, DC, January 27. Available at Northwest Labor Press website, www.nwlaborpress.org/2005/GOPSSStrategy.pdf.

Howard, Christopher. 1997. *The Hidden Welfare State: Tax Expenditures and Social Policy in the United States.* Princeton, NJ: Princeton University Press.

———. 2006. *The Welfare State Nobody Knows: Debunking Myths about US Social Policy.* Princeton, NJ: Princeton University Press.

Howard, Christopher, and Edward D. Berkowitz. 2008. "Extensive but Not Inclusive: Health Care and Pensions in the United States." In *Public and Private Social Policy: Health and Pension Policies in a New Era*, edited by Daniel Béland and Brian Gran, 70–91. Basingstoke, UK: Palgrave Macmillan.

Hsiao, William. 1988. *A National Study of Resource Based Relative Value Scales for Physician Services: Final Report.* Boston: Harvard School of Public Health.

Huber, Evelyne, and John D. Stephens. 2001. *Development and Crisis of the Welfare State: Parties and Policies in Global Markets.* Chicago: University of Chicago Press.

Immergut, Ellen M. 1998. "The Theoretical Core of the New Institutionalism." *Politics and Society* 26:5–34.

Jacobs, Alan M. 2009a. "How Do Ideas Matter? Mental Models and Attention in German Pension Politics." *Comparative Political Studies* 42, no. 2: 252–79.

———. 2009b. "Policymaking as Political Constraint: Institutional Development in the US Social Security Program." In *Explaining Institutional Change: Ambiguity,*

Agency, and Power, edited by James Mahoney and Kathleen Thelen, 94–131. New York: Cambridge University Press.

———. 2011. *Governing for the Long Term: Democracy and the Politics of Investment.* New York: Cambridge University Press.

Jacobs, Lawrence. 2005. "Health Disparities in the Land of Equality." In *Healthy Wealthy and Fair: Health Care and the Good Soci*ety, edited by James Morone and Lawrence Jacobs, 37–63. New York: Oxford University Press.

———. 2011. "America's Critical Juncture: The Affordable Care Act and Its Reverberations," *Journal of Health Politics, Policy and Law,* 36, no 3: 625–31.

Jacobs, Lawrence, and Robert Shapiro. 2002. "Politics and Policymaking in the Real World: Crafted Talk and the Loss of Democratic Responsiveness." In *Navigating Public Opinion: Polls, Policy and the Future of American Democracy,* edited by Jeff Manza, Fay Lomax Cook, and Benjamin Pages, 54–75. New York: Oxford University Press.

Jacobs, Lawrence, and Theda Skocpol. 2010. *Health Care Reform and American Politics: What Everyone Needs to Know.* New York: Oxford University Press.

Jaenicke, Douglas, and Alex Waddan. 2006a. "President Bush and Social Policy: The Strange Case of the Medicare Prescription Drug Benefit." *Political Science Quarterly* 121, no. 2: 217–40.

———. 2006b. "Recent Incremental Health Care Reforms in the US: A Way Forward or False Promise?" *Policy and Politics* 34, no. 2: 241–64.

Jenson, Jane. 1989. "Paradigms and Political Discourse: Protective Legislation in France and the United States before 1914." *Canadian Journal of Political Science* 22:235–58.

John, David A. 1999. "Clinton's Bait-and-Switch Social Security Plan," *Heritage Foundation,* Executive Memorandum #570, February 5, www.heritage.org/research /reports/1999/02/clintons-bait-and-switch-social-security-plan.

———. 2005. "Add-On Accounts: At Best, a Bad Fix for Social Security," *Heritage Foundation,* WebMemo #686, March 14, www.heritage.org/research /reports/2005/03/add-on-accounts-at-best-a-bad-fix-for-social-security.

Johnson, Dirk. 1995. "Welfare in Transition: States Are Already Providing a Glimpse at Welfare's Future; Wisconsin: Big Cuts Already, and More Ahead." *New York Times,* September 21.

Johnson, H., and D. Broder. 1997. *The System: The American Way of Politics at Breaking Point.* Boston: Little, Brown.

Justice, Glen. 2005. "Groups that Clashed in the Campaign Are Facing Off Again. *New York Times,* April 12.

Kaiser Family Foundation. 2009. "Health Insurance Coverage of Total Population: States (2008–2009), US (2009)." StateHealthFacts.org, www.statehealthfacts.org /comparebar.jsp?ind=125&cat=3.

———. 2010. "Summary of Key Changes to Medicare in 2010 Health Reform Law," *Kaiser Family Foundation,* www.kff.org/healthreform/upload/7948-02.pdf.

Kamarck, Elaine. 1992. "The Welfare Wars." *New Democrat,* July 12–15.

Katz, Michael. 1986. *In the Shadow of the Poorhouse: A Social History of Welfare in America*. New York: Basic Books.

———. 1989. *The Undeserving Poor: From War on Poverty to War on Welfare*. New York: Pantheon Books.

———. 1993. The *Underclass Debate: Views from History*. Princeton, NJ: Princeton University Press.

Katznelson, Ira. 1981. "A Radical Departure: Social Welfare and the Election." In *The Hidden Election: Politics and Economics in the 1980 Presidential Campaign*, edited by Thomas Ferguson and Joel Rogers, 313–40. New York: Pantheon.

Kaus, Mickey. 1995. *The End of Equality*, 2nd ed. New York: Basic Books.

Kay, Adrian. 2005. "A Critique of the Use of Path Dependency in Policy Studies." *Public Administration* 8, no. 3: 553–71.

———. 2007. "Tense Layering and Synthetic Policy Paradigms: The Politics of Health Insurance in Australia." *Australian Journal of Political Science* 42, no. 4: 579–91.

———. 2009. "Understanding Policy Change as a Hermeneutic Problem." *Journal of Comparative Policy Analysis* 11, no. 1: 47–63.

King, Anthony. 1973. "Ideas, Institutions and the Policies of Governments: A Comparative Analysis: Part III." *British Journal of Political Science* 3, no. 4: 409–23.

King, Desmond. 1995. *Actively Seeking Work? The Politics of Unemployment and Welfare Policy in the United States and Great Britain*. Chicago: University of Chicago Press.

———. 2005. "Making People Work: Democratic Consequences of Welfare". In *Welfare Reform and Political Theory*, edited by Lawrence M. Mead and Christopher Beem, 65–81. New York: Russell Sage Foundation.

King, Desmond, and Randall A. Hansen. 1999. "Experts at Work: State Autonomy, Social Learning and Eugenic Sterilization in 1930s Britain." *British Journal of Political Science* 20:77–107.

Kingdon, John W. 1995. *Agendas, Alternatives, and Public Policies*, 2nd ed. New York: HarperCollins.

Kingson, Eric R. 1984. "Financing Social Security: Agenda-Setting and the Enactment of the 1983 Amendments to the Social Security Act." *Policy Studies Journal* 13, no. 1: 131–55.

Klein, Jennifer. 2003. *For All These Rights: Business, Labor, and the Shaping of America's Public–Private Welfare State*. Princeton, NJ: Princeton University Press.

Kosterlitz, Julie. 2004. "The Ownership Society." *National Journal* 36, no. 4: 230–37.

Krugman, Paul. 2008. "It's a Different Country." *New York Times*, June 9.

———. 2011. "Ludicrous and Cruel." *New York Times*, April 7.

Lakoff, George. 2002. *Moral Politics: How Liberals and Conservatives Think*. Chicago: University of Chicago Press.

Lambrew, Jeanne, and Karen Davenport. 2006. "Has Medicare Been Privatized? Implications of the Medicare Modernization Act, Beyond the Drug Benefit," *Center for American Progress*, www.americanprogress.org/kf/medicare_privatization.pdf.

Lawlor, Edward F. 2003. *Redesigning the Medicare Contract: Politics, Markets and Agency*. Chicago: University of Chicago Press.

Leavitt, Michael. 2006. "Welfare Reform a Success, But More Must Be Done." *Salt Lake Tribune*, August 21.

Lecours, André, ed. 2005. *New Institutionalism: Theory and Analysis*. Toronto: University of Toronto Press.

Leff, Mark H. 1983. "Taxing the 'Forgotten Man': The Politics of Social Security Finance in the New Deal." *Journal of American History* 70, no. 2: 359–79.

Lemieux, Jeff. 2004. "The Kolbe-Stenholm Social Security Plan." Available at *Centrist.org*.

Leonhardt, David. 2010. "In Health Bill, Obama Attacks Wealth Inequality." *New York Times*, March 23.

Lewis, Oscar. 1961. *The Children of Sanchez*. New York: Random House.

———. 1966. *La Vida: A Puerto Rican Family in the Culture of Poverty—San Juan and New York*. New York: Random House.

———. 1969. "The Culture of Poverty." *In On Understanding Poverty: Perspectives from the Social Sciences*, edited by Daniel P. Moynihan, 187–220. New York: Basic Books.

Lieberman, Robert C. 2002. "Ideas, Institutions, and Political Order: Explaining Political Change." *American Political Science Review* 96, no. 4: 697–712.

Light, Paul C. 1995. *Still Artful Work: The Continuing Politics of Social Security Reform*. New York: McGraw-Hill.

Lindblom, Charles. 1959. "The Science of Muddling Through." *Public Administrative Review* 19 (Spring): 74–88.

Liu, John C., and Robert E. Moffit. 1995. "A Taxpayer's Guide to the Medicare Crisis," *The Heritage Foundation*, September 27, www.heritage.org/research/reports/1995/09/a-taxpayers-guide-to-the-medicare-crisis.

Lower-Basch, Elizabeth. 2010. "A New Conversation on Women and Poverty." Testimony to Senate Finance Committee, September 21, www.clasp.org/admin/site/publications/files/CLASP-Finance-Committee-testimony-for-the-record.pdf.

Mahoney, James. 2003. "Strategies of Causal Assessment in Comparative Historical Analysis." In *Comparative Historical Analysis in the Social Sciences*, edited by James Mahoney and Dietrich Rueschemeyer, 337–72. New York: Cambridge University Press.

Mahoney, James, and Kathleen Thelen, eds. 2009. "A Theory of Gradual Institutional Change." In *Explaining Institutional Change: Ambiguity, Agency, and Power*, 1–37. New York: Cambridge University Press.

Maioni, Antonia. 1998. *Parting at the Crossroads: The Emergence of Health Insurance in the United States and Canada*. Princeton, NJ: Princeton University Press.

Mann, Kirk. 1994. "Watching the Defectives: Observers of the Underclass in the USA, Britain and Australia." *Critical Social Policy* 14, no. 2: 79–99.

Marcus, R., and D. Balz. 1994. "Clinton Outlines Plan to Break Welfare Cycle." *Washington Post*, June 15, A1.

Marier, Patrik. 2008. *Pension Politics: Consensus and Social Conflict in Ageing Societies*. London: Routledge.

———. 2009. "The Power of Institutionalized Learning: The Uses and Practices of Commissions to Generate Policy Change." *Journal of European Public Policy* 16, no. 8: 1204–23.

Marmor, Theodore R. 2000. *The Politics of Medicare*, 2nd ed. New York: Aldine de Gruyter.

Marmor, Theodore, and Jacob S. Hacker. 2005. "Medicare Reform and Social Insurance: The Clashes of 2003 and Their Potential Fallout." *Yale Journal of Health Policy, Law and Ethics* 5 (January): 479–85.

Marmor, Theodore R., and Jerry L. Mashaw. 2006. "Understanding Social Insurance: Fairness, Affordability, and the 'Modernization' of Social Security and Medicare." *Health Affairs* 25, no. 3: 114–34.

Martin, Isaac. 2008. *The Permanent Tax Revolt: How the Property Tax Transformed American Politics*. Palo Alto, CA: Stanford University Press.

Mayhew, David R. 1974. *Congress: The Electoral Connection*. New Haven, CT: Yale University Press.

McGurn, William. 2008. "Obama Talks Nonsense on Tax Cuts." *Wall Street Journal*, October 21.

Mead, Lawrence M. 1986. *Beyond Entitlement: The Social Obligations of Citizenship*. New York: Free Press.

———. 1987. "The Obligation to Work and the Availability of Jobs: A Dialogue between Lawrence M. Mead and William Julius Wilson." *Focus* 10, no. 2: 11–19.

———. 1988. "The New Welfare Debate." *Commentary* 85, no. 3: 44–52.

———. 1992. *The New Politics of Poverty: The Nonworking Poor in America*. New York: Basic Books.

———. 1997a. "Citizenship and Social Policy: T. H. Marshall and Poverty." In *The Welfare State*, edited by E. F. Paul, F. D. Miller, and J. Paul, 197–230. Cambridge: Cambridge University Press.

———. 1997b. *The New Paternalism*. Washington, DC: Brookings Institution Press.

———. 2004. *Government Matters: Welfare Reform in Wisconsin*. Princeton, NJ: Princeton University Press.

Mebane, Felicia E. 2000. *Medicare Politics: Exploring the Roles of Media Coverage, Political Information, and Political Participation*. New York: Garland Publishing.

Mehta, Jal. 2011. "The Varied Roles of Ideas in Politics: From 'Whether' to 'How.'" In *Ideas and Politics in Social Science Research*, edited by Daniel Béland and Robert Henry Cox, 23–46. New York: Oxford University Press.

Merrien, François-Xavier. 1997. *L'État-providence*. Paris: Presses Universitaires de France.

———. 2001. "The World Bank's New Social Policies: Pensions." *International Social Science Journal* 53:537–50.

Moffit, Robert. 2008. "The Success of Medicare Advantage Plans: What Seniors Should Know," *The Heritage Foundation*, Backgrounder No. 2142, June 13, www.heritage.org/Research/Reports/2008/06/The-Success-of-Medicare-Advantage-Plans-What-Seniors-Should-Know.

Moffit, Robert, and Alison Acosta Fraser. 2008. "Washington Must Pull the Trigger to Contain Medicare Spending," *The Heritage Foundation*, WebMemo No. 1796, February 4, www.heritage.org/research/reports/2008/02/congress-must-pull-the-trigger-to-contain-medicare-spending.

Moon, Marilyn. 2006. *Medicare: A Policy Primer*. Washington, DC: Urban Institute Press.

Moore, Stephen. 2004. *Bullish on Bush: How George Bush's Ownership Society Will Make America Stronger*. Lanham, MD: Madison Books.

Moran, Michael. 2000. "Understanding the Welfare State: The Case of Health Care." *British Journal of Politics and International Relations* 2, no. 2: 135–60.

Morgan, Kimberly J. 2010. "Medicare, Deservingness, and Cost Containment." In *The New Politics of Old Age Policy*, edited by Robert Hudson, 275–302. Baltimore: John Hopkins University Press.

Morris, Dick. 1997. *Behind the Oval Office: Winning the Presidency in the Nineties*. New York: Random House.

Moynihan, Daniel P. 1973. *The Politics of a Guaranteed Income: The Nixon Administration and the Family Assistance Plan*. New York: Random House.

———. 1995. "The Devolution Revolution." *New York Times*, August 6.

Munnell, Alicia H., and Steven A. Sass. 2006. *Social Security and the Stick Market: How the Pursuit of Market Magic Shapes the System*. Kalamazoo, MI: W. E. Upjohn Institute.

Murray, Charles. 1984. *Losing Ground: American Social Policy, 1950–1980*. New York: Free Press.

———. 1987. "In Search of the Working Poor." *Public Interest* 89:3–19.

Myers, Robert J. 1993. *Social Security*, 4th ed. Philadelphia: Pension Research Council University of Pennsylvania Press.

Myles, John. 1988. "Postwar Capitalism and the Extension of Social Security into a Retirement Wage." In *The Politics of Social Policy in the United States*, edited by Margaret Weir, Ann Shola Orloff, and Theda Skocpol, 265–84. Princeton, NJ: Princeton University Press.

Myles, John, and Paul Pierson. 1997. "Friedman's Revenge: The Reform of 'Liberal' Welfare States in Canada and the United States." *Politics and Society* 25, no. 4: 443–72.

———. 2001. "The Comparative Political Economy of Pension Reform." In *The New Politics of the Welfare State*, edited by Paul Pierson. 305–33. Oxford: Oxford University Press.

Myles, John, and Jill Quadagno. 2002. "Political Theories of the Welfare State." *Social Service Review* 76, no. 1: 34–57.

Nagourney, Adam. 2009. "Politics and the Age Gap." *New York Times*, September 13.

National Commission on Fiscal Responsibility and Reform. 2010. *The Moment of Truth: The Report of the National Commission on Fiscal Responsibility and Reform*. December. Washington, DC: The White House. www.fiscalcommission.gov/sites/fiscalcommission.gov/files/documents/TheMomentofTruth12_1_2010.pdf.

Nather, David, and Rebecca Adams. 2003. "Medicare Rewrite." *Congressional Weekly Quarterly*, July 5, p. 1696.

Nix, Kathryn. 2010. "Top 10 Disasters of Obamacare," *Heritage Foundation* WebMemo no. 2848, March 30, http://thf_media.s3.amazonaws.com/2010/pdf/wm_2848.pdf.

Nixon, Richard M. 1978. *The Memoirs of Richard Nixon*. New York: Grosset and Dunlap.

Nonnemaker, Lynn K. 2009. "Medicare Cost Sharing Requirements for 2009," AARP Public Policy Fact Sheet, *AARP Public Policy Institute*, http://assets.aarp.org /rgcenter/health/fs151_medicare.pdf.

Novelli, Bill. 2001. "Statement by AARP CEO Bill Novelli in Response to the Expected Recommendations of the Commission to Strengthen Social Security," December 10, AARP press release, available at http://seniorjournal.com/NEWS /SocialSecurity/12-11-1AARPSays.htm.

Obama, Barack. 2009. "Remarks by the President in Town Hall Meeting, University of New Orleans." Washington, DC: Office of the Press Secretary (October 15).

———. 2010. "Executive Order—National Commission on Fiscal Responsibility and Reform." Washington, DC: Office of the Press Secretary (February 18).

Oberlander, Jonathan. 2003. *The Political Life of Medicare*. Chicago: University of Chicago Press.

———. 2007. "Through the Looking Glass: The Politics of the Medicare Prescription Drug, Improvement, and Modernization Act." *Journal of Health Politics, Policy and Law* 32, no. 2: 187–219.

O'Connor, Alice. 2001. *Poverty Knowledge: Social Science, Social Policy, and the Poor in Twentieth Century US History*. Princeton, NJ: Princeton University Press.

OECD. 2009. "OECD Health Data 2009—Comparing Health Statistics across OECD Countries." Paris: OECD. www.oecd.org/document/54/0,3746,en_21571361 _44315115_43220022_1_1_1,00.html.

Olasky, M. 1992. *The Tragedy of American Compassion*. Wheaton, IL: Crossway.

Oliver, Thomas, Philip Lee, and Helene Lipton. 2004. "A Political History of Medicare and Prescription Drug Coverage." *Milbank Quarterly* 82, no. 2: 283–354.

Olson, Laura Katz. 2010. *The Politics of Medicaid*. New York: Columbia University Press.

Orenstein, Mitchell A. 2008. *Privatizing Pensions: The Transnational Campaign for Social Security Reform*. Princeton, NJ: Princeton University Press.

Orloff, Ann Shola. 1993. *The Politics of Pensions: A Comparative Analysis of Canada, Great Britain and the United States, 1880–1940*. Madison: University of Wisconsin Press.

———. 2002. "Explaining US Welfare Reform: Power, Gender, Race and the US Policy Legacy." *Critical Social Policy* 22:97–119.

Orloff, Ann Shola, and Bruno Palier, eds. 2009. "Special Issue on Culture, Ideas and Discourse in the Emergence of New Gendered Welfare States." *Social Politics* 16, no. 4: 405–581.

Orren, Karen, and Stephen Skowronek. 2004. *The Search for American Political Development*. Cambridge: Cambridge University Press.

Padamsee, Tasleem. 2009. "Culture in Connection: Re-Contextualizing Ideational Processes in the Analysis of Policy Development." *Social Politics* 16, no. 4: 413–45.

Page, Benjamin, and Robert Shapiro. 1992. *The Rational Public: Fifty Years of Trends in Americans' Policy Preferences*. Chicago: University of Chicago Press.

Page, Susan, and Oren Dorell. 2005. "President Touts 'Progressive Indexing' Plan." *USA Today*, April 28.

Pal, Leslie, and R. Kent Weaver. 2003. *The Government Taketh Away: The Politics of Pain in the United States and Canada*. Washington, DC: Georgetown University Press.

Palazzolo, Daniel J. 1999. *Done Deal: The Politics of the 1997 Budget Agreement*. New York: Chatham House.

Palier, Bruno. 2002. *Gouverner la sécurité sociale*. Paris: Presses Universitaires de France.

———. 2005. "Ambiguous Agreements, Cumulative Change: French Social Policy in the 1990s." In *Beyond Continuity: Institutional Change in Advanced Political Economies*, edited by Wolfgang Streeck and Kathleen Thelen, 127–44. New York: Oxford University Press.

Palmer, John. 1988. *Income Security in America: The Record and the Prospects*. Washington, DC: Urban Institute Press.

Park, Edwin, Robert Greenstein, and Richard Kogan. 2004. "Overlooked Element of the Medicare Trustees' Report Could Spell Trouble for Beneficiaries in Future Years." Washington, DC: Center on Budget and Policy Priorities.

Parrot, Sharon. 1998. *Welfare Recipients Who Find Jobs: What Do We Know about Their Employment and Earnings?* Washington, DC: Center on Budget and Policy Priorities.

Parsons, Christi, and Andrew Zajac. 2009. "The Next Healthcare Battle: Medicare Subsidies." *Los Angeles Times*, August 19, A1.

Parsons, Craig. 2002. "Showing Ideas as Causes: The Origins of the European Union." *International Organization* 56, no. 1: 47–84.

———. 2007. *How to Map Arguments in Political Science*. Oxford: Oxford University Press.

Patashnik, Eric. 2000. *Putting Trust in the US Budget: Federal Trust Funds and the Politics of Commitment*. Cambridge: Cambridge University Press.

Patterson, J. T. 1994. *America's Struggle against Poverty 1900–1994*. Cambridge, MA: Harvard University Press.

Pavetti, LaDonna. 2009. "Testimony before the House Subcommittee on Income Security and Family Support." October 8, www.cbpp.org/files/10-8-09testimony.pdf.

Pavetti, LaDonna, and Dottie Rosenbaum. 2010. "Creating a Safety Net that Works When the Economy Doesn't: The Role of the Food Stamp and TANF Programs." Washington, DC: Center on Budget and Policy Priorities.

Pavetti, LaDonna, Danilo Trisi, and Liz Schott. 2011. "TANF Responded Unevenly During Downturn." Washington DC: Center on Budget and Policy Priorities.

PBGC. 2003. "Pension Insurance Data Book 2003." *Pension Benefit Guaranty Corporation*. www.pbgc.gov/Documents/2003databook.pdf.

Pear, Robert. 1995. "Democrats See Virtue in Shift to the Right on Welfare." *New York Times*, March 17.

———. 1996a. "Clinton Endorses the Most Radical of Welfare Trials." *New York Times*, May 19.

———. 1996b. "Clinton Wavers after Backing Welfare Plan." *New York Times*, June 15.

———. 1996c. "Senate Passes Welfare Measure, Sending It for Clinton's Signature." *New York Times*, August 2.

———. 2002. "House Passes a Welfare Bill with Stricter Rules on Work." *New York Times*, May 17.

———. 2003a. "Medicare Plan Raises the Cost for the Affluent." *New York Times*, October 6.

———. 2003b. "3 Big Issues Stump Negotiators in a Bill to Revamp Medicare." *New York Times*, November 14.

———. 2004. "AARP Opposes Bush Plan to Replace Social Security with Private Accounts." *New York Times*, November 12.

———. 2005. "As Deadline Nears, Sorting out the Medicare Drug Plan." *New York Times,* October 11.

———. 2009a. "Medicare Officials to Let Insurers Warn Recipients about Pending Health Bills." *New York Times*, October 17.

———. 2009b. "Senator Tries to Allay Fears on Health Overhaul." *New York Times*, September 23.

———. 2011a. "G.O.P Blueprint Would Remake Health Policy." *New York Times*, April 4.

———. 2011b. "Democrats See Perils on Path to Health Cuts." *New York Times*, September 13.

Pear, Robert, and Jackie Calmes. 2010. "Medicare Stronger, Social Security Worse in Short Run, Report Finds." *New York Times*, August 5.

Pear, Robert, and Erik Eckholm. 2006. "A Decade after Welfare Overhaul, a Shift in Policy and Perception." *New York Times*, August 21.

Pear, Robert, and David Herszenhorn. 2009. "Democrats Push Health Care Plan While Issuing Assurances on Medicare." *New York Times*, July 29.

Pear, Robert, and Chris Hulse. 2003. "Senate Removes Two Roadblocks to Drug Benefit." *New York Times*, November 25.

Pear, Robert, and Robin Toner. 2003. "Medicare Plan Covering Drugs Backed By AARP." *New York Times*, November 18.

Perkins, Frances. 1946. *The Roosevelt I Knew*. New York: Viking.

Peters, Guy B., Jon Pierre, and Desmond S. King. 2005. "The Politics of Path Dependence: Political Conflict in Historical Institutionalism." *Journal of Politics* 67, no. 4: 1275–1300.

Peterson, Mark. 1998. "The Politics of Health Care Policy: Overreaching in an Age of Polarization." In *The Social Divide, Political Parties and the Future of Activist Government*, edited by Margaret Weir, 181–229. Washington, DC: Brookings Institution Press.

Petrocik, John R. 1996. "Issue Ownership in Presidential Elections, with a 1980 Case Study." *American Journal of Political Science* 40, no. 3: 825–50.

Pierson, Paul. 1992. "Policy Feedbacks and Political Change: Contrasting Reagan and Thatcher's Pension-Reform Initiatives." *Studies in American Political Development* 6:359–90.

———. 1994. *Dismantling the Welfare State? Reagan, Thatcher, and the Politics of Retrenchment*. New York: Cambridge University Press.

———. 1996. "The New Politics of the Welfare State." *World Politics* 48, no. 1: 143–79.

———. 1998. "The Deficit and the Politics of Domestic Reform." In *The Social Divide, Political Parties and the Future of Activist Government*, edited by Margaret Weir, 126–78. Washington, DC: Brookings Institution Press.

———. 2000. "Increasing Returns, Path Dependence, and the Study of Politics." *American Political Science Review* 94, no. 2: 251–67.

———. 2001. "Coping with Permanent Austerity." In *The New Politics of the Welfare State*, edited by Paul Pierson, 410–56. Oxford: Oxford University Press.

———. 2004. *Politics in Time: History, Institutions, and Social Analysis*. Princeton, NJ: Princeton University Press.

Pierson, Paul, and R. Kent Weaver. 1993. "Imposing Losses in Pension Policy." In *Do Institutions Matter? Government Capabilities in the United States and Abroad*, edited by R. Kent Weaver and Bert A. Rockman, 110–50. Washington, DC: Brookings Institution Press.

Piñera, José. 1999. "A Real Solution to the Social Security Crisis: Testimony of José Piñera before the US House Committee on Ways and Means," February 11. Available at Cato Institute, www.cato.org/testimony/ct-jp021199.html.

Piven, Francis F., and Richard Cloward. 1971. *Regulating the Poor: The Functions of Public Welfare*. New York: Pantheon Books.

Pratico, Dominick. 2001. *Eisenhower and Social Security: The Origins of the Disability Program*. New York: Writers Club Press.

Pratt, Henry J. 1993. *Gray Agendas: Interest Groups and Public Pensions in Canada, Britain, and the United States*. Ann Arbor: University of Michigan Press.

President's Commission to Strengthen Social Security. 2001. "Strengthening Social Security and Creating Personal Wealth for All Americans," December. http://govinfo.library.unt.edu/csss/reports/Final_report.pdf.

Quadagno, Jill. 1988. *The Transformation of Old Age Security: Class and Politics in the American Welfare State*. Chicago: University of Chicago Press.

———. 1994. *The Color of Welfare: How Racism Undermined the War on Poverty*. New York: Oxford University Press.

———. 1999. "Creating a Capital Investment Welfare State." *American Sociological Review* 64, no. 1: 1–10.

———. 2005. *One Nation, Uninsured: Why the US Has No National Health Insurance*. New York: Oxford University Press.

Quadagno, Jill, and J. Brandon McKelvey. 2008. "The Transformation of American Health Insurance." In *Health at Risk: America's Ailing Health System and How to Heal It*, edited by Jacob Hacker, 10–31. New York: Columbia University Press.

Quadagno, Jill, and Debra Street. 2006. "Recent Trends in US Social Welfare Policy: Minor Retrenchment or Major Transformation?" *Research on Aging* 28, no. 3: 303–16.

Rabinovitz, J. 1995. "US Opposing Welfare Rules in Connecticut." *New York Times*, December 9.

Reagan, Ronald. 1984. "Remarks on Signing the Social Security Amendments of 1983." In *Public Papers of the Presidents, Reagan, 1983*, 560–62. Washington, DC: United States Government Printing Office.

———. 1986. "Address before a Joint Session of the Congress Reporting on the State of the Union." February 4. Janda.org. http://janda.org/politxts/state%20of%20 union%20addresses/1981-1988%20Reagan/RWR86.html.

———. 1988. "Address before a Joint Session of the Congress Reporting on the State of the Union." January 25. Janda.org.http://janda.org/politxts/state%20of%20 union%20addresses/1981-1988%20Reagan/rwr88.html.

Rector, Robert. 1992. "Requiem for the War on Poverty: Rethinking Welfare after the Los Angeles Riots." *Policy Review*, (Summer): 40–46.

———. 1996. "God and the Underclass." *National Review*, July 15, 30–33.

Reed, Bruce. 2004. "Bush's War against the Wonks: Why the President's Policies Are Falling Apart." *Washington Monthly*, March 4, www.washingtonmonthly.com /features/2004/0403.reed.html.

Riccio, J., D. Friedlander, and S. Freedman. 1994. *GAIN: Benefits, Costs, and Three-Year Impacts of a Welfare-to-Work Program*. New York: Manpower Demonstration Research Corporation.

Rice, Thomas. 2011. "A Progressive Turn of Events." *Journal of Health Policy, Politics and Law* 36, no. 3: 491–94.

Rice, Thomas, Katherine Desmond, and Jon Gabel. 1990. "The Medicare Catastrophic Coverage Act: A Post Mortem." *Health Affairs* 9, no. 3: 75–87.

Richards, Raymond. 1994. *Closing the Door to Destitution: The Shaping of the Social Security Acts of the United States and New Zealand*. University Park: Pennsylvania State University Press.

Robertson, A. Haeworth. 1997. *The Big Lie: What Every Boomer Should Know about Social Security and Medicare*. Washington, DC: Retirement Policy Institute.

Rochefort, David A., and Roger W. Cobb, eds. 1994. *The Politics of Problem Definition: Shaping the Policy Agenda*. Lawrence: University Press of Kansas.

Rogers, Jean. 1999. "Statement of J. Jean Rogers, Administrator Wisconsin Department of Workforce Development, Madison, Wisconsin, Testimony before the Subcommittee on Human Resources of the House Ways and Means Committee on Ways and Means, Hearings on the Effects of Welfare Reform," May 27.

Rogers-Dillon, Robin H. 2004. *The Welfare Experiments: Politics and Policy Evaluation*. Stanford, CA: Stanford University Press.

Rose, Richard. 2004. *Learning Lessons in Comparative Public Policy: A Guide to Analysis*. London: Routledge.

Rosenbaum, David E. 2003a. "A Final Push in Congress: The Savings Plan; Tax Free Accounts Drew Years from the Wary." *New York Times*, November 23.

———. 2003b. "Bush Signs Law to Cover Drugs for the Elderly." *New York Times*, December 9.

———. 2005a. "Few See Gains from Social Security Tour." *New York Times*, April 3.

———. 2005b. "Lawmakers Postponing Bush Priority on Benefits." *New York Times*, July 15.

Rosenbaum, S., K. John, C. Sonosky, A. Markus, and C. DeGraw. 1998. "The Children's Hour: The State Children's Health Insurance Program." *Health Affairs* 17, no. 1: 75–89. doi:10.1377/hlthaff.17.1.75.

Ross, Fiona. 2007. "Policy Histories and Partisan Leadership in Presidential Studies: The Case of Social Security." In *The Polarized Presidency of George W. Bush*, edited by George C. Edwards III and Desmond S. King, 419–46. Oxford: Oxford University Press.

Ross, Stanford, and David Walker. 2010 "Misled on Medicare." *New York Times*, August 14.

Rovner, Julie. 1987a. "Democratic Leaders Slow Pace of Medicare Bill." *Congressional Quarterly Weekly Report*, July 4, p. 1437.

———. 1987b. "New Medicare Plan May Include Drug Coverage." *Congressional Quarterly Weekly Report*, May 23, p. 1082.

———. 1989. "Both Chambers in Retreat on 1988 Medicare Law." *Congressional Quarterly Weekly Report*, October 7, pp. 2635–38.

Ruggie, Mary. 1996. *Realignments in the Welfare State: Health Policy in the United States, Britain, and Canada*. New York: Columbia University Press.

Rutenberg, Jim, and Jackie Calmes. 2009. "False 'Death Panel' Rumor Has Some Familiar Roots." *New York Times*, August 14.

Sabatier, Paul A. 1988. "An Advocacy Coalition Framework of Policy Change and the Role of Policy-Oriented Learning Therein." *Policy Sciences* 21:129–68.

Sack, Kevin. 2000. "Gore and Bush Trade Jabs on Pensions and Spending." *New York Times*, November 2.

Saldin, Robert. 2010. "Healthcare Reform: A Prescription for the 2010 Republican Landslide?" *The Forum* 8, no. 4: Article 10.

Sanders, Daniel S. 1973. *The Impact of Reform Movements on Social Policy Change: The Case of Social Insurance*. Fair Lawn, NJ: R. E. Burdick.

Sass, Steven A. 1997. *The Promise of Private Pensions: The First Hundred Years*. Cambridge, MA: Harvard University Press.

Sawhill, Isabel. 1995. "Distinguished Lecture on Economics in Government: The Economist vs. Madmen in Authority." *Journal of Economic Perspectives* 9, no. 3: 3–13.

Schickler, Eric. 2001. *Disjointed Pluralism: Institutional Innovation and the Development of the US Congress*. Princeton, NJ: Princeton University Press.

Schieber, Sylvester J., and John B. Shoven. 1999. *The Real Deal: The History and Future of Social Security*. New Haven, CT: Yale University Press.

Schlesinger, Arthur. 1959. *The Coming of the New Deal*. Boston: Houghton-Mifflin.

Schlesinger, Mark. 2002. "On Values and Democratic Policy Making: The Deceptively Fragile Consensus around Market-Oriented Medical Care." *Journal of Health Policy, Politics and Law* 27, no. 6: 889–925.

Schmidt, Vivien A. 2002. "Does Discourse Matter in the Politics of Welfare State Adjustment?" *Comparative Political Studies* 35, no. 2: 168–93.

———. 2011. "Reconciling Ideas and Institutions through Discursive Institutionalism." In *Ideas and Politics in Social Science Research*, edited by Daniel Béland and Robert Henry Cox, 47–64. New York: Oxford University Press.

Schön, Donald A., and Martin Rein. 1994. *Frame Reflection: Toward the Resolution of Intractable Policy Controversies*. New York: Basic Books.

Schott, Liz, and LaDonna Pavetti. 2010. "Walking Away from a Win, Win, Win: Subsidized Jobs Slated to End Soon Are Helping Families, Businesses, and Communities Weather the Recession." Washington, DC: Center on Budget and Policy Priorities.

Schram, Sanford F., Joe Soss, and Richard C. Fording, eds. 2003. *Race and the Politics of Welfare Reform*. Ann Arbor: University of Michigan Press.

Schwartz, David. 2010. "Social Security a Big Issue for Sharron Angle and Harry Reid, but Few Ideas." *Las Vegas Sun*, June 15. www.lasvegassun.com/news/2010/jun/15/social-security-big-issue-few-ideas/

Schwarz, John E. 1983. *America's Hidden Success: A Reassessment of Twenty Years of Public Policy*. New York: W. W. Norton.

Serafini, Marilyn W. 2002. "An Rx for the Democrats." *National Journal*, June 22.

———. 2005. "One More for the Ownership Society." *National Journal* 37, no. 11: 783.

———. 2010. "Health Care Law's Medicare Trims Altering Seniors' Views." *USA Today*, October 26.

Shafer, Byron E. 2003. *The Two Majorities and the Puzzle of Modern American Politics*. Lawrence: University Press of Kansas.

Shafer, Byron E., and William Claggett. 1995. *The Two Majorities: The Issue Context of Modern American Politics*. Baltimore: John Hopkins University Press.

Sherman, Emily. 2008. "Candidates Ignoring Coming Social Security Crisis, Critics Say." CNN Website, October 23. www.cnn.com/2008/POLITICS/10/23/social.security/index.html.

Shklar, Judith. 1991. *American Citizenship: The Quest for Inclusion*. Cambridge, MA: Harvard University Press.

Sinclair, Barbara. 2006. *Party Wars: Polarization and the Politics of National Policy Making*. Norman: Oklahoma University Press.

Skidmore, Max J. 1999. *Social Security and Its Enemies*. Boulder, CO: Westview.

Skocpol, Theda. 1990. "Sustainable Social Policy: Fighting Poverty without Poverty Programs." *The American Prospect* 1, no. 2: 58–70.

———. 1992. *Protecting Soldiers and Mothers: The Political Origins of Social Policy in the United States*. Cambridge, MA: The Belknap Press of the Harvard University Press.

———. 1997. *Boomerang: Health Care Reform and the Turn against Government*. New York: W. W. Norton.

Skogstad, Grace, ed. 2011. *Policy Paradigms, Transnationalism and Domestic Politics*. Toronto: University of Toronto Press.

Skowronek, Stephen. 1997. *The Politics Presidents Make: Leadership from John Adams to Bill Clinton*. rev. ed. Cambridge, MA: Harvard University Press.

Small, Melvin. 1999. *The Presidency of Richard Nixon*. Lawrence: University of Kansas Press.

Smith, David. 2002. *Entitlement Politics: Medicare and Medicaid 1995–2001*. New York: Aldine de Gruyter.

Social Security Online. 2011. *Supplemental Security Income*. www.ssa.gov/ssi/.

Somers, Margaret, and Fred Block. 2005. "From Poverty to Perversity: Ideas, Markets, and Institutions over 200 Years of Welfare Debate." *American Sociological Review* 70, no. 2: 260–87.

Soss, Joe, and Sanford Schram. 2007. "A Public Transformed? Welfare Reform as Policy Feedback". *American Political Science Review* 101, no. 1: 111–27.

Staff of the *Washington Post*. 2010. *Landmark: The Inside Story of America's New Health-Care Law and What It Means for Us All*. New York: Public Affairs.

Starr, Paul. 1994. *The Logic of Health Care Reform: Why and How the President's Plan Will Work*, rev. ed. New York: Penguin Books.

Steensland, B. 2006. "Cultural Categories and the American Welfare State: The Case of Guaranteed Income Policy." *American Journal of Sociology* 111, no. 5: 1273–326.

———. 2008. *The Failed Welfare Revolution: America's Struggle over Guaranteed Income Policy*. Princeton, NJ: Princeton University Press.

Steinhauer, Jennfier. 2010. "Ads Use Medicare Cuts as Rallying Point". *New York Times*, October 30.

Steinmo, Sven. 2010. *The Evolution of Modern States: Sweden, Japan, and the United States*. New York: Cambridge University Press.

Steinmo, Sven., Kathleen Thelen, and Frank Longstreth, eds. 1992. *Structuring Politics: Historical Institutionalism in Comparative Analysis*. Cambridge: Cambridge University Press.

Steinmo, Sven, and John Watts. 1995. "It's the Institutions, Stupid! Why the United States Can't Pass Comprehensive National Health Insurance." *Journal of Health Politics, Policy and Law* 20, no. 2: 329–72.

Stephanopoulos, George. 1999. *All Too Human: A Political Education*. Boston: Little, Brown.

Stevens, Beth. 1988. "Blurring the Boundaries: How the Federal Government Has Influenced Welfare Benefits in the Private Sector." In *The Politics of Social Policy in the United States*, edited by Margaret Weir, Ann Shola Orloff, and Theda Skocpol, 123–48. Princeton, NJ: Princeton University Press.

Stevenson, Richard W. 2001a. "Bush Panel Outlines 3 Plans for Social Security Overhaul." *New York Times*, November 30.

———. 2001b. "Social Security Panel Presents Options but No Unified Plan." *New York Times*, December 11.

Stevenson, Richard W., and Elisabeth Bumiller. 2005. "Bush Cites Plan That Would Cut Social Security Benefits." *New York Times*, April 29.

Stockman, David A. 1986. *The Triumph of Politics: How the Reagan Revolution Failed*. New York: Harper and Row.

Stone, Deborah. 1997. *Policy Paradox: The Art of Political Decision Making*. New York: W. W. Norton.

Streeck, Wolfgang, and Kathleen Thelen, eds. 2005. *Beyond Continuity: Institutional Change in Advanced Political Economies*. Oxford: Oxford University Press.

Stryker, Robin, and Pamela Wald. 2009. "Redefining Compassion to Reform Welfare: How Supporters of 1990s US Federal Welfare Reform Aimed for the Moral High Ground." *Social Politics* 16, no. 4: 519–57.

Sundquist, James L. 1968. *Politics and Policy: The Eisenhower, Kennedy, and Johnson Years*. Washington, DC: Brookings Institution Press.

Surel, Yves. 2000. "The Role of Cognitive and Normative Frames in Policy-Making." *Journal of European Public Policy* 7, no. 4: 495–512.

Svahn, John A., and Mary Ross. 1983. "Social Security Amendments of 1983: Legislative History and Summary of Provisions." *Social Security Bulletin* 46, no. 7: 3–48.

Svihula, Judie, and Carroll L. Estes. 2007. "Social Security Politics: Ideology and Reform." *The Journals of Gerontology: Social Sciences* 62B, no. 2: S79–S89.

———. 2008. "Social Security Privatization: An Ideologically Structured Movement." *Journal of Sociology & Social Welfare* 1:75–104.

Tanner, Michael. 2004. *Social Security Time Bomb, and the Candidates Aren't Talking*, April 4. *Cato Institute*, www.cato.org/pub_display.php?pub_id=2633.

———. 2011. "Government Health Care Is Already on Life Support—Here's How to Save It." *New York Post*, April 9.

Taylor-Gooby, Peter, ed. 2005. *Ideas and Welfare State Reform in Western Europe*. Houndmills, UK: Palgrave.

Teles, Steven M., 1996. *Whose Welfare: AFDC and Elite Politics*. Lawrence: University of Kansas Press.

———. 1998. "The Dialectics of Trust: Ideas, Finance, and Pension Privatization in the US and the UK." Paper presented at the Annual Meeting of the Association for Public Policy Analysis and Management, October, New York City.

Thelen, Kathleen. 2003. "How Institutions Evolve: Insights from Comparative–Historical Analysis." In *Comparative–Historical Analysis: Innovations in Theory and Method*, edited by James Mahoney and Dietrich Rueschemeyer, 208–40. New York: Cambridge University Press.

———. 2004. *How Institutions Evolve: The Political Economy of Skills in Germany, Britain, the United States, and Japan.* Cambridge: Cambridge University Press.

Thomas, Landon, Sr. 2004. "Wall St. Lobby Quietly Tackles Social Security." *New York Times*, December 21.

Thompson, Derek. 2010. "The Disappointing Liberal Reaction to the Deficit Commission." *The Atlantic*, November 11, www.theatlantic.com/business/archive/2010/11/the-disappointing-liberal-reaction-to-the-deficit-commission/66434/#.

Titmuss, Richard M. 1958. *Essays on the Welfare State.* London: Allen and Unwin.

Tobin, J. 1968. "Raising the Incomes of the Poor." In *Agenda for the Nation: Papers on Domestic and Foreign Policy Issues*, edited by K. Gordon. 77–116. Washington, DC: Brookings Institution Press.

Tocqueville, Alexis de. 1955. *The Old Regime and the French Revolution.* New York: Anchor Books.

Tolchin, Martin 1989a. "Expansion of Medicare is Painful for Congress." *New York Times*, August 27.

———. 1989b. "Retreat in Congress: The Catastrophic Care Debacle." *New York Times*, October 9.

Toner, Robin 1995. "The Ad Campaign: Attacking the G.O.P.'s Plan for Medicare." *New York Times*, November 4.

———. 1996. "Battered by Labor's Ads, Republicans Strike Back Published." *New York Times*, July 15.

———. 2000. "The 2000 Campaign: The Ad Campaign; Battle on Prescription Drugs." *New York Times*, September 21.

Trilling, Richard J. 1976. *Party Image and Electoral Behavior.* New York: Wiley.

Tuohy, Carolyn. 2003. "Controlling Health Care Costs for the Aged." In *The Government Taketh Away: The Politics of Pain in the United States and Canada*, edited by Leslie Pal and R. Kent Weaver, 71–105. Washington, DC: Georgetown University Press.

Twight, Charlotte. 1997. "Medicare's Origin: The Economics and Politics of Dependency." *The Cato Journal* 16, no. 3, www.cato.org/pubs/journal/cj16n3-3.html.

Tynes, Sheryl R. 1996. *Turning Points in Social Security: From "Cruel Hoax" to "Sacred Entitlement."* Stanford, CA: Stanford University Press.

US Census Bureau. 1971. "Statistical Abstract of the United States." Washington, DC: US Government Printing Office.

———. 2009a. "Table 459: Federal Outlays by Detailed Function, Statistical Abstract of the US." Washington, DC: US Census Bureau. www.census.gov/compendia/statab/2008/tables/08s0459.pdf.

———. 2009b. "Table HIA-2: Health Insurance Coverage Status and Type of Coverage All Persons by Age and Sex 1999 to 2007," Current Population Survey Annual Social and Economic Supplements. Washington, DC: US Census Bureau.

———. 2011a. "Table HI01: Health Insurance Coverage Status and Type of Coverage by Selected Characteristics: 2010 All Races," Current Population Survey. Washington DC: US Census Bureau, www.census.gov/hhes/www/cpstbles/032011/health/h01_001.htm.

———. 2011b. "Income, Poverty and Health Insurance Coverage in the United States 2010." Washington DC: U.S Department of Commerce, www.census.gov/pro/2011pubs/p60-239.pdf.

US Congress. 1994. US House of Representatives. Committee on Ways and Means. 1994. "1994 Green Book: Background Material and Data on Programs within the Jurisdiction of the Committee on Ways and Means." Washington, DC: US Government Printing Office.

———. 1996. "1996 Green Book: Background Material and Data on Programs within the Jurisdiction of the Committee on Ways and Means." 104th Congress, 2nd session. WMCP: 104-14. Washington, DC: US Government Printing Office. http://aspe.hhs.gov/96gb/contents.htm.

———. 1998. "1998 Green Book, Background Material and Data on Programs Within the Jurisdiction of the Committee on Ways and Means." 105th Congress, 2nd session. WMCP: 105-7. Washington, DC: US Government Printing Office.

US Department of Health and Human Services. 2006. "The Next Phase of Welfare Reform: Implementing the Deficit Reduction Act of 2005." US Department of Health and Human Services.

———. 2009. "Medicare Part B Monthly Premiums in 2009." Medicare.gov, https://questions.medicare.gov/cgi-bin/medicare.cfg/php/enduser/std_adp.php?p_faqid=2099.

US Department of Labor, Office of Policy Planning and Research. 1965. "The Negro Family: The Case for National Action." Washington, DC: US Government Printing Office.

US National Advisory Commission on Civil Disorders. 1968. Report of the President's Commission on Civil Disorders. New York: Bantam Books.

US President's Commission on Income Maintenance Programs. 1969. "Report of the President's Commission on Income Maintenance Programs: Poverty amid Plenty." Washington, DC: US Government Printing Office.

Varian, Hal R. 2005. "Two Issues Face Social Security, and Applying One Answer to Both Is Risky." New York Times, February 10.

Vladeck, Bruce. 2004. "The Struggle for the Soul of Medicare." Journal of Law, Medicine and Ethics 32, no. 3: 410–15.

Waddan, Alex. 1997. The Politics of Social Welfare: The Collapse of the Centre and the Rise of the Right. Cheltenham: Edward Elgar.

———. 1998. "A Liberal in Wolf's Clothing: Nixon's Family Assistance Plan in the Light of 1990s Welfare Reform." Journal of American Studies 32, no. 2: 203–18.

———. 2002. Clinton's Legacy? A New Democrat in Governance. Basingstoke, UK: Palgrave.

Walsh, James I. 2000. "When Do Ideas Matter? Explaining the Successes and Failures of Thatcherite Ideas." Comparative Political Studies 33, no. 4: 483–516.

Wawro, Gregory, and Eric Schickler. 2006. Filibuster: Obstruction and Lawmaking in the US Senate. Princeton, NJ: Princeton University Press.

Weaver, Carolyn L. 1982. *The Crisis of Social Security: Economic and Political Origins.* Durham, NC: Duke Press Policy Studies.

Weaver, Kent. R. 1986. "The Politics of Blame Avoidance." *Journal of Public Policy* 6, no. 4: 371–98.

———. 1988. *Automatic Government: The Politics of Indexation.* Washington, DC: Brookings Institution Press.

———. 1996. "Deficits and Devolution in the 104th Congress." *Publius: The Journal of Federalism* 26, no. 3: 45–86.

———. 2000. *Ending Welfare as We Know It.* Washington, DC: Brookings Institution Press.

———. 2005. "Public Pension Reform in the United States." In *Ageing and Pension Reform around the World: Evidence from Eleven Countries,* edited by Giuliano Bonoli and Toshimitsu Shinkawa, 230–51. Cheltenham: Edward Elgar.

———. 2010. "Paths and Forks or Chutes and Ladders: Negative Feedbacks and Policy Regime Change." *Journal of Public Policy* 30, no. 2: 137–62.

Weaver, Kent R., and Bert Rockman, eds. 1993. *Do Institutions Matter? Government Capabilities in the US and Abroad.* Washington, DC: Brookings Institution Press.

Weaver, Kent R., Robert Y. Shapiro, and Lawrence R. Jacobs. 1995. "The Polls— Trends: Welfare." *Public Opinion Quarterly* 59: 606–27.

Weaver, W. 1970. "Welfare Plan Stirs Job Rules Dispute." *New York Times,* May 1, 1.

Weiner, Terry. 2007. "Touching the Third Rail: Explaining the Failure of Bush's Social Security Initiative." *Politics & Policy* 35, no. 4: 872–97.

Weir, Margaret. 1992. *Politics and Jobs.* Princeton, NJ: Princeton University Press.

Weisman, Jonathan. 2005a. "GOP Lawmakers Acknowledge Uphill Fight on Social Security." *Washington Post,* May 30, A4.

———. 2005b. "Social Security Legislation Could Be Shelved." *Washington Post,* September 16, A5.

Weisman, Jonathan, and Jim VandeHei. 2005. "Exit Strategy on Social Security Is Sought." *Washington Post,* June 16, A9.

Weisman, Jonathan, and Ben White. 2005. "Bush's Social Security Plan Assumes Much from Stocks." *Washington Post,* February 9, E1.

Weyland, Kurt. 2008. "Toward a New Theory of Institutional Change." *World Politics* 60 (January): 281–314.

White, Joseph. 2001. *False Alarm: Why the Greatest Threat to Social Security and Medicare Is the Campaign to "Save" Them.* Baltimore: Johns Hopkins University Press.

———. 2007a. "Markets and Medical Care: The United States, 1993–2005." *Milbank Quarterly* 85, no. 3: 395–448.

———. 2007b. "Protecting Medicare: The Best Defense Is a Good Offense." *Journal of Health Politics, Policy and Law* 32, no. 2: 221–46.

Wilsford, David, and Lawrence D. Brown. 2010. "Path Dependency: A Dialogue." *Journal of Health Politics, Policy and Law* 35, no. 4: 681–88.

Wilson, William J. 1987a. "The Obligation to Work and the Availability of Jobs: A Dialogue between Lawrence M. Mead and William Julius Wilson." *Focus* 10, no. 2: 11–19.

———. 1987b. *The Truly Disadvantaged: The Inner City, the Underclass, and Public Policy*. Chicago: University of Chicago Press.

———. 1997. *When Work Disappears: The World of the New Urban Poor*. New York: Vintage Books.

Wincott, Daniel. 2011. "Ideas, Policy Change and the Welfare State." In *Ideas and Politics in Social Science Research*, edited by Daniel Béland and Robert Henry Cox, 143–66. New York: Oxford University Press.

Wiseman, Michael, and Martynas Yčas. 2008. "The Canadian Safety Net for the Elderly." *Social Security Bulletin* 68, no. 2: 53–67.

Witte, Edwin E. 1962. *The Development of the Social Security Act*. Madison: University of Wisconsin Press.

Zedlewski, Sheila R., and Linda Giannarelli. 1997. *Diversity among State Welfare Programs: Implications for Reform*. Washington, DC: Urban Institute Press.

Zelizer, Julian E. 1998. *Taxing America: Wilbur D. Mills, Congress, and the State, 1945–1975*. New York: Cambridge University Press.

———. 2007. "Seizing Power: Conservatives and Congress since the 1970s." In *The Transformation of American Politics: American Government and the Rise of Conservatism*, edited by Paul Pierson and Theda Skocpol, 105–34. Princeton, NJ: Princeton University Press.

Zelman, Walter. 1994. "The Rationale behind the Clinton Health Reform Plan." *Health Affairs* 14 (Spring): 9–29.

Zittoun, Philippe. 2009. "Understanding Policy Change as a Discursive Problem." *Journal of Comparative Policy Analysis* 11, no. 1: 65–82.

Index

Aaron, Henry, 140

Affordable Care Act (ACA) (2010), 17–18, 113–19, 174, 177; cuts in payments to health care providers, 115–16; and income-related premiums, 118; and the Independent Payment Advisory Board, 117–18; and Medicare Advantage plans, 114–16, 118–19; and the Medicare Trustees report on financial projections, 116, 124n30; and Obama administration, 76, 113, 114–17, 118–19, 121, 177; partisan political divisions, 113–19; as policy reversal of the MMA, 113–19; and so-called "death panels," 76, 116

AFL-CIO, 151

African Americans: and the FAP, 33–34; Moynihan report (1965) on family structure and AFDC, 39, 42; and welfare politics, 33–34, 39, 42, 48

Agnew, Spiro, 33

Aid to Dependent Children (ADC), 26

Aid to Families with Dependent Children (AFDC), 9, 25–30, 35, 36–38, 43–44, 46, 68–71; the AFDC-UP program, 25, 29, 45; Clinton's early legislative agenda and the WRA, 49–50; and conservatives' ownership on welfare issue, 69–70; creation of, 25, 26; expansion in the 1960s, 29–30, 32; explanations for successful conservative reform of, 68–71; and the "feminization of poverty," 38; historical overview, 25–30, 35, 36–38, 46; minimum income figures and AFDC benefits, 33–34; the 1967 amendments and recipients' transition to the workforce, 43; and Nixon's FAP, 33–34; numbers of recipients by late 1980s/early 1990s, 46; policy legacies, 27–28, 70–71; and PRWORA, 24, 61–62, 66–68; and Reagan's attack on social welfare-spending, 36–37; and

Reagan's OBRA reforms, 43–44; research on welfare policy and longevity of welfare receipt, 57–58; state-to-state variations in benefit levels, 27, 29–30, 52; state waiver provisions, 51–55, 69, 71; and Supreme Court decisions on federal welfare policy, 29–30; work requirements (welfare-to-work), 43–44

Alliance for Worker Retirement Security, 152, 153

Altman, Nancy, 159

Altmeyer, Arthur, 127–28

American Association for Labor Legislation (AALL), 76–77

American Association of Retired Persons (AARP): and Medicare, 90, 92, 106, 117, 151; and Social Security, 126, 131, 140, 146, 151, 153

American Conservative Union, 33

American Enterprise Institute, 109, 115, 140

American Medical Association (AMA), 77, 80, 83

American Political Development, 3

American Recovery and Reinvestment Act (ARRA), 67–68, 168

Americans for Tax Reform, 146–47

Angle, Sharron, 160

Antos, Joseph, 109, 115

Baer, Kenneth, 114

Balanced Budget Act (BBA) (1997), 94, 99–101

Balanced Budget Refinement Act (1999), 100

Ball, Robert, 127–28, 130–31, 137, 140, 142

Bane, Mary Jo, 57–58

Banfield, Edward, 31

Barbour, Haley, 98

Barnes, Fred, 110, 147

Bartlett, Bruce, 106

Baucus, Max, 104, 150

Beck, Glenn, 116

Benefits Improvement and Protection Act
(2000), 100
Bentsen, Lloyd, 45, 72n7
block grants, 57, 61–62
Blyth, Mark, 8
Boehner, John, 116
Bonior, David, 63
Bowen, Otis, 90
Bradley, Bill, 64
Breaux, John, 100–101, 104, 140, 152
Brookings Institution, 140
Brown, Jerry, 37
Burke, Thomas, 91
Bush, George H. W./Bush administration, 32,
72n7; and the MCCA, 91; and Medicare,
88–89, 91; and OBRA, 89; and welfare
"crisis," 46
Bush, George W./Bush administration:
Commission to Strengthen Social
Security, 143–46; conservative ideology
of demographic pessimism and financial optimism, 152–53; *Decision Points*,
150; and the DRA, 64, 65–66; on health
savings accounts (HSAs), 110; Helping
Hands proposals, 105; Medicare reform
and prescription drug benefits, 76, 102–
6, 108, 110, 112, 151; and "ownership society," 146–48, 161–62; and PRWORA
reauthorization debate, 64–65; second
term, 149–51, 156–57; Social Security
privatization and personal savings
accounts, 142–57, 161–62, 176; Social
Security privatization and public relations drive ("town hall meetings"), 153–
55; the 2000 presidential campaign, 103,
142–43; the 2004 presidential debates,
148–49; the 2004 State of the Union
address, 147–48; the 2005 State of the
Union address, 152–53; and welfare
reform issue, 64–66; and widespread liberalization of 401(k)s and IRAs, 136. *See
also* Social Security privatization
Business Roundtable, 152
Butler, Stuart, 134–35
Byrnes, John, 80

California state and welfare policy: Governor
Reagan and the attack on AFDC, 36–37;
Proposition 13 (1978), 37; Riverside's
"work first" approach, 53
Campbell, Andrea Louise, 170
Card, Andrew, 151
Carter, Jimmy/Carter administration: and
1977 amendments to the Social Security
Act, 129; and the PBJI, 35, 36; welfare
policy and politics, 35, 36, 69
Cato Institute, 136, 140, 152, 163
Center for Economic and Policy Research,
140
Center on Budget and Policy Priorities, 140
Clinton, Bill/Clinton administration: as
Arkansas governor, 45–46, 69–70,
72n14; and the BBA, 94, 99–101; campaign promise to "end welfare as we
know it," 10, 49, 66; and health insurance reform, 76, 82, 94–102, 121; and the
HSA, 95–96, 103; long-standing interest
in welfare reform, 28–29, 46, 48–49, 63;
the 1999 State of the Union address, 141–
42, 159; the 1998 State of the Union message, 139–40; and PRWORA, 60–63, 176;
and Social Security, 137–42; and welfare
reform/welfare policy, 10, 12, 28–29, 36,
42–43, 45–55, 60–63, 69–70, 174, 176; and
the WRA, 42–43, 49–51, 59. *See also* welfare reform (PRWORA)
Clinton, Hillary, 62, 65, 67, 73n24
Cloward, Richard, 33
Club for Growth, 112
Coalition for Medicare Choices, 108
Coalition to Modernize and Protect America's
Social Security, 152
Colmer, William, 34
*A Community of Self-Reliance: The New
Consensus on Family and Welfare* (1987
report of the Working Seminar on
Family and American Welfare Policy),
41
Concord Coalition, 140
Congress: Medicare package (1965), 80; and
Medicare reform, 90–91, 102, 104–6,
110–11, 123n19; and Social Security
reforms, 130–32, 134, 140–41, 144, 150–52,

156–57, 161; and welfare reform, 44–46, 55–60, 62–65

Congressional Budget Office (CBO), 82, 108, 149, 177

conversion (mechanism of incremental change), 6, 8, 171

Council of Economic Advisors (CEA), 1964 report, 31

D'Amato, Alfonse, 63

Daschle, Tom, 63

Davis, Tom, 150

Deal, Nathan, 59

Deal bill, 59

Dean, Howard, 57, 61

"death panels," 76, 116

Deficit Reduction Act (2005), 64, 65–66

defined-benefit pensions/defined-contribution pensions, 134, 157–58, 166n44, 169

DeLay, Tom, 150

Democratic Leadership Council, 48

Democratic National Committee, 98

Democrats: Medicare issue ownership, 75–76, 91, 93, 94–98, 116–17, 121–22, 173–74; Social Security issue ownership, 11–12, 128–29, 130, 132, 134, 141, 148–49, 150, 155, 160, 161, 162, 173–74

Department of Health, Education and Welfare (HEW), 37

Department of Health and Human Services (HHS), 51, 66

Dionne, E. J., 147

"displacement" (comprehensive legislative revision), 6, 23n12

Dole, Robert: and the 1996 presidential campaign, 54, 61; and Reagan's Greenspan Commission, 130; and welfare reform, 45, 54, 59–60, 61

Douthat, Ross, 116–17

Earned Income Tax Credit (EITC), 36, 44

Edwards, John, 67

Eisenhower, Dwight D., 128

Ellwood, David: Clinton welfare reforms and welfare time limits, 42–43, 50–51, 57–58; Poor Support, 42

Employee Benefit Research Institute, 111

Employee Retirement Income Security Act (1974), 135

Engler, John, 56

Family Assistance Plan (FAP), 25, 31–36, 47; hybrid ideological thinking, 31–32, 35–36, 47; liberals' complaints about the minimum income figures, 33–34, 35–36; and the so-called negative income tax (NIT) scheme, 31–32, 33, 72n6; and the work requirement, 32, 35

Family Support Act (FSA), 45–46

fee-for-service (FFS) Medicare, 99–100, 108–9, 115

Feinstein, Dianne, 108

"feminization of poverty," 38

Foster, Richard, 124n30

401(k) plans, 135–36, 137

Frenzel, Bill, 144

Friedman, Milton, 31, 128, 134

Frist, Bill, 105

Furman, Jason, 154

Galbraith, John Kenneth, 31

Gephardt, Dick, 58–59, 63

Germanis, Peter, 134–35

Gilder, George, 38–39; Wealth and Poverty, 38

Gilens, Martin, 48

Gillon, Steven, 138–39

Gingrich, Newt: and Clinton's health care reform efforts, 94, 97–98, 123n14; and Clinton's welfare reforms (the WRA), 51; Contract with America, 55–57; and health savings accounts, 111; and Republican attacks on the ACA (Medicare reform), 117; and Social Security reform, 138–39; welfare reform debate and House Republicans, 55–57, 58–59

Goldwater, Barry, 128, 134, 163n5

Goodman, John, 117

Gordon, Linda, 71n4

Gore, Al: and the Clinton welfare plan, 49; and prescription drug benefits for the elderly, 102–3; and PRWORA reauthorization debate, 64; and Social Security debate over personal savings accounts,

Gore, Al (cont'd)
143; the 2000 presidential campaign, 64,
102–3, 143
government health care. *See* Medicaid and
Medicare reform
Gramlich, Edward M., 138
Gramm, Phil, 59–60, 101
Greater Avenues to Independence (GAIN), 53
Greenberg, Stanley, 95
Greenspan, Alan: and Clinton's Social
Security reform ideas, 142; and Reagan's
bipartisan commission on Social
Security, 130–32, 134, 144, 161
Greenspan Commission, 130–32, 134, 144, 161
Gregg, Judd, 140

Hacker, Jacob, 4, 22n4, 135
Harrington, Michael, 31
Haskins, Ron, 41, 55–56, 72n12
Hastert, Dennis, 104, 105
Health Care Financing Administration
(HCFA), 98, 123n14
health care reform. *See* Medicare reform
Health Insurance and Portability
Accountability Act (HIPAA) (1996),
110–11
health maintenance organizations (HMOs), 99
health savings accounts (HSAs), 109–11, 122,
124n24, 176
Health Security Act (HSA), 95–96, 103
Heinemann Commission (Johnson's
Commission on Income Maintenance
Programs), 32
Heritage Foundation: and Medicare, 96, 108,
112, 123n17; and Social Security reform,
140, 152; and welfare policy, 48, 55–56
historical institutionalism, 3–5, 19, 22n2, 169
Hobbs, David, 105
Horn, Wade, 65
House Ways and Means Subcommittee: and
Medicare reform, 79, 92, 108; and wel-
fare policy, 41, 43
Humana, 114–15
Humphrey, Hubert, 33

ideas and policy change, 7–10, 172–73, 175–78;
and coalition building, 8; ideological

frames, 10; integrated framework and
the role of ideas, 2, 12–15, 175–78; and
issue ownership, 10–12, 173–74; and the
nonideational approaches of Mahoney
and Thelen, 7, 23n13; and policy paradigms, 9, 14, 178; and political ideologies, 23n19; and strategic choices of
actors, 9–10, 13–14, 172; and the three
incremental mechanisms, 8, 172–73
incrementalism: and conservatives' Social
Security privatization, 134–36; mechanisms (conversion, layering, and policy drift), 6, 8, 171; Medicare reform
and conservative ideas, 99–101, 107; and
path-departing change outside "critical junctures," 5, 6, 13–14, 15–18; postwar
Social Security expansion, 127–29
Independent Payment Advisory Board
(IPAB), 117–18
individual retirement accounts (IRAs), 135–
36, 137
institutions, 3–5, 169–71; factors and strategic choices of actors, 13–14; factors creating constraints and opportunities, 13;
historical institutionalism, 3–5, 19, 22n2,
169; institutional fragmentation and lack
of formal party discipline, 3, 70–71, 169;
and path-departing policy change, 16;
policy layering, 6, 8, 51–55, 69, 71, 137,
171; and the "political context," 7; welfare reform and institutional dynamics,
61–63, 70–71
integrated framework for understanding policy change, 1–23; basic analytical statements, 13–14; data and analysis, 18–19;
empirical observations, 18–19; insights
the integrated framework can provide
for scholars, 14–15; "process tracing"
approach, 19; recognizing existence of
asymmetrical power relations, 13; and
the role of ideas, 2, 12–15, 172–73, 175–78;
systematic comparisons of the three case
studies, 18–19. *See also* path-departing
policy change
issue ownership, 10–12, 14, 173–74; Medicare
reform, 11–12, 75–76, 91, 93, 94–98, 102–
6, 116–17, 121–22, 173–74; Social Security

issue, 11–12, 128–29, 130, 132, 134, 141,
    148–49, 150, 155, 160, 161, 162, 173–74;
    welfare policy and politics, 11–12, 28–29,
    46–49, 54, 60, 69–70, 72n16, 173–74

Jacobs, Lawrence R., 47
Jeffords, Jim, 104
Job Opportunities and Basic Skills training
    program (JOBS), 45
Johnson, Lyndon B./Johnson administration:
    and Medicare, 80, 81; welfare policy and
    politics, 30–31, 32, 69
Johnson, Nancy, 108

Keane, Kevin, 53
Kennedy, Edward, 105, 108, 112
Kennedy, John F., 78–79
Kerner Commission, 32
Kerr, Robert, 79
Kerrey, Bob, 101, 123n15
Kerr-Mills proposal, 79–80, 81–82
Kerry, John, 148–49
King, Desmond, 45
Kingdon, John W., 9
Kingson, Eric, 159
Kirkland, Lane, 130
Kolbe, Jim, 150
Kristol, William, 95
Krugman, Paul, 67

Lake, Celina, 49
Landrum, Phil, 34
layering. See policy layering
Lewis, Oscar, 31
Long, Russell, 34
Lott, Trent, 106

Mahoney, James, 6–7
Malthus, Thomas, 42
managed care plans, 99–100, 103, 107–9,
    114–16
Manpower Demonstration Research
    Corporation, 52
Matsui, Bob, 51
MCCA. See Medicare Catastrophic Coverage
    Act (MCCA)
McCain, John, 106, 117, 159

Mead, Lawrence, 33, 40–41, 45, 55, 72n16
Medicaid: creation of, 80; and the disabled,
    83, 122n6; spending and coverage, 82,
    122nn6–7
medical inflation (health care costs), 85–86
Medicare Advantage (MA) program, 108–9,
    114–16, 118–19, 122
Medicare Catastrophic Coverage Act
    (MCCA), 88, 89–94, 121; and congres-
    sional Democrats, 90–91; George H.
    W. Bush and, 91; and Medicare Part B,
    91; and prescription drug benefits, 91,
    103, 123n13; and Reagan administration,
    89–92; repeal and aftermath, 93; self-
    funding mechanism, 92; seniors' opposi-
    tion, 90–93
Medicare Modernization Act (MMA) (2003),
    19, 20–21, 102–12, 121, 176; the ACA as
    policy reversal of, 113–19; and the battle
    for issue ownership, 76, 102–6, 121–22;
    Bush administration and, 76, 102–6,
    108, 110, 112, 151; the congressional vote,
    105, 110–11, 123n19; conservative opposi-
    tion, 105–6, 123n17; conservative policy
    layering, 74, 106–12, 121; contradictory
    ideologies, 74; demonstration projects
    and fiscal trigger mechanism, 111–12;
    and health savings accounts (HSAs),
    109–11, 122; higher estimated/projected
    costs, 105–6; and income-related premi-
    ums, 108, 118, 124n23; the MA program
    (Medicare Advantage), 108–9, 114–16,
    122; as Part D of Medicare, 104–5, 114,
    121, 168; partisan ideological divisions,
    102, 104–6, 123n19; and private insur-
    ance/private managed care plans, 107–9,
    114–16; and seniors' rising costs/out-of-
    pocket costs, 103; the so-called "donut
    hole," 105, 114, 118, 121
Medicare Preservation Act (1995), 97
Medicare reform, 5, 17–18, 20–21, 74–124, 168,
    176; the ACA (2010), 17–18, 113–19, 174,
    177; barriers to universal health insur-
    ance reform, 83–84; the BBA (1997), 94,
    99–101; George H. W. Bush administra-
    tion, 87–89, 91; George W. Bush admin-
    istration and the MMA, 19, 76,

Medicare reform (cont'd)
102–6, 108, 110, 112, 151; Clinton and the
Democrats, 94–102, 121; and Clinton's
welfare reform, 94–95; and conservative policy ideas, 87–89, 93–94, 96–101,
105–6, 119, 120–21; conservative policy
layering, 74, 106–12, 114–16, 121, 171; and
contrary/contradictory long-term policy
legacies, 74, 76, 84–87, 119–20, 168; and
the disabled, 83, 122n6; and Gingrich,
94, 97–98, 123n14; and health savings
accounts (HSAs), 109–11, 122, 124n24,
176; the historical development of government health insurance, 76–80, 119–
20; ideological contradictions of cost
control in the 1980s, 87–94; ideological divisions and political partisanship,
74–76, 95–96, 102, 104–6, 113–19, 120–21,
168; income-testing/income-related premiums, 108, 118, 124n23; issue ownership, 11–12, 75–76, 91, 93, 94–98, 102–6,
116–17, 121–22, 173–74; the Kerr-Mills
proposal and program, 79–80, 81–82;
managed care plans, 99–100, 103, 107–
9, 114–16; the MCCA, 88, 89–94, 121;
Medicaid, 80, 82, 83; and medical inflation, 85–86; the Medicare Advantage
(MA) program, 108–9, 114–16, 118–19,
122; the MMA and prescription drug
benefits, 20–21, 74, 76, 102–12, 121; MMA
demonstration projects and fiscal trigger mechanism, 111–12; the National
Bipartisan Commission on the Future of
Medicare, 100–101, 103; Obama administration, 76, 113–19, 121, 176; original
funding arrangements and failure to
expand on the original benefits, 84–87;
Part A (Hospitalization Insurance), 80,
81, 86–87, 97; Part B (Supplementary
Medical Insurance), 80, 81, 84–85, 86–87,
89, 91, 103, 108, 118, 124nn23–24; Part
C (Medicare+Choice (M+C)), 99–101,
103, 107, 108–9, 114; Part D, 104–5, 114,
121, 168; payment methodologies and
reimbursement, 88–89, 93–94; and
physicians/health care providers, 86,
88–89, 93–94, 115–16; postwar period,
77–80; and private insurance sector, 78,
83–84, 85, 100, 107–9, 114–16; the prospective payment system (PPS), 88–89;
Reagan administration, 87–92, 93; and
Republican budget wars, 96–101, 119;
and seniors as political constituency,
90–93, 170; and seniors' out-of-pocket
costs, 85, 103; the so-called "donut hole,"
105, 114, 118, 121; and Social Security
oversight and funding model, 81, 86–87;
statistics on American uninsured, 84;
supplementary packages and Medigap
policies, 4, 85; traditional fee-for-service
(FFS) Medicare, 99–100, 108–9, 115; and
Truman, 77–78, 80, 83; Trustees report
on financial projections (2010), 116,
124n30; and universal health insurance
in other countries, 78; US health care
spending compared to other countries,
84; and "welfare medicine," 81, 82
Menendez, Robert, 116
Mills, Wilbur, 79
Moffit, Robert, 108
Moore, Stephen, 112
Morris, Dick, 62, 98
Moynihan, Daniel Patrick: as advisor to
Nixon and issue of the FAP, 32–33, 35;
Moynihan report (1965), 39, 42; and
Senate vote on PRWORA, 63; and Social
Security, 144, 152, 164n11; and welfare
reform issue, 32–33, 35, 39, 42, 45, 54, 63
Mundt, Karl, 80
Murray, Charles, 10, 39–40, 41–42, 48; Losing
Ground, 39; "perversity thesis," 10, 42;
and the Working Seminar on Family
and American Welfare Policy, 41

National Association of Manufacturers, 152
National Bipartisan Commission on the
Future of Medicare, 100–101, 103
National Commission on Fiscal
Responsibility and Reform (2010), 159,
160, 163
National Commission on Social Security
Reform (Greenspan Commission), 130–
32, 134, 144

National Committee to Preserve Social
Security and Medicare (NCPSSM),
92, 140
National Federation of Federal Employees, 131
National Governors Association (NGA),
45–46, 61
National Organization for Women, 151
National Welfare Rights Organization
(NWRO), 33–34, 69
negative income tax (NIT) scheme, 31–32, 33,
72n6
Nelson, Bill, 115
New Deal, 1; federalism and public health
insurance, 76–77; and Social Security
system, 126–27, 128
New Democrats: and health care reform,
94–95; and welfare policy, 48–49, 50–51
New Poor Law (1830s Britain), 25–26
New Republic, 36
New York Times, 65, 106, 117, 149
The 1996 Green Book, 24–25
Nixon, Richard/Nixon administration: and
the FAP, 32, 47, 72n7; and Social Security
expansion, 127, 128; universal health
insurance issue and 1960 presidential
campaign, 79; and welfare reform, 25,
31–36, 47, 69
Norquist, Grover, 146–47
Novelli, William, 106, 146

OASDI (federal Old-Age, Survivors, and
Disability Insurance), 126
Obama, Barack/Obama administration: the
ACA, 113, 114–17, 118–19, 121, 174, 177;
extension of 2001 tax cuts, 176–77;
Medicare reform, 76, 113–19, 121, 176;
and PRWORA, 67; reform challenges, 1;
Social Security reform issue, 158–60, 163;
welfare reform issue, 66–68
Office of Management and Budget, 47, 69, 114
Old Age and Survivors Insurance (OASI)
trust fund, 130–31; OASI Trustees Report
(2010), 133
Omnibus Budget Reconciliation Act (OBRA),
43–44, 89
O'Neill, Thomas P., 130

Organization for Economic Co-operation and
Development (OECD), 84
"ownership society," 146–48, 161–62

Palin, Sarah, 116
Panetta, Leon, 62
paradigms, policy, 9, 14, 178
path-departing policy change, 5–8, 15–18,
167–69; actors' motivations and strategic choices, 7, 9–10, 13–14, 17, 23n24, 172;
comprehensive legislative revision ("displacement"), 6, 23n12; feedback effects,
3–5, 7; ideas, 7–10, 172–73, 175–78; incremental changes outside critical junc-
tures/external shocks, 5, 6, 13–14; issue
ownership, 10–12, 14, 173–74; mechanisms, 5–8, 171–73; and Social Security
privatization, 133, 168–69; the three
cases/three distinct patterns of policy
change, 17–18; welfare reform, 15, 17–18,
24, 25–26, 28, 167–68, 171; what is meant
by "change," 16–17
PBJI. See Program for Better Jobs and Income
(PBJI)
Pelosi, Nancy, 106
Penn, Mark, 62
Penny, Tim, 144, 152
Pepper, Claude, 90, 130
Personal Responsibility Act (PRA), 56–57
Personal Responsibility and Work
Opportunity Reconciliation Act
(PRWORA). See welfare reform
(PRWORA)
personal savings accounts: accounts "carved
out" of the payroll tax, 138, 140–43,
145–46; arguments against, 146, 151,
153, 154–55; Bush administration and
Social Security privatization, 142–57,
161–63; and shift from defined-benefit to
defined-contribution pensions, 134, 157–
58, 166n44, 169. See also Social Security
privatization
Physician Payment Review Commission
(PPRC), 89
Pierson, Paul, 4–5, 22n4, 107
Piñera, José, 140
Piven, Francis Fox, 33

policy change. *See* integrated framework for
understanding policy change; path-
departing policy change
policy drift: as mechanism of incremental
change, 6, 8; Social Security and the
American pension system, 158, 172; welfare policy, 37–38
policy feedback: and failed Social Security
privatization, 161; historical institutionalism and concept of, 3–5; and policy
legacies, 7
policy layering, 6, 8, 171–72; as mechanism of
incremental change, 6, 8, 171; Medicare
reform, 74, 106–12, 114–16, 121, 171; Social
Security privatization, 137, 172; welfare
reform, 51–55, 69, 71, 171
policy legacies, 170–71, 173; and feedback
effects, 7; and historical institutionalism,
4–5; Medicare reform, 74, 76, 84–87, 119–
20, 168; path-departing policy change
and complexity of, 17; welfare policies,
27–28, 70–71
poverty and dependency (and welfare
debate), 31, 37–42, 44, 47–48, 69–70;
and African Americans, 39, 48; deserv-
ing/undeserving poor, 36, 45–46, 48;
"feminization of poverty," 38; Gilder on
poverty and family structure, 38–39;
Lewis's "culture of poverty," 31; Murray
and, 10, 39–40, 41–42, 48; public opinion and popular polls on welfare and
morality, 47–48; Reagan rhetoric of welfare dependency, 44, 69–70; report of
the Working Seminar on Family and
American Welfare Policy, 41
Pozen, Robert C., 154
prescription drug benefits: and Clinton, 102;
and the MCCA, 91, 103, 123n13; and the
MMA, 20–21, 74, 76, 102–12, 121. *See also*
Medicare Modernization Act (MMA)
(2003)
presidential campaigns: and Medicare reform,
102–3; 1960, 79; 1980, 37, 129; 1996, 54,
59–60, 61; Social Security reform issue,
129, 142–43, 148–49, 158–59; 2000, 64,
102–3, 142–43; 2004, 148–49; 2008, 158–
59; universal health insurance issue, 79;

welfare policy and reform, 37, 54, 59–60,
61, 64
President's Commission on Income
Maintenance Programs (Heinemann
Commission), 32
President's Commission to Strengthen Social
Security (Bush administration), 143–46
private insurance sector and Medicare, 78,
83–84, 85, 100, 107–9, 114–16; managed
care plans and the MMA's prescription drug benefits, 107–9, 114–16; and
Medicare+Choice (M+C), 100; supplementary health insurance and Medigap
policies, 4, 85
private plans and Social Security. *See* personal
savings accounts
Program for Better Jobs and Income (PBJI),
35, 36
PRWORA (Personal Responsibility and Work
Opportunity Reconciliation Act). *See*
welfare reform (PRWORA)

Quadagno, Jill, 15

Reagan, Ronald/Reagan administration:
bipartisan Greenspan Commission,
130–32, 134, 144, 161; and Iran-Contra
affair, 90, 91; Medicare financing and
reform, 87–92, 93; the 1980 presidential campaign, 37, 129; the 1986 State of
the Union, 44; and OBRA, 43–44; and
Social Security system, 129–32, 134, 144,
161; welfare policy and politics, 33, 36–37,
43–44, 51, 69–70
Rector, Robert, 40, 48, 56
Reed, Bruce, 50–51, 62, 106
Reid, Harry, 159–60
Reischauer, Robert, 41
Republican National Committee, 98
Republicans: Medicare reform and budget
wars, 96–101, 119; and welfare policy
issue ownership, 11–12, 28–29, 46–49, 54,
60, 69–70, 72n16, 174; welfare reform bill
(HR 3500), 55–57
retrenchment, 4–5, 15
Rivlin, Alice, 41

Rogers, Jean, 64
Roosevelt, Franklin D., 77, 127, 128, 174
Rostenkowski, Dan, 91
Rother, John C., 117, 151
Roth IRAs, 135
Rove, Karl, 147, 150, 156–57
Ryan, Paul, 110, 119

Santorum, Rick, 104
Sawhill, Isabel, 47
Schieber, Sylvester, 137
Schram, Sanford, 72n16, 73n26
Schweiker, Richard, 129–30
Senate Finance Committee (SFC): and Nixon's
    FAP, 31, 34–35; and OBRA, 43; and
    PRWORA reauthorization debate, 65
Shalala, Donna, 62
Shapiro, Robert Y., 47
Shaw, E. Clay, Jr., 66, 156
Social Security Act (1935): and AFDC, 25, 26;
    amendments and the politics of auster-
    ity, 129, 131–32, 134–35; and health insur-
    ance, 77, 81; and the "maternalist welfare
    state," 71n4; the 1939 amendments, 130;
    the 1977 amendments, 129; the 1983
    amendments, 125, 131–32, 134–35; and
    OASDI, 126; the postwar amendments
    and expansion of the system, 127
Social Security Administration (SSA): over-
    sight and funding model for Medicare,
    81, 86–87; and postwar expansion of
    Social Security, 130, 137
Social Security Advisory Council's 1997 report
    and recommendations, 137–38, 140
Social Security privatization, 18, 20–21, 125–
    66, 176; and "add-on accounts," 138, 141–
    42; Advisory Council's 1997 report and
    recommendations, 137–38, 140; after-
    math to 2005 failure/factors explain-
    ing, 157–63; Bush administration and
    personal savings accounts, 142–57, 161–
    63; Bush's Commission to Strengthen
    Social Security, 143–46; Bush's "own-
    ership society," 146–48, 161–62; Bush's
    public relations drive and "town hall
    meetings," 153–55; Bush's second term

agenda priority, 149–50, 165n36; Bush's
    2004 State of the Union address, 147–48;
    Bush's 2005 State of the Union address,
    152–53; and business coalitions, 152; and
    Clinton, 137–42; Clinton's congressio-
    nal hearings, 140–41; Clinton's rhetoric
    about "saving" Social Security, 139–40;
    Clinton's White House Conference on
    Social Security, 140; Congress and Bush's
    attempted reforms, 150–52, 156–57; con-
    servative ideology of demographic pes-
    simism and financial optimism, 152–53;
    conservative incrementalism, 134–36;
    conservative "Leninist strategy," 134–35,
    158; conservative supporters of Bush's
    plan, 151–52; defined-benefit private pen-
    sion plans/defined-contribution plans,
    134, 157–58, 166n44, 169; emergence of
    privatization idea, 132–42; fiscal out-
    look (2010), 159, 160, 163; fiscal situa-
    tion of the trust funds and the surpluses,
    132; ideological debates, 133–36, 150–55,
    161–63; ideological logic grounded in
    individualistic and promarket ideas,
    15, 134–35, 146–48, 154, 161–62; institu-
    tional layering, 137, 172; issue ownership
    (Democrats), 11–12, 128–29, 130, 132, 134,
    141, 148–49, 150, 155, 160, 161, 162, 173–
    74; long-term fiscal challenges related to
    demographic changes and population
    aging, 132–33; Obama presidency, 158–
    60; opposition and arguments against
    personal savings accounts, 146, 151, 153,
    154–55; "partial privatization," 134; and
    path-departing reforms, 133, 168–69; and
    personal savings accounts "carved out"
    of the payroll tax, 138, 140–43, 145–46;
    and policy drift, 158, 172; policy feed-
    back, 161; the "progressive indexation"
    idea, 154, 156; Republicans forging bipar-
    tisan coalitions, 128–29, 161, 162; savings
    schemes such as IRAs and 401(k)s, 135–
    36, 137; and stock market return rates,
    137; and think tanks, 140, 152; the 2000
    presidential campaign, 142–43; the 2004
    presidential debates, 148–49; the 2008

Social Security privatization (cont'd)
presidential campaign, 158–59; the 2010
midterm elections, 159–60
Social Security system (historical background and development), 126–32; ben-
efits/contributions, 127; benefits/federal
expenditures, 74; Carter and the 1977
amendments, 129; disability insurance,
127, 128; Eisenhower administration, 128;
enduring popularity, 126–29, 161; fiscal problems and shift to the politics of
austerity (late 1970s and early 1980s),
129–32; the flawed automatic indexation scheme, 127, 128, 129, 163n6; as
institutional legacy of the New Deal,
126–27, 128; Nixon administration, 127,
128; OASDI, 126; postwar politics of
expansion, 127–29; Reagan's bipartisan
Greenspan Commission, 130–32, 134,
144, 161; Reagan's bipartisan strategy and
the 1983 amendments, 131–32, 134–35;
Supplemental Security Income (SSI),
126, 158
Soss, Joe, 72n16, 73n26
Stark, Fortney "Pete," 92, 110
State Children's Health Insurance Program
(SCHIP, now CHIP), 82, 101
states and welfare policy: Clinton as Arkansas
governor, 45–46, 69–70, 72n14; late
1980s, 44–46; Reagan and AFDC in
California, 36–37; Riverside, California's
"work first" approach, 53; state experimentation and AFDC waiver provisions,
51–55, 69, 71; state-to-state variations in
benefit levels, 27, 29–30, 52; Wisconsin,
53–55
Stenholm, Charles, 150, 161
Stephanopoulos, George, 62
Street, Debra, 15
Supplemental Security Income (SSI), 126, 158

Talent, James, 56
Tax Equity and Fiscal Responsibility Act
(1982), 88–89
Temporary Assistance to Needy Families
(TANF), 24, 61–62, 67–68, 168
Thatcher, Margaret, 147

Thelen, Kathleen, 6–7, 172
think tanks and Social Security, 140, 152
Thomas, Bill, 100–101
Thompson, Tommy, 53–54, 56, 61, 105
Tocqueville, Alexis de, 15–16
Townsend Plan, 77
Trudeau, Garry, 155
Truman, Harry: and Medicare signing cere-
mony, 80, 83; and national public health
insurance, 77–78; and Social Security, 128

US Chamber of Commerce, 117
US Supreme Court decisions on federal welfare policy, 29–30

Vladeck, Bruce, 74–75

Wall Street Journal, 150
Waxman, Henry, 93
Weaver, Carolyn, 137, 140
Weaver, Kent R., 47
Weaver, W., 45
welfare policy and politics, 24–55; AFDC,
9, 25–30, 35, 36–38, 43–44, 46, 68–71;
"blame the victim" discourse, 41–42;
block grants, 57, 61–62; Carter's PBJI,
35, 36; Clinton's early legislative agenda,
49–51; Clinton's promise to "end welfare as we know it," 10, 49, 66; Clinton's
recasting of issue ownership, 12, 46–49,
70, 72n16, 174; conservative agendas
and marriage/families, 25, 38–39, 65;
the Deal bill, 59; deserving/undeserv-
ing poor dichotomies, 36, 45–46, 48; the
EITC, 36, 44; explanations for the success of conservative reforms, 68–71;
FSA in the late 1980s, 45–46; George H.
W. Bush administration, 46; George W.
Bush administration, 64–66; Gingrich
and House Republicans, 55–57, 58–59;
ideology and conservative discourse, 9,
24–25, 27–28, 37–43, 47–48, 57–58, 70;
incremental change (late 1980s), 44–46;
issue ownership (conservative), 11–12,
28–29, 46–49, 54, 60, 69–70, 72n16,
173–74; Johnson administration, 30–31,
32, 69; the lead-up to the 1996 reforms,

55–60; liberal responses to conservative discourse, 41–43, 57–58; Nixon's FAP, 25, 31–36, 47; Obama era, 66–68; OBRA in the 1980s, 43–44, 89; policy drift, 37–38; and policy layering, 51–55, 69, 71, 171; policy legacies, 27–28, 70–71; politics of a government-guaranteed income, 30–36, 47; poverty and dependency discussions, 31, 37–42, 44, 47–48, 69–70; PRWORA and Clinton's reform effort, 20, 24, 55–71, 176; PRWORA reauthorization debate, 64–65, 168; public opinion on welfare and morality, 47–48; Reagan administration, 33, 36–37, 43–44, 51, 69–70; Republican bill (HR 3500), 55–57; selective interpretation of data and research evidence, 52–55, 57–58; state experimentation and waiver provisions, 51–55, 69, 71, 171; and state governors, 36–37, 44–46, 53–54, 56–57, 61; state-to-state variations in implementation and benefits, 27, 29–30, 52; TANF, 24, 61–62, 67–68, 168; time limits, 42–43, 50–51, 57–58, 59–60, 62; work requirements and welfare-to-work, 32, 35, 41, 43–44, 46, 52–53, 65, 66; the WRA, 42–43, 49–51, 59. *See also* welfare reform (PRWORA)
welfare reform (PRWORA), 20, 24, 55–71, 176; aftermath, 63–66; and block grants to states, 61–62; and Bush administration, 64–66; Clinton policy advisors and debate over signing, 62, 176, 178n3; Clinton's initial vetoes, 60–61; Clinton's motives and embrace of welfare reform, 63, 66; as comprehensive reform taking place in absence of "external shock," 5; electoral calculations, 61, 62–63; and the government shutdowns, 60–61; and health care reform, 94–95; House Democrats and the vote on, 62–63; impact on AFDC entitlement, 24, 61–62, 66–68; lead up to, 55–60; and 1996 presidential campaign, 61; and Obama era, 66–68; passage, 61–63, 68; as path-departing conservative policy change, 15, 17–18, 24, 25–26, 28, 167–68, 171; reauthorization debate, 64–65, 168; and retrenchment, 5, 15; and TANF, 24, 61–62, 67–68, 168; and the 2000 presidential campaign, 64; viewed as policy success, 63–64, 67; work requirements and the caseload reduction credit, 65, 66
"welfare state," 22n4
Wellstone, Paul, 63
White House Conference on Social Security (1998), 140
Wiley, George, 33–34
Wilson, William Julius, 42
Wisconsin state welfare policies, 53–55
Witte, Edwin, 26, 27
Wofford, Harris, 94
Work and Responsibility Act (WRA), 42–43, 49–51, 59
Working Seminar on Family and American Welfare Policy, 1987 report, 41
Wright, Jim, 91

Zelman, Walter, 95
Zittoun, Philippe, 23n24